THE LIFE AND ADVENTURES
OF
JOHN A. MURRELL
THE GREAT WESTERN LAND PIRATE

THE LIFE AND ADVENTURES
OF
JOHN A. MURRELL
THE GREAT WESTERN LAND PIRATE

H.R. HOWARD

NEW INTRODUCTION BY
KEVIN D. McCANN

BRAYBREE
VINTAGE EDITION

This 2014 Edition published by
BrayBree Publishing Company LLC
P.O. Box 1204
Dickson, Tennessee 37056-1204
Visit our website at www.braybreepublishing.com

Originally published in 1847

BrayBree Vintage Edition of *The Life and Adventures of John A. Murrell, the Great Western Land Pirate*
Copyright © 2014 BrayBree Publishing Company LLC
Introduction copyright © 2014 Kevin D. McCann

No part of this book may be reproduced, stored in or introduced into a retrieval system or transmitted in any form by any means (electronic, mechanical, photocopying, recording, or otherwise) without the prior written permission of the copyright owner.

ISBN-13: 978-1-940127-08-8
FIRST EDITION 2014
Printed in the United States of America

Front cover and frontspiece:
Taken from *The Life and Adventures of John A. Murrell, the Great Western Land Pirate, with Twenty-One Spirited Illustrative Engravings* (1847)

*About the
BrayBree Vintage Edition series*

Many works in the public domain are available online in print and e-book versions. However most are of inferior quality, printed with generic covers irrelevant to the subject matter and little effort made to give the reader a clean, presentable book.

Each book in the BrayBree Vintage Edition series has a unique cover design relative to the subject. The original edition is reproduced in its entirety, with spelling and grammatical errors left intact. The new edition includes a new introduction, index, or other supplemental material.

Titles are chosen for the BrayBree Vintage Edition series based on their historical significance to the local and regional history of the state of Tennessee.

INTRODUCTION.

Never let the truth get in the way of a good story.
—Mark Twain

Outlaws have long been a source of fascination in American culture. Memories of the Old West evoke images of such colorful men as Jesse James, Wyatt Earp, and Billy the Kid. One notorious figure who predates them all is John A. Murrell, the "Great Western Land Pirate" of the Old Southwest. According to renowned author Mark Twain, he was the worst of them all. "[Jesse] James was a retail rascal; Murrel, wholesale," he wrote in *Life on the Mississippi*.[1]

A Virginia native who was raised in Williamson County, Tennessee and later moved to the Denmark community in southwest Madison County, Murrell

---

1. Mark Twain, *Life on the Mississippi* (Boston: James R. Osgood and Company, 1883): 312.

(pronounced *Mer-uhl*) was a known horse thief and counterfeiter who was tried and convicted of slave stealing in 1834. But it was the testimony and subsequent tell-all pamphlet of Virgil A. Stewart that created the Murrell legend and his reputation as a cold-blooded killer and the leader of a secret criminal organization called the Mystic Clan of the Confederacy. According to Stewart, Murrell conceived a plot to incite a slave insurrection as a diversion for widespread thievery by himself and his cohorts, some of whom occupied positions of prominence in Southern society.

The legend of John A. Murrell made a good story. But it was one in which truth was embellished and exaggerated from its very conception. Over fifty years later, historian James Phelan wrote that Stewart's tale "was so filled with glaring inconsistencies and even contradictions that it is safe to accept only that which coincides with known facts." He added, "It is probable…that Stewart elaborated the idea [of a slave insurrection] in order to attract attention, for notoriety was the breath of his nostrils."[2]

Still, the exploits of John A. Murrell were popular with many nineteenth-century readers. In addition to Stewart's initial account published in 1835 entitled *History of the Detection, Conviction, Life and Designs of John A. Murrell, the Great Western Land Pirate, Together with His System of Villainy, and Plan of Exciting a Negro Rebellion, and a Catalogue of the Names of Four Hundred and Forty-Five of His Mystic Clan, Fellows and Followers, and Their Efforts for the Destruction of Mr. Virgil A. Stewart, the Young Man Who Detected Him, to Which*

---

2. James Phelan, *History of Tennessee: Making of a State* (Boston: Houghton, Mifflin and Company, 1888): 350, 351.

Tennessee Historical Marker for John Murrell on U.S. Highway 70, near Jackson, Tennessee

is Added a Biographical Sketch of Mr. Virgil A. Stewart, another Murrell book appeared a year later written by H.R. Howard that focused on Stewart himself: *The History of Virgil A. Stewart and His Adventure in Capturing and Exposing the Great "Western Land Pirate" and His Gang, in Connexion with the Evidence; Also of the Trials, Confessions, and Execution of a Number of Murrell's Associates in the State of Mississippi During the Summer of 1835, and the Execution of Five Professional Gamblers by the Citizens of Vicksburg, on the 6th July, 1835.*

Little is known about the literary career of H.R. Howard. In the mid 1840s, he was a writer for the *National Police Gazette,* a publication that featured sensationalized stories about crime and what would now be considered tabloid style journalism. He wrote a series of articles about noteworthy rogues and criminals for the *Police Gazette*—including Murrell—that were the basis for many of his subsequent books.

Howard's articles about Murrell were published by T.B. Peterson and Brothers of Philadelphia in 1847 and sold as a paperback pamphlet for twenty-five cents. *The Life and Adventures of John A. Murrell, the Great Western Land Pirate* was the first biography of the outlaw and became a popular book that went through several printings. In addition to recounting his life and criminal activities, it also featured interesting woodcut illustrations depicting those scenes.

It will be obvious to readers of *Life and Adventures* that it is more a fanciful dime novel than a true biography of Murrell. While some incidents like the account of his 1834 trial are based on fact, others clearly rely on Howard's vivid imagination to fill the narrative gaps. Historian James Lal Penick Jr. wrote: "Murrell now entered directly into the penny-dreadful genre that in the decades after the 1840s did so much to formulate the mythology of the American frontier before the era of the motion picture. This was the full-blown legend."[3] Still it still makes for interesting reading, and is presented in this BrayBree Vintage Edition as an example of nineteenth-century dime novel literature.

KEVIN D. MCCANN

---

3. James Lal Penick Jr., *The Great Western Land Pirate: John A. Murrell in Legend and History* (Columbia, MO: University of Missouri Press, 1981): 170

THE LIFE AND ADVENTURES
OF
JOHN A. MURRELL
THE GREAT WESTERN LAND PIRATE

THE LIFE AND ADVENTURES
OF
JOHN A. MURRELL
The Great Western Land Pirate.
With 22 Elegant and Spirited Engravings.

The Publishers take the opportunity of saying that the above work is at once a correct, authentic, and graphic account of the deeds of one of the most daring and prominent men that ever figured in the records of crime. In the South and West, he is still spoken of as without an equal for the energy, capacity, tact and perseverance, which he exhibited in carrying out his stupendous villanies. It is but justice to the author to say, that the interest of the work is sustained without a moment's flagging, from the first to the last page of this exciting history.

Philadelphia:
T. B. PETERSON & BROTHERS, 306 CHESTNUT STREET.

PRICE, TWENTY-FIVE CENTS.

NEW BOOKS JUST PUBLISHED:

KIT CLAYTON; or, The Hero of the Road,	price 25 cents.
BILL HORTON; or, The Mysterious Highwayman,	price 25 cents.
NED HASTINGS; or, The Terror of the Road,	price 25 cents.
THE RIVER PIRATES,	price 25 cents.
NAT BLAKE; or, The Doomed Highwayman	price 25 cents.

THE
LIFE AND ADVENTURES
OF
JOHN A. MURRELL,
THE
GREAT WESTERN LAND PIRATE,

WITH TWENTY-ONE SPIRITED ILLUSTRATIVE ENGRAVINGS.

Philadelphia:
T. B. PETERSON AND BROTHERS,
306 CHESTNUT STREET.

PREFACE.

To those who are not familiar with the gradual settlement of the West, the remarkable events chronicled in the following pages may appear more like the illusions of a romance than the sober passages of history; but to those who have marked the degrees of its redemption into civilization, the existence of the terrific drama in which John A. Murrell figured as the main actor, will easily be recognised as no improbable event.

For the first quarter of the present century, the whole border of the Mississippi river, and its tributaries were lined with dense forests, almost impervious canebrakes, and tangled chapparal, forming retreats, which, like the mountain fastnesses of the Abruzzi and the Pyrennees, teemed with hordes of fugitive criminals and unprincipled adventurers. The sympathetic elements of this social refuse, joined, of course, in many instances together, and the result was the production of numerous marauding bands which were equally the terror of the honest resident, the solitary traveller, the river and the Indian trader. The principal of these bands at the commencement of the present century was under the command of the famous Joseph Thompson Hare, or, as he has been named, "the Rinaldo Rinaldini of America." The successes of this robber chieftain and his men were such as to inspire numbers to his example, and numerous adventurers succeeded him, who, plunging into the primeval jungles and haunting the swamps, soon infested the valley region throughout its length and breadth.

This exuberant ruffianism was, however, desultory in its character and aims, until the appearance of John A. Murrell, who, studying brigandism as a science, devoted the ascendancy which he had acquired among the marauders by his genius and his exploits, to confederating all the various elements of the region into a single combination, to be waged against law and order with the methodised strife of an opposing system.

The manner in which this aspiring villain sought to carry out these views, and the extraordinary consequences which their agitation produced, it is the task of the following pages to explain; the publishers, therefore, will not attempt to anticipate the narrative, or to delay the reader further than to give the assurance, that the most implicit reliance may be placed upon the accuracy of the entire of the details.

As a conclusive evidence of this, it is, perhaps, enough to say, that the work was prepared with great care by the editors of the "National Police Gazette" of this city, and compiled from a multiplicity of sources, comprising the current newspapers of the time spoken of, the records of the trial, the correspondence of one of the counsel engaged in the case, the recollections of old inhabitants of Tennessee, the narrative of the young man who delivered Murrell up to justice, and the prison gossip of the" Massaroni of the West" himself.

As an interesting illustration of the remarkably faithful development of Murrell's character by the author of the within work, we herewith subjoin a phrenological sketch of his mental qualities, as taken by the celebrated professor, O.S. Fowler,[1] in the year 1835. It was taken by Mr. Fowler before any history of Murrell had been compiled, and remained unpublished in that gentleman's possession until the singular agreement of the author's delineation of the robber chieftain with the mental chart induced Mr. Fowler to produce it fill the sake of coincidence. This circumstance is the more worthy of consideration from the fact, that the author is known to be skeptical of all the more elaborate refinements of phrenology, and that he has, nevertheless, by his shrewd and practical analysis of human character in this instance, unconsciously established tho extreme of the claims which he, in other modes, disputes.

Sketch of the Phrenological Developments of JOHN A. MURRELL, *as given by Professor O. S. Fowler, in the State Prison at Nashville, Dec., 1835.*

JOHN A. MURRELL has a very strong Constitution; is well formed, tall, active, muscular, very fond of motion, and works and moves with more ease than most men.

---

1. Orson Squire Fowler (1809–1887) was a leading proponent of the science of phrenology, the belief that the shape and contours of the human skull determined intellectual traits and personality.

His Phrenological organization indicates a marked character. His head is high and long, and his brain of full size, which, with a predominance of mental and motive temperaments, gives clearness, activity, and strength of mind. One of the leading points in his character is Energy, arising from large Combativeness and Destructiveness. He is uncommonly forcible and executive, and is prepared to go through thick and thin to accomplish his purposes. He never stops at trifles, and has any amount courage and presence of mind in times of danger. He is fond of excitement, and not at all daunted by opposition.

His Acquisitiveness is fully developed, giving rather a strong desire for property, yet it is not a ruling passion. Secretiveness is quite large, enabling him to exercise a high degree of tact and management, and also giving him perfect command over his countenance and ability to conceal his real feelings, and act in disguise, if necessary. Cautiousness is only moderate, hence, he is bold, daring, and hasty. Approbativeness only average, with large and active self-esteem, making him manly, dignified, and authoritative, and more than polite, affable, and familiar. He is disposed and qualified to take the lead, instinctively commands respect, and easily secures an influence over others, and, at the same time, acts regardless of their opinions. He is prepared to take any amount of responsibility upon himself, if necessary, to carry out his plans. He would make a superior general in time of action.

His Firmness is very large and active, giving great strength of will, determination, and perseverance. This is another most distinct feature of his character, and to it he is indebted, in a great degree, for his success and influence.

His sense of Justice is not so small, naturally, as might be supposed; yet it is not large. If he had been educated under different circumstances, this faculty might have been as active and influential as in the majority of men. His Hope is quite prominent, and with Combativeness, Destructiveness, Self-esteem, and Firmness, gives him an uncommon degree of enterprise, and disposes him to large plans and to anticipate great results. He has fair Marvellousness, rather large Veneration, and full Benevolence; hence, under religious influences, he would be capable of sustaining a religious character, which would, comparatively speaking, do credit to the profession.

As to his social feelings, some of them, namely, Amativeness, Philoprogenitiveness, are well developed, but Adhesiveness is not large. He is a friend so long as it is his interest, but no longer. His Concentrativeness is large, giving him great power of application and continuity of thought. He has considerable ingenuity, scope of mind, and sense of the witty, and under favorable circumstances, would show them in character to quite an extent.

Intellectually, he has great powers of observation. He is forcible and clear as a reasoner, and quite safe in planning; he is seldom at a loss for ways and means to accomplish his purposes. His most successful manner of reasoning is by analogy and comparison. He is neat and systematic, has a good mechanical eye, superior practical judgment, and good general memory. He is a decidedly matter-of-fact man, and uncommonly quick and accurate in his judgment of the character and motives of others.

His Language, Individuality, Eventuality, and Comparison, enable him to entertain company agreeably, relate many anecdotes, and show off to the best advantage.

His notorious rascality does not depend so much upon a bad Phrenological organization, as upon the wrong direction of his mind when young, as history will probably show. He has natural ability, if it had been rightly called out and directed, for a superior scholar scientific man, a lawyer, or a statesman.

O.S. Fowler.

CHAPTER I.

Murrell's parents—His mother learns him to steal—Robbery of the pedlar—He evinces a literary taste and turns his attention to the law—Leaves home at the age of seventeen to seek his fortune—His villany at Nashville—His flight—He falls in with a highwayman and enters into a deep wood with him—What takes place between him and the highwayman while there.

John A. Murrell, the terrible marauder whose sanguinary bands and bloody deeds for years spread consternation throughout the western country, was born in Middle Tennessee in the year 1804.[1] His parent were poor but intelligent people, and his father bore

---

1. John Andrews Murrell was actually born in Lunenburg County, Virginia, the second of four sons (eight children in all) born to Jeffrey and Zilpha (Andrews) Murrell. The family moved to Williamson County, Tennessee in 1806. James Lal Penick Jr., *The Great Western Land Pirate: John A. Murrell in Legend and History* (Columbia, MO; University of Missouri Press, 1981): 9–11.

a very good reputation among his neighbors and associates. His mother, however, did not stand so fair. Though from an unexceptionable family, she was a coarse and immodest woman, and in addition to setting an example of of licentious conduct to her children, she, according to the confessions of her son, even taught him to steal. The father endeavored to stem this corrupting influence, but being a timid and irresolute man, was unable to put in force the sharp control requisite to correct the evil.

The bad woman had her way, and John A. Murrell may be said to have drawn his barbarous and vicious nature from his mother's breast. Deprived thus early of the protection of a good example, and nurtured upon baseness, the children reeled headlong into vice, and in a short time after the unhappy father's death, went astray in various ways.

As early as the age of ten, the subject of our present history was quite a proficient in the art of stealing, and just at the point of the above period, for the purpose of evincing the degree of his abilities, committed a depradation in his father's house upon a pedlar who had applied for lodging for the night. Young Murrell stood gazing with wishful eyes upon the treasures of the pack, as the travelling vender displayed them piece by piece to the family before going to bed, and as he saw them laid away, resolved on making himself possessor of that portion of the contents of the budget which had most challenged his admiration. With a view of carrying out his purpose, he officiously lighted the pedlar to his room, and hung about the door till he saw where he laid his pantaloons which contained his keys. Having accomplished this first purpose, he waited till the salesman got asleep; then creeping softly in at a window at one end of the room, crawled to the bedside, got the keys, and selected such articles as he had previously coveted. He took these to the window and dropped them out; then returning, locked the trunk, replaced the keys in the sleeper's pockets, and finally left the room as noiselessly as he had entered. His work, however, was not yet done, for he was obliged to conceal his booty before he returned to bed, but having done this he sought his couch and sunk into a gratified repose. The pedlar went away without discovering his loss, but Murrell's exploit was discovered by his mother on the second day, and the result was that he received a severe beating for having privately disposed of a portion of the plunder without her knowledge or consent.

This punishment, though it did not inculcate in his youth's heart a sense of justice to his parent, taught him at least the danger of provoking her rage by any act of deception; and when a similar chance to rob a guest occurred a few months afterwards, he wisely made her the accomplice of his crime. The latter adventure did not result so successfully as the first for the young thief, for just as he was opening the sleeper's trunk, the latter awoke, sprang out of bed, and seized him by the neck. Finding himself detected, Murrell burst out in the most piteous complaints, accompanied by sighs and tears against his mother's cruelty, and falling on his knees, with admirable dissimulation begged the stranger to protect him from her fury. Rubbing his eyes, the amazed occupant of the room next heard the angry tones of his mother's voice as if in pursuit of the boy, and in the moment afterward saw her face appear at the window, demanding the young scamp, that she might finish the lesson just commenced upon his back, for staying out from home beyond his time. The well played scene completely duped the traveller, and from an indignant complainant he became an assiduous intercessor for the boy. Having at length secured a truce, the good natured stranger passed the youngster out of the window to the custody of his parent, and betook himself to bed totally unconscious of the secret history of the scene. Unluckily the affair was not ended with the guest's retirement, for the keys which had been extracted from his pocket were in the trunk, and the lock was turned. It was a dangerous enterprise indeed to venture again upon the broken repose of such a sleeper, but yielding to the necessity of the task, the boy was obliged to mount the shed again, and after having locked the trunk to replace the keys in the pocket of the owner. He performed the exploit successfully, and having descended received his reward in a portion of the contents of a bottle with which his mother was soothing her agitation beneath the window.

We give these early scenes as they were related by the criminal himself in an idle conversation with a chance acquaintance, as they serve to account for his early debasement and for his subsequent bent of mind and character.

With all his knavery and hardihood, Murrell was intelligent and industrious, and by a keen application to his studies at school, and a passion for reading every thing which fell in his way, he very rapidly attained a comprehensive degree of intelligence. Most singular of all—he appeared to have a taste for the study of the law, and whenever he could get a volume of legal lore would pore over it with all the eagerness evinced by the most ardent reader of romance.

He explained this taste as an artificial one entirely, which had grown out of his determination to follow the pursuits of a highwayman. "If I had never intended to follow the profession I am in," said Murrell, "I never should have cared about the law, but as soon as I had made up my mind to the 'cross,' I resolved to acquaint myself with all the dangers that laid in the way of success and of escape, and in the course of time, by reading. I became a pretty good lawyer."

At the age of sixteen Murrell's father died,[2] and shortly after that, having a severe quarrel with his mother, he resolved to leave home and seek his fortune on his own hook. To accomplish this purpose in a proper manner it was necessary that he should have money; so having set a night for his departure, he broke open his mother's bureau drawer and drew from it an amount of fifty dollars, and then effected a burgularous entrance into a grocery store in the neighborhood and obtained an amount of thirty-seven dollars more. With this sum he left his native town and took the direction of Nashville. Though not yet seventeen, Murrell, when he entered the capital city of Tennessee, was a man in stature and appearance, and possessed a most gracious and athletic form. He was not aware of these personal advantages, and in due concession to an ordinary degree of personal conceit, he made it his first business, on entering the city, to go directly to a fashionable tailor's shop and attire himself in the most becoming garb. He then enquired for the best hotel, engaged a room, and sat himself down to await the first opportunity that should offer to profitably

---

2. Jeffrey Murrell died in 1824. Lal Penick, *Great Western Land Pirate*, 22–23.

exercise the rules which he had deliberately adopted for his future course of life.

The first thing which attracted his especial notice at this place, was a very interesting and beautiful young lady, who with her father and brother were putting up at the same hotel. He effected an acquaintance with the brother, and through him gained access to the sister. For a few days, by representing himself as the son of a wealthy man in Eastern Tennessee, and by spending the remainder of his money profusely, he managed in ingratiate himself to no small degree with the young man, and also succeeded in making a favorable impression upon the sister.

Pushing his fortune like an old campaigner, he soon, by secret assiduities, deepened the the impression into a sentiment which romantic young ladies who are very desirous of getting married are but too apt to mistake for love. This continued for the period of two weeks, during which time though Murrell was rapidly progressing in the girl's affections, he was more rapidly running out of money. Feeling at length the pecuniary crisis pressing too closely on him, he was obliged to lead his young friend into a debauch, and pick his pocket during his intoxication of his wallet containing a sum of forty three dollars. With a portion of this amount he purchased an elegant trinket for the sister, and ere a week more had run round, the villain had by duplicity and artful promise accomplished her ruin. Through the incaution of youthful passion the parties were at length detected by a female servant, who with a prudence common among women immediately cautioned every one of her associates to secrecy on the subject. Bad news flies quick, and it was not long before this intelligence spread to where it was most dangerous to have it known. Murrell by some means got hint that the secret of his villainy was out, and to avoid the inevitable consequences, precipitately fled, not however without first seizing a valuable broach which belonged to his mistress, before he left her presence for the last time.

Obtaining a horse he took a south-westerly direction and rode hot foot away from the town, and it was not until he had scampered over ten miles of the road that he hauled up with a feeling of any safety. It was near evening, and feeling the effects of his sharp journey, he stopped at an inn by the roadside to refresh his horse and afford himself a little rest. His first intention was to stop for the night, but learning from a traveller, whose horse was also at the door, that there was a commodious hotel a few miles farther on, to which he himself was bound, he concluded to join his company. He considered this movement as judicious, moreover, as it would put a little more distance between him and his foes at Nashville, and if they should pursue him, why he might also have a hand to help him. When the horses were sufficiently breathed, Murrell and the stranger mounted, and as they rode easily away they fell into a familiar conversation. Our adventurer following the inclination of young men, just entering upon the world, commenced boasting of his family and wealth, and spoke with so much apparent earnestness, that he evidently impressed his companion with the opinion that he had at that time a large sum of money on his person. They had ridden almost three miles in this manner when they struck the edge of a heavy wood, through which the stranger said they would be obliged to ride for the distance of a mile. Shrinking a little from the somber avenue, which looked more dark and gloomy from the contrast of the faint grey light of the moonless sky above, the young adventurer followed his companion's horse into the jungle. They proceeded slowly for about ten minutes, when suddenly the stranger drew his horse across the road, and as Murrell looked up to inquire the meaning of the motion, he saw the muzzle of a pistol within a few inches of his head, and at the same time received a peremptory order to dismount.

Thunderstruck at such conduct in his new acquaintance, the young thief attempted to expostulate but the highwayman was imperative and down he was obliged to get, and to stand with his hands above his head, until his *friend* also dismounted and put himself, as he loosely remarked, upon an equal footing with his captive. The robber then proceeded deliberately to bind the young man's hands, conversing with him very pleasantly the while, and assuring him in the blandest tones, that if he attempted to show resistance, or make the slightest noise, he would be under the painful necessity of blowing out his brains. Having at length made his prisoner perfectly secure, the highwayman commenced searching his person, but lo, instead of finding the sum which the boaster had pretended to possess, he reaped no richer harvest than six or seven dollars. Chagrined beyond measure at his mean reward, the robber cursed the duplicity of the young liar without stint, and taunted his conceit as the occasion of his loss. It was in vain that Murrell protested—it was in vain he assured the robber he was one of his own calling; the experienced depredator had been deceived in his first representations, when he had no interest to lie, and bluntly told him he would not believe him now. With this rebuff he bound the youngster to a tree and rode off, leaving him to curse the stupid vanity which had aroused the acquisitiveness of a man who otherwise might not have considered him worth robbing.

"Well, never mind," said Murrell after his rage had somewhat subsided through the influence of an hour's reflection. "I've got the worst of his turn, and it will pass for a good lesson, any how, but if *my* chance ever comes with that fellow, if I don't make every thing a little more than square, then I hope to die on this tree!"

CHAPTER II.

Fast bind, fast find—Reflections under a tree—A friend—Sequel to the robber of the pedlar—The log house—Its inmates—The robber and the robbed—Re-union—The robbers spend a pleasant day, and Murrell at night gives them a proof which dispels all doubt of his character.

When the grey dawn, which drove the reluctant shadows from the sky, had stolen its way through the dusky foliage of the wood, it still found Murrell bound like an Indian sacrifice to a tree, which his horse, which the careful highwayman had tethered opposite, stretched out his nose towards his whilom master, as if to inquire the reason of his singular hostelry, and still more singular delay. The young robber had fretted and cursed himself into a sullen silence, and perceiving no assured hope of release, had doggedly resigned himself to the chances of accidental succor. In addition to his loss, and the grievous inconvenience he had been put to, he felt a deep chagrin at having been so easily duped, misled, and beaten at his own game; and while he secretly acknowledged his imprudence in trusting himself so carelessly with a stranger, he bitterly resolved to avenge himself on the first victim who should fall into his clutches.

The morning advanced; the uncertain dawn gave place to a clear and penetrating light, and the topmost foliage of the gigantic trees around waved in the rich glow of the uprising sun.

"Damnation! Is a man to die here like a dog!" bitterly exclaimed the young desperado, twitching at his bands again—"Damnation!"—but here he paused, and inclining his ear to the air which sifted through the trees from the south, he thought he heard the sound of crackling branches and a distant whistle.

"Hello! Hello-o-o!" shouted the captive.

No sound replied.

"Hullo! Hullo-o-o-o-o!" again shouted Murrell.

"Hillo-o-o!" returned a clear loud voice, in the direction of the first sound, and in a few minutes after, a horseman plunged through the surrounding thicket, and stood in the presence of the prisoner. The newcomer was a middle-sized man, thick set, and strongly built, with a ruddy, but weather-beaten complexion, half concealed by a pair of whiskers, which clothed his face from the centre of his cheek down to the line of the wisp-like black neck-handkerchief, which encircled his neck. He had a large blue eye, full of intelligence and resolution, and his mouth, though it betrayed a line or two of humor as he gazed upon the woeful picture of the captive, expressed strong will and strength of character.

"Hello! hello!" said the stranger, "what the devil is afoot now! There's been some foul play here, I guess. What's the matter, young man? How long have you been here?"

"All night, and am likely to remain here till the day of judgment, unless you do me the favour to cut these cords," replied Murrell.

"Well, that shall be done before you can say Jack Robinson," said the horseman, springing to the ground with practiced agility. "There," said he, drawing the keen edge of a mischievously heavy knife over the toughened cords, "There—give yourself a shake, now, and see how you feel."

"Stiff, weary, cold, hungry, and dry," said Murrell, swinging to and fro for a moment, to restore the circulation in his limbs, and then casting himself heavily on the ground.

"Two of your complaints I can cure out of hand, then," remarked the stranger, putting his hand into the side pocket of his moleskin surtout—"here's a flask of the pure stuff, that never paid tribute to the customs. Take a pull at all, and see what it'll do for you."

Scarcely pausing to thank his philanthropic acquaintance, Murrell seized the flask and took a heavy draught, then pausing for a moment for breath, followed it by another, somewhat lighter in its character, and then handed it back.

"Well, you're not troubled with an impediment in your swallow, any how," said the stranger, dryly, looking into the flask, and then shaking it doubtfully beside his ear. "But never mind, it's better in your belly than in my bottle, and besides that, there's more than enough left yet for me. Now, I'll give you a toast. Here's to *luck*, always good, however it comes, but best when it's *forced*!"

"Well, that's a nice toast for me to drink just now," said Murrell, dryly.

"I don't want you to drink it just now," said the stranger, with a smile, as he put the bottle, for better security, back into his pocket, "but no man can respond to a better sentiment. All the world looks for luck—fools wait for it with their mouths wide open, but brave men take it by storm. But never mind that now," continued he, taking a seat on the ground, beside the young man, "let's have the why and the wherefore of this 'ere." The stranger accompanied this latter remark by pointing to the cords which he had cut from Murrell's arms. The latter, loosened from his taciturnity by the genial cordial that now began coursing through his veins, commenced his story, and gave the stranger a complete recital of the occurrence which obliged him to fly from Nashville, and also of his subsequent rencontre with the highwayman, and its results.

"Robbed you of every cent, eh?" said the stranger, reflectingly, "well, how much had you?"

"Four hundred dollars, a gold watch, and a diamond broach."

"Well, well, that was too bad!" But why didn't you say you was a robber yourself? It would have been no harm, you know."

"I did tell him so," said Murrell, "but he wouldn't believe it; but I'll make him believe it, if I ever meet him, or else I don't understand myself."

"Good blood, my boy! Come, I like that. That shows spirit!" said the stranger approvingly, then looking at the youth very closely for a few moments, he suddenly remarked—"It strikes me that I have seen you before."

"I think not," said Murrell, somewhat uneasily.

"My life upon it, I'm right," said the stranger. 'It is some six or seven years ago, and you were a mere boy, but I recollect you now, perfectly. Your name is Murrell."

"You are mistaken, sir," said the young robber, coldly, but with some embarrassment.

"That's all very well," replied the stranger, determinately. "It's all very well and very prudent for you to deny it, but you'll lose nothing by my acquaintance. I admire your character and your qualities, more particularly as I have had the leisure of testing the latter by having been robbed by you once upon a time."

"Robbed by me, sir?" said Murrell, in unfeigned astonishment. "I never saw you in my life before, sir."

"Oh, yes," returned the stranger, earnestly, "don't you recollect the pedlar that put up at your house this summer seven years ago, who you robbed of a bolt of linen and some gilt trinkets? I was travelling in disguise at that time, and the pack I had with me I had taken from a pedlar, whom I overhauled on the Smithville road. You can now understand the reason why you never saw me come back to complain of the loss afterwards. Oh yes," continued the speaker, reflectingly, "I saw the old woman the next spring, explained the matter to her privately, and all in good nature, and she made every thing right with me, and told me the whole story. I said then that you was a smart promising boy, and wanted her to let me have you, but could not get her consent. She's a very

LIKENESS OF JOHN A MURRELL.

clever woman, is your mother. But do tell me how she's getting along? I haven't seen her now this four years."

Finding that it was no longer of any use to attempt to conceal his identity, and being moreover well disposed to form the acquaintance of a man evidently deeply skilled in the mysteries of a profession in which he himself as yet was an unskilled amateur, Murrell replied frankly to the latter interrogatory, and thus commenced a confidence, the mutual revelations of which proved that the two new acquaintances were beings eminently worthy of each other.

In the course of the colloquy, Crenshaw,[1] (for that was the stranger's name,) informed his young companion that the man who robbed and bound him to a tree the night before, was his own accomplice, and that on being informed of the circumstances of the exploit by his partner, and the fact that the young man whom he had robbed had claimed to belong to the profession, he resolved to satisfy himself upon the subject by paying him a visit on his own hook. To this result, he informed Murrell, he owed his release, and also the return of the seven *dollars*, which would be restored to him as soon as they should all meet together.

Mutually pleased with each other, these amiable companions then mounted their horses, and turned in the direction which the first highwayman had taken on his departure the night before.

A few hours' journey brought them to a small but <u>comfortable log</u> house, which stood on the edge of a

1. Murrell identifies him as Harry Crenshaw, though historians believe him to be Daniel Crenshaw, a local horse thief in Williamson County, Tennessee at the time of Murrell's residence there. La Penick, *Great Western Land Pirate*, 21–22.

wood about two miles from the main road. Here they dismounted, and after knocking at the door two or they times, they were admitted by a black boy, who upon recognising Crenshaw, told him to wait a moment and he would call his master. The boy then disappeared, and in a moment afterwards an elderly man, of middle size and respectable appearance, entered the room and politely expressed his gratification at seeing his visitors.

"I've brought a young friend of mine here to see you, Harris," said Crenshaw, pointing to Murrell with his riding "whip," "who is desirous of becoming one of us, and who is already a tolerable dabster in our line.—He's a son of Mrs. Murrell of whom you've heard me speak," continued he, as he observed the old man eyeing the new disciple from head to foot, "and is as staunch as he is good looking."

"Happy to see you, Mr. Murrell, take a seat, sir," said Harris, with dignified suavity, at the same time setting out a couple of chairs, "be seated, gentlemen."

"Where's Joe," said Crenshaw, throwing his hat on the table, and making himself perfectly at home by kicking off his heavy boots.

"He'll be here in a few minutes if every thing is all right," replied Harris, again significantly eyeing Murrell.

"Yes, every thing is all right," somewhat tartly returned Crenshaw, impatient at this challenge of his discretion—"every thing is all right; so just call him in, and then let's have something to eat, for I'm hungry as a tiger, and my young friend here is more hungry still."

Being thus summoned, the party spoken of entered the room, and Murrell beheld in the new comer, his travelling companion of the night before.

Murrell rose to his feet with a smile which told that every thing had been explained to him, and as the robber and the victim shook hands, Crenshaw crowned the odd reconciliation with a hearty laugh.

The greatest good humor at once prevailed among the inmates of the room, and in ready concession to the raging appetites of the two recent comers, a substantial meal was soon spread upon the table. Miller and Harris having already been to breakfast, did not join the meal, but they shared profusely in the contents of a bottle that graced the feast, and that was filled with the same nervous beverage that Crenshaw had imparted to his companion in the forest.

During the meal, the subject that was principally discussed and laughed over, was the incident of the previous night, and Murrell was not a little bantered, by both Miller and Crenshaw, upon his extravagant representations as to his money and his connections. Notwithstanding that Murrell took all these hits in good part, and laughed along, his conceit was wounded at the idea that all the fun and all the advantage should be on the other side; and as the liquor mounted to his brain, he chafed at their derision and inwardly resolved to turn the tables upon Miller, as well out of a lingering feeling of revenge for the suffering he had made him undergo, as to establish his ability at a higher mark than the conduct of the appeared willing to accord. Concealing his intentions, he demanded the privilege of retiring to bed shortly after he had eaten, which request being granted, he refreshed himself with a sleep of five or six hours' duration. He then got up, and on going down stairs, found Crenshaw and Miller playing at cards with some five or six hundred dollars in gold and silver lying on the table between them, and the everlasting brandy bottle in the centre. Harris sat looking on, watching the chances of the game, and only sharing in that portion of the amusements of the other two which was comprehended in the emptying of the flask. Murrell was not asked to take a hand, as he was known to be without money; and the two gamblers, hardly looking up from the excitements of the game to notice his coming down stairs, kept playing on. The strife for the gold lasted through a period of five hours, at the end of which time, chance, which had been regularly wavering from side to side, struck wholly in favor of Miller, and made him winner of all upon the board. A supper was then set out and soon disposed of, when the whole party adjourned for bed.

Miller, Crenshaw and Murrell were all consigned to a single room, and the two former, quite drunk and excessively fatigued, cast themselves carelessly upon the floor, leaving the latter the sole possessor of the only bed the room contained. Crenshaw and Miller soon fell fast asleep, but Murrell, watchful from his late repose, and animated by his purpose, did not close his eyes.

As soon as the measured and heavy respiration of his companions convinced him the untruthful robber that they were sound, he stealthily arose, unbuckled from around Miller's body the belt, into which he had put (with his own) all the gold he had won from Crenshaw, buckled it round his own waist, thew his clothes out of the window, and was on the point of following himself, when a thought struck him, and he drew himself again inside. He then went carefully down into the room where the gambling had taken place, and taking a piece of chalk that had been used to score the game, returned, and wrote on the floor, beside Miller, the following words: "For the purpose of robbing me, you refused to believe my character. I now give you proof you cannot doubt. You have had the laugh at me to-day, but it will be my turn to-morrow. Good bye!"

Having written this, he dropped out of the window to the ground, dressed himself speedily, went to the stable, selected Crenshaw's horse, ham-strung Miller's and his own to guard against immediate pursuit, and then mounting, walked at a slow pace until he considered himself at a safe distance when rising in his stirrups, and taking his final look at the house where lay the sleepy robbers, he burst into a laugh, struck his heels against the sides of his spirited steed, and went off at a sharp gallop, eight hundred dollars richer than the night before.

CHAPTER III.

Continuation of flight—Running a negro—The uncertainty of white men—Arrives in Memphis—Meets with an old acquaintance, and makes new ones—Sets out on a fresh enterprise—The burglary at Randolph—Becomes associated with counterfeiters, and extends his connections—His success—Strange rencontre at Cincinnati—A backward glimpse—Crenshaw's story—The Kentucky horse thieves—Crenshaw and Murrell set out for Georgia.

Swiftly and unceasingly did Murrell ride through the five hours between him and the dawn, and gallantly and cheerfully did the noble beast which he bestrode, obey his bidding.

Day broke upon a broad and open path, and as the heavy mists arose from the dark surface of the earth into the more elastic atmosphere above, the youthful adventurer saw the clustering cottages of a comfortable village looming in the distance.

"Thank Heaven," said Murrell, with a feeling of gratification, as he threw himself off his wearied steed, in front of a large swinging sign that promised entertainment for man and horse; "here's rest and something to eat, at last."

Murrell gave his nag in charge of a boy, who came, rubbing his eyes, out of the stable door, and then turning to the landlord, who was engaged in opening the shutters, he ordered breakfast. To the questions which the inquisitive proprietor assailed him with in relation to his business, he answered, that he was in pursuit of a fugitive slave, and then seeking for information in his turn, learned that the mail for the southwest, via Centreville,[1] would pass through the village at eight o'clock. He resolved, upon learning this, to abandon the wearied animal which had borne him throughout the night, and to transfer himself to the latter and more sure mode of conveyance.

Having come to this conclusion, he sought to dispose of his horse, and finally succeeded, after half an hour's chaffering, to get an advance of fifty dollars on a price set at double that amount.

He then set out in the stage, with the intention of pursuing a directly onward course, until he struck the Tennessee river, at Perryville.[2] Having arrived at Perryville, however, he did not consider it yet quite safe to halt so near to the scene of his recent exploits, and after a pause of but a single day, he took his line of travel

---

1. Centerville, Tennessee, the county seat of Hickman County, located 80 miles southwest of Nashville.

2. Perryville, Tennessee, the county seat of Perry County, located on the east bank of the Tennessee River 112 miles southwest of Nashville.

again for Lexington.[3] Merely remaining in Lexington until the following morning, he again set out in the direction of the south-west, deciding to make Memphis, on the river, his ultimate destination. This choice was owing partly to the stories he had heard of its advantages for an adventurer like himself, and partly to the fact, that a young fellow, who belonged to his own village, and who had run away three years before, for stealing, had located himself, there, pursued a series of professional speculations in the neighborhood with great success. Murrell promised himself a very pleasurable meeting with his old acquaintance; and as he meditated forming a connection with him, he resolved to introduce himself fresh from some exploit that would make a favorable impression of his abilities.

On the afternoon of the fourth day after his departure from Lexington, he stopped at a small village on the road, where, from the comforts exhibited by the principal inn, he resolved to put up for a few hours, and if necessary, to remain all night. Giving no further evidence of his intentions, than might be surmised from his putting up his horse and ordering a meal, he sat down upon the stoop fronting the road, to enjoy the luxury of a segar, while the repast was in course of preparation. While thus engaged, a tall athletic negro slave, mounted on a stout gray gelding, drove up before the door, and got off to deliver to the landlord a parcel from his master, who was a wealthy planter of the county. Murrell gazed upon the negro's fine proportions with an eye of admiration, and having learned that he had recently been severely punished by

---

3. Lexington, Tennessee, the county seat of Henderson County, located 114 miles southwest of Nashville.

his master for some act of disobedience, he determined to turn the disaffection to account, and to make him his own property. With this view he approached the slave's horse, as he was about remounting, and pretending to admire the animal's proportions, asked him the location of his home, and made an agreement that he should meet him on the road at nine o'clock that evening. The negro's habitation was five or six miles distant, so that Murrell started on his expedition before the night had well set in. As he approached the plantation which had been indicated to him, he drew his horse up to a walk, and having slowly traversed the distance of about half a mile, he at length saw the object of his search, leaning over the fence which bordered the road. Beckoning the negro to his side, Murrell told him that he had heard he had a hard master, and that the reason why he wished to see him, was to know whether he couldn't do something to soften his condition. The negro, easily caught at this unusual sympathy, enlarged upon his miseries, but concluded with a despondent disbelief in any amelioration of his condition.

"Oh! Never say that," said Murrell, "there are friends enough of the coloured man in this country, who will do well by him and take care of him, if he can only be got into a northern State. I am one of the slaves' friends, and if you want to be free, and to have plenty of money to buy lands and horses, and to live like a white man, I'll put you in the way of doing it." The negro stood bewildered with the view, and the subtle white man perceiving that he had upset his simple mind, clenched the impression he had made, by handing him out a flask of brandy, and inviting him to take a drink. The negro did not show much reluctance to this unusual courtesy, and taking a deep draught, passed the bottle back to his philanthropic friend. Murrell then continued his proposals, and to the slave's inquiry as to how he could safely accomplish his release, he told him that if would agree to let him carry him off, and sell him in the next town, and carry him off again, and perform the same operation for five or six times in succession, he would ensure that they would make enough money to divide three or four thousand dollars between them in a few weeks, when he would finally slip him into a northern State, where he could live like a gentleman ever afterwards.

The slave was intoxicated with this alluring view, and yielded without any further hesitation to the white man's temptations, declared himself ready to accompany him any where, and in whatever manner he might choose. Murrell then directed him to mount behind him, when , after tying his hands behind his back, he bound him to his own body to give him the appearance of a recovered fugitive, and then drove the spurs to his strong gelding, to make the most of what was left of the night.

The negro stealer and his voluntary captive, arrived in Raleigh[4] just before the break of dawn, where the former succeeded in selling his prize to a planter about starting that very morning for Kentucky. Having accomplished this fortunate transfer, and received an advance of five hundred dollars on the negro's value, he left at once for Memphis, where he arrived the same afternoon, and concealed himself under an assumed name.

---

4. Raleigh, Tennessee was established in 1826. At this time, it was the county seat of Shelby County. (Memphis superseded it as county seat in 1866.)

On the following day, he found the friend he sought, keeping a tavern near the water's edge, and apparently doing a very thriving business. This man, whose name was Roberts, welcomed Murrell warmly to his house; and after hearing a relation of his exploits, and their results, introduced him with admiration to several of his friends. He advised Murrell however not to stay in Memphis for fear of the inquiries that would be inevitably started after the man who had decoyed away the slave. The mode in which that piece of business had been done, Roberts informed him, though creditable to his ingenuity and daring, was of a character that would lay him open to suspicion, and the best thing he could do, would be to take a share in an enterprise that was going up the river that very night for the robbery of a store at Randolph.[5] Murrell agreeing to this, was next told by Roberts that he would see the two hands who were going into the job, and ask them if they were willing to let him in a third, and at what rate. The application resulted favourably for Murrell, who on paying down fifty dollars bonus for admission to the speculation, was acquainted with all its particulars, and entitled to a fair proportion of its avails. He then set out with his two new associates that very evening, by steamboat, up the river. They landed at Randolph early in the morning, and concealing themselves in the woods all day, entered the town at night fall and reconnoitered the premises on which they <u>had their design</u>. Withdrawing then again, they waited

5. Randolph, Tennessee was located on the second Chickasaw Bluff of the Mississippi River in Tipton County, north of Memphis. Because of its close proximity to the mouth of the Hatchie River, it was a more prominent river port than Memphis in the 1830s. Eastin Morris, *The Tennessee Gazetter* (Nashville, TN: W. Hasell Hunt & Co., 1834. Reprinted 1971): 241.

MURRELL RUNNING A SLAVE.

until eleven o'clock, when they returned, and by the aid of a well assorted lot of skeleton keys, they effected an entrance, and robbed the store of twelve hundred dollars worth of goods, and one hundred and thirty-seven dollars in money. This plunder was immediately conveyed to the river side, and put on board of a good sized flat boat, that was seized for the purpose, and which, after receiving its freight, was stepped into by the robbers and shoved out into the stream. Having floated with the current for about fifteen miles, the robbers directed the boat to the Arkansas shore, where, after unloading it, the shoved it back into the river, so that her stopping place might not indicate the spot of their debarkation. The goods were then shouldered, and being carried for about half a mile, were deposited in the house of an Irish tavern keeper, whose unostentatious and uninviting establishment served as an admirable receptacle for stolen goods.

At this place Murrell remained from three to four weeks, by the advice of Roberts; at the end of which time he entered into a connection with some southern counterfeiters, and went with them on an expedition up the Mississippi and Ohio rivers, stopping at Cincinnati a few weeks, and afterward pursuing the route as far as Wheeling.

Murrell remained principally in this part of the country for the ensuing three years, during which time, by his continual activity, and the great variety of his exploits, he became well known to every rogue in the west, and also became generally acknowledged as the most capable man of his age in the profession. At different times, during this period of his career, he was in possession of several thousand dollars; but being addicted to gaming and debauchery, he would frequently be despoiled of every dollar, by these conjunctive wastes, and thus be driven by actual necessity, into active crime again. In 1825 he was in Cincinnati with the sum of four thousand dollars at his command, when he was unexpectedly accosted in the street by name, by a man, whose emaciated appearance and mean apparel, betokened extreme poverty as well as recent sickness. The well-dressed robber looked with surprise at the attenuated form being him, and, in the gaunt features of its owner, sought, without avail, the recognition of a familiar lineament.

"I saw you yesterday," said the invalid, "and hailed you, but you did not hear me. The fever has left me neither voice nor limbs, and I see now, by your not recognizing me, that it has left nothing of old times even upon my face. I do not believe that my best acquaintance would find a trace in this wasted form of what used to be Harry Crenshaw."

"What, my old friend, the pedlar!" cried Murrell, seizing the shadow by the hand, then standing off at arm's length, and surveying him again, he continued, "Well, sure enough, there's little of your outside left. But come, that's to mend—every thing's to mend. I'm deeply in your debt, and must make up what passed at Harris's six years ago. Fortunately, I'm able to do it, and what's better still, I'm willing. Where do you stop?"

"About half a mile on the back road. I walked down here expressly for the chance of seeing you, because I did not want to send you a message."

Murrell here interrupted Crenshaw by handing him a roll of notes, and directing him to stop at a tailor's and purchase a suit of clothes, on his road home. He then bid him adieu, after having promised to call upon him at nine o'clock on that evening, at the house where he resided. Murrell kept his word, and found Crenshaw at the miserable dwelling of a poor labourer, whose sterling humanity, though trammeled and circumscribed by want, would not deny to the invalid the shelter of his roof and a portion of his fare, even though all prospects of remuneration for his care had failed in the second week of his boarder's illness.

In the conversation that ensued between the two robbers, at this second meeting, Crenshaw gave Murrell a description of the consternation of Miller when he found himself stripped of all his money by the green young man whom he had bantered so unmercifully on the previous day. He was in a torrent of passion when he read the taunt which the absent depredator had written by his side; but when, on flying to the stable, for the purpose of pursuit, he found both remaining horses disabled, his rage knew no bounds. "Your act proved beneficial to us both, though," added Crenshaw; "for in an hour afterward, two officers, from Franklin,[6] arrived at the house, and arrested us both, on charge of the robbery of the very money of which you deprived us, and the fact of its not being on the premises, or in our possession, was all that saved us subsequently from conviction. As it was, we were taken to Franklin, but got off, as I said, for want of evidence against us. This affair turned us up in the neighbourhood, and being obliged to change our location, Miller and I left old Harris, and worked our way down to New Orleans, where we got along tolerably

---

6. Franklin, Tennessee was the county seat of Williamson County, situated on the southwest bank of the Harpeth River.

well, till we killed a man on the Levee, for which we were pursued and arrested. We remained in prison for four months, on this charge, when, by the aid of some instruments which Miller's girl brought in to him, we broke jail and escaped. We ran down to Barataria,[7] where we found a pretty good lot of fellows, with a fine clipper brig, bound for the Isle of Pines and the open sea, and, thinking there was better weather ahead than behind, we joined with them. We had not been but a week out, before Miller had a drunken quarrel with an Irishman on board, who drew his dirk and stabbed him to the heart. I interfered, and got badly wounded in the shoulder, and, indeed, only had my life saved by the timely interference of the commander. That very night a violent storm arose, which took both masts out of us, and laid us upon the sea a helpless, tumbling hulk. The prospects of the enterprise were now ruined, and all we had to do, when the tempest lulled, was to rig a jury mast, and make for the nearest port. We made Santa Cruz the second day after our misfortune, when, foreseeing no further advantage in remaining with the crowd, I left, and got away by myself, a few days afterward, in a brig that was bound for Mobile. I was penniless when I arrived in that town, and feeling the necessity of doing something at once, I stopped a man on the road, and took three hundred dollars from him. I was caught, however, the next day, and taken to prison. Fortunately, the man himself, who was the only positive witness against me, died before the trial came on, and the jury not agreeing on the testimony that was left, I got off again. From Mobile I worked <u>my way through</u> the country up to this place, about four

7. Barataria, Louisiana

months ago, when I was seized with a fever, which has reduced me to the condition in which you see me now. But, thank fortune, the consuming heat has left me at last, and now, that my mind is more at ease, I shall soon regain my strength, and be fit for action."

"From this time out I shall do nothing without you," said Murrell. "I have plenty of funds on hand, and I can wait till you are yourself again."

"I understand that you are at the head of an extensive band in these parts," said Crenshaw. "I heard of your fame in the south and southwest, and the very purpose of my northward journey was to see you."

"No," replied Murrell, "I have no regular company as yet, though, to say the truth, I can count friends in all directions. I have been reflecting a good deal lately upon an organization, but now that I have met with you, I shall postpone any action upon the subject, until you are strong enough to be an active counsellor."

Here the conversation ended, and after leaving an ample sum with Crenshaw to pay all his previous expenses, and to handsomely reward his charitable host, Murrell bade the invalid good night.

In a few days after this interview, Murrell left Cincinnati, and took a trip to Kentucky, promising Crenshaw to be back in a few days. He went to make a bargain in relation to several horses which had been stolen by some of his associates in the latter state. Meeting the horse thieves at the place appointed, he bought all that had been taken, which was four in number, and stipulated to pay a certain price for them in case they were delivered to him at an appointed time and place in Middle Tennessee. Having made this arrangement in view of certain designs, which were then just breaking in upon his scheming mind, he returned to Cincinnati, in the fourth week after his departure therefrom, and, to his surprise, found Crenshaw in an almost robust state of health. Congratulating him upon his improved condition, Murrell then broke to Crenshaw his designs for the regular organization of a band, which should count among its members every class of depredators, and which could have a systematised plan of arrangement that would be mutually beneficial to, and protective of the whole. To set this scheme properly on foot, it was necessary to have a conference with certain parties of influence and deserved renown in Georgia, and it was with a view of this journey that he had ordered the horses to be sent from middle Tennessee, that he and Crenshaw might proceed to the former state under the character of horse traders, and by the disposal of the animals, cover their enterprise as well as defray the expenses of their expedition.

Crenshaw heartily approved of all Murrell's plans, and in three days afterward the two robbers set out for Tennessee. They found their horses at the appointed place, and without suffering any delay in taking possession of them, they continued directly onward to their ultimate destination.

CHAPTER IV.

The mountain path—The bloody deed—The traveller's horse—
Arrival at Jasper—The cry of blood—The Alabama line—The
friend of Crow Creek—Close concealment—Separation of the
Ruffians—Murrell in Mobile—The tragedy of the gaming table—
The unfortunate winner.

In crossing the Cumberland mountains they fell in with a young South Carolinian trader, named Woods, who had been to Tennessee to buy a drove of hogs, but who, having found the animals too much advanced in price, had declined to purchase, and was now returning home with all his money in his pocket. These facts were soon ascertained by the two robbers through a conversation started for the purpose, when it was at once decided that they should make themselves the masters of the gold. There was but one safe way to accomplish this, and that was by his death. A brief debate decided them upon this course, and, having come to this conclusion, Murrell proposed that the deed should be done at once; but Crenshaw, who had previously travelled on the road, demanded a delay until they should reach a certain place upon the mountain path which he regarded as peculiarly fitted for their atrocious purpose.

The travellers jogged pleasantly along together, and the young trader, unconscious of his impending doom, sought with all the cheerfulness of a frank and amiable nature, to soften the tedious time with pleasant road-side gossip. The robbers seconded his cheerful mood with a conversation equally gay and friendly, and Murrell with a ready invention, for which he was remarkable, rattled off several amusing but fabulous adventures in return. Thus two pleasant hours ran round, and the young man appeared to increase in spirits, in proportion as he approached the scene in which he was to be made a sacrifice to a bloody thirst for gold. At length the road took a sudden turn, and twisted abruptly up a rugged ascent that curved along the edge of a deep ravine. This was the spot that Crenshaw had inwardly selected for the murder, and beckoning to Murrell to fall behind the trader, he whispered to him that the moment had arrived, and took from him his heavy loaded whip, for the commission of the deed. He then directed Murrell to ride ahead, and when he got upon the point of ground which commanded the open view of the South, to make a pause, and call the attention of his companion to the beauty of the scenery; he then would ride up on the other side and knock out his brains.

These suggestions chimed so well with Murrell's views that he did not offer an amendment to the plan, but rode straight on, and accosting the trader as he came up, by a careless remark, kept on with him to the apex of the hill. Then drawing up his horse, and sweeping the southern horizon with his hand, he pointed out the various beauties of the scene.

The unsuspecting trader obeyed the treacherous direction; but, alas! unhappy man, just as he was about to express his admiration of the grand expanse that was doomed to be his parting view of the beauties of this earth, a deadly bludgeon, swung by the ruthless hand of Crenshaw, crushed deep into his skull, and he reeled from his saddle to the ground a dead man.

So fatal was the blow, that he did not even groan; and so helpless did he fall, that the horse that bore him evinced no more alarm than if his master were descending regularly from the saddle. The miscreants at once dismounted and hastily set about plundering the body. This they speedily accomplished, and after having obtained from it a sum of twelve hundred and sixty two dollars, next debated on the best method of its disposal.

"We'll throw him down the rocks," said Crenshaw, "that's the best way to dispose of him. When he reaches the bottom it will be a hard matter to tell how he met his death, and it's ten to one he;s never seen again.—Do you catch hold of his legs, and I'll take him by the shoulder. So now this way, to the edge of that rock. There! Now, *one*! *two*! *three*! and let go!"—and as the elder murderer gave the final word, they swung the ghastly body of their victim far beyond the crag, and in a moment more,

MURDER OF WOODS, THE SOUTH CAROLINIAN

all that remained of its brave humanity, was a mangled mass of bloody flesh and splintered bones.

"Well, thank God, *that's* over!" said Murrell, with a long drawn breath of relief, as he arose from the bending position in which he had watched the body plunge into the recesses of the jungle. "Poor fellow! I'm sorry to bid him so sad a good bye! But what's done can't be helped."

"He had but one fault that I know of, and that was his money," said Crenshaw. "However, every man must have his faults."

"Well, we have shrived him of that sin, at any rate," said Murrell, recovering his spirits upon Crenshaw's joke, "and now we must look to ourselves, and see that we do not suffer for the christian service. I think we had better tumble his saddle over after him; it might be recognized, and we must run no risks for trifles."

Having, by the disposal of this latter article, taken, as they thought, every precaution against detection, the murderers remounted, and with the dead man's horse added to their own, pushed on their journey, apparently with as small concern as if no extraordinary incident had happened.

Through free from apprehension of pursuit, it was, nevertheless, clearly the policy of the ruffians to place as great a distance between them, and the scene of their fiendish crime, as was possible in a given time; so pushing on at a brisk pace, and maintaining it with an unabated ardor throughout the afternoon, they accomplished a distance of sixteen miles before the evening shadows had blotted out their path. Overcome, then, with the fatigue occasioned by their sharp and extended travel, a fatigue somewhat enhanced, moreover, by the excitement, which even their practised and almost stoical brutality was not proof against, they hailed with pleasure, the prospect of a good night's rest, which was promised them by a tavern, in a little village, a few miles from Jasper.[1]

While taking their supper at this place, Murrell accidentally observed the host, and two men, suspiciously regarding them from the shadow of the door of an adjoining room, and, also, noticed that their narrow scrutiny was accompanied by a low and earnest colloquy. Sharpened by the apprehension natural to the situation, he attentively inclined his ear, without appearing to do so, and managed to catch a portion of their conversation. His pains were soon rewarded, and his alarm may be imagined when he detected the name of the murdered man frequently repeated in their discourse, and further learnt, by a few leading words, that he was not only well known at the place, but that his horse, then in their possession, had also been recognized as an old acquaintance. A sudden chill ran through the murder's veins as he made this terrible discovery, and for a moment he was unnerved and irresolute what course to follow. His mind, in its uncertain satisfaction, conjured up a thousand fears, and forgetting, in the first confusion of the moment, that their speed had outran all tidings of their crime, he imagined that the body of the slaughtered man had been discovered, and that they would, in the next moment, hear an accusation of his murder. A moment's reflection, however, relieved him of this dread, and regaining his self-possession at the thought, he instantly decided on his course.

---

1. Jasper, Tennessee, the county seat of Marion County, located north of the Tennessee River and 112 miles southeast of Nashville.

He felt assured that there could exist, against them, nothing graver than a mere suspicion, and felt convinced, also, that that suspicion found its extremest measure in a doubt of their honest possession of the animal. Though young in years, his stirring life had deeply skilled Murrell in the history of human nature, and he had had occasion, long before, to learn that the only way to defeat a curiosity, the prosecution of which might be dangerous, was to swerve it from its course by a voluntary ingenuousness, which should appear to explain the very points which are the objects of the most eager inquiry.

Acting upon this philosophy, he rose cheerfully from the table, at the conclusion of his supper, and after passing a word or two with different persons about the bar-room, politely invited the whole company up to drink. This opened a general conversation, and standing carelessly with his back against the counter and his glass in his hand, he fell, apparently without design, into a rattling relation of his life and experience as a horse-dealer, amusing his audience, occasionally, with well told anecdotes, and occasionally dilating on the qualities of stock, in a manner which placed his knowledge of the business beyond a doubt. He told his name; he told his friend's name (fictitious of course); he informed them of his residence, and gave a history of his father's exploits during the war, until finding that he had worked his hearers up to the proper pitch of confidence and admiration, he returned again to his vocation, spoke of his stock, and boldly enlarged upon the virtues and qualities of the dead traveller's horse.

"He's a noble animal; a noble animal!" remarked the robber, with an emphasis which bespoke the degree of his satisfaction at its possession. "I prize him above all the rest, and well I may, for he cost me a good round sum. I bought him from a young Carolinian trader, in Nashville, who had come on to Tennessee to buy a drove of hogs—his name, I believe, was Woods: yes, Woods. He was very loth to part with him, but I had set my mind upon the animal, and I tell you what, it's a pretty hard thing for a man to get away from me, when I'm determined on a bargain."

This produced a climax, and as the speaker saw its satisfactory effect upon the countenances of his auditory, he clenched the result, by clapping his nearest listener upon the back, and inviting the whole company to take a parting drink with him and his friend before their retirement to bed. The proposed courtesy was of course readily accepted, and after it had been duly recognized with all the honours, the landlord assiduously waited upon the robbers to their room.

"I say, Harry," said Murrell, in a cautious whisper, after listening till the retreating step of the landlord had faded from his ear, "I say, Harry, there's danger in this place. I begin to fear we may have left something in sight on the hill. If it should be so, a single day's delay might ruin us. We must be on the road again at day-break, and keep our heels at work till we cross the line. There's danger here, I tell you!"

"I see it all!" said Crenshaw. "If the body is found, we're sure to be pursued. Damn the horse, I say!"

"Well, never mind the horse now. We must strike for Jasper at day-break, sell our horses, give a false scent, and change our course for Alabama."

"It is the very plan I was about to propose," replied Crenshaw; "So we'll have no disagreement upon that point; and now that that is settled, let's go to bed, for I'm dying for some sleep."

At dawn the robbers were preparing for a start, and ere the sun was fairly up, they had bidden good bye to their deluded host. In another hour they were in Jasper. The pressing necessity of the case lent Murrell a double energy, and by ten o'clock he had disposed, at a tolerable price, of all his horses, but the ones which he and his companion rode. Having done this, he purchased two coarse suits of clothes, and giving out that they were going into Georgia, took the road for that State. Having arrived at a wood, a few miles from the town, they secreted themselves, put on their new disguise, buried their old garments, remounted and turned backward towards Alabama, and rode, almost without intercession, until they crossed the line.

Good cause had they for haste; for it was not three hours after their departure from Jasper, before news arrived from the village where the ruffians had passed the previous night, that some travellers had discovered the body of a man in a jungle on the mountain, who, from all the circumstances, was supposed to have been recently murdered. The attention of those who had found the body had first been attracted by an empty wallet, which Crenshaw, while riffling the body, had thoughtlessly thrown upon the ground, and which, being of the same colour as the earth, had escaped his notice when he was disposing of the trader's hat and saddle.

Not knowing how to account for the presence of such an article, in such a place, without a serious conclusion, the discoverers commenced searching for something which might explain the mystery. At length, looking over the edge of the rock, they perceived a fragment of muslin hanging from a limb, and also saw some broken branches of the bushes at the bottom of the jungle, which, though they did not stand apart, yet showed a cragged gap, as if some heavy object, which, perhaps, lay concealed beneath, had forced a sudden passage through. Pursuing their inquiry, they at length found the body of the murdered victim, and though they perceived no special wound upon the mangled mass, to attribute to a violent hand, they could not hesitate to ascribe its presence there to human agency. This news was brought to the village where the robbers had put up, and as soon as the innkeeper heard the story, he declared his guests of the previous night to be the murderers.

It was but an hour after noon, and the villains had but a short start, so saddling his horse, the innkeeper and a couple of his neighbours posted off to town. Alas, they were too late. The murderers had made no stay in Jasper, but four hours before noon had taken the road to Georgia. No time was lost in hesitation. The cry of blood was up, and upon every avenue, both north and south, voluntary squads of horsemen soon scoured the country round.

Meanwhile Murrell and Crenshaw, as if conscious of the danger which pursued them, pushed on without intermission, for even two hours after dark, when striking the banks of Crow Creek, they turned up an unfrequented road that ran along its banks, and led to the cabin of a member of the northern gang named Parmer, with whom Crenshaw had made an acquaintance a year before. This man welcomed the two congenial spirits with a warm professional reception, and on hearing their condition, advised them to remain with him until he could learn if there was any danger in venturing directly on.—This proposition agreeing exactly with the desires of the fugitives, they closed with it at once, and bade their host to consider them as his thankful guests.

In the morning, Parmer started out for news, and returned at noon with an account that the chase was up in all directions for the two men who had left Jasper on the day before. This decided the course of the murderers, and for two weeks they remained concealed at Parmer's house.

At the end of that time they considered it safe to start again, and receiving new suits of disguises from their hospitable friend, they left their horses with him to dispose of, and taking a boat at nightfall near his door, dropped down the creek till it met the Tennessee river, and then followed the course of that stream to the limit of its southern bend, in the vicinity of Bellefont,[2] where they abandoned it for the land again. By pursuing a cautious course, sleeping in the woods during the day time, and travelling only at night, the murderers at length arrived in safety at Tuscaloosa, the capital of the State, where they found many friends, and were enabled to throw off the restraints which they had been obliged latterly to submit to, for the purpose of preventing a trace being obtained of their destination.

Murrell remained in Tuscaloosa for about three weeks, when having seen all the *speculators* in the neighbourhood,

---

2. Bellefont, Alabama, then the county seat of Jackson County in the northeast part of the state

and explained to them an outline of his plans, he sent Crenshaw south-east in the direction of Montgomery, while he himself was to follow the course of the Tombigbee, to Mobile. Both were again to meet in the latter city, as soon as Crenshaw could accomplish a series of visits to the resident depredators in the eastern portion of the State.

On his arrival in Mobile, Murrell, whose recent danger had forced him into a circumspect career, gave way to all the vicious temptations of the town, and losing sight for the time, of all professional views, plunged into a course of riotous enjoyment that soon brought his stock of funds to an alarming ebb. This result he mainly owed to the hazards of the gaming table, and following that fascination to its end, he went, in the third week after his arrival, to make a final venture of his capital of twenty dollars, in the vain hope to retrieve all his former losses.—He commenced the game, and from the start his hazards were attended with success. His capital of twenty dollars rose by degrees until it grew to nineteen hundred, when desiring only to make it square two thousand, he put down what he intended to be his last bet, let chance go as it would. The bet lost; out unable to contemplate the unpleasant gap which the mishap had taken from the symmetrical amount he had designed to win, he put down a sum of two hundred to retrieve the deficit. This venture followed the fate of the previous wager, and from this moment he began to lose so fast, that in half an hour from the declension of his luck, he saw himself completely bankrupt, and without a dollar. Springing to his feet when his last bet went by the board, as if he had been stung, he dashed the champagne bottle beside him on the floor, and gnashing his teeth with rage, glared for a moment on the bankers and the delusive table, as if about to seize it and toss it upside down. Restraining his passion, however, he contented himself with a curse, and flinging himself moodily down in a chair, watched sullenly the further operations of the game.

There was one player at the table who was more fortunate than himself, and who appeared to have caught the tide of his luck from the moment it had begun to turn, and to have profited just in proportion as the success of the observer had declined. Indeed, the respective alternations were so regular in degree, that it appeared to Murrell to be a mere transfer of his winnings to the pocket of the fortunate gamester.

The coincidence was fatal to the player, for as he cashed in his heaps of winnings, Murrell fixed his fierce and burning eyes upon him with a jealous gaze, which spoke a bloody and a desperate resolve.

He left the house, and secreted himself near the door, and as the devoted winner came forth he glided behind him up the solitary street, until he reached a spot suited to his purpose, when he drew his knife, rushed upon him and clove his skull in twain. The miserable victim fell lifeless to the earth, upon the blow, and the avaricious ruffian knelt beside the quivering body to rifle it of its envied gains. But to his astonishment and rage, instead of the treasure that he sought upon the person of the corpse, he found but a five dollar note, and a few silver shillings.—He had mistaken in the character of his victim, who instead of having been a bona fide player, was merely a secret accomplice, or "capper in" of the gamblers, whose regular business it was to pretend to play and to win, for the purpose of decoying and leading others on.

The gains, therefore, which had excited Murrell's brutal avarice, had all been illusory, and the deluded ruffian had laid murder on his soul for a sum which h e would have disdained to steal.

As he rose from the body he spurned it spitefully with his foot, and was about turning disgustfully away, when he felt the sudden fall of a heavy hand upon his shoulder.

CHAPTER V.

The recognition—Crenshaw's precaution against witnesses for the prosecution—Professional reconnoissance—The hospitable mate—The bag of gold—Robbery of the brig—Departure from Mobile—The slave insurrection—Fiendish contrivance of Murrell's—Detection of the black incendiary—His doom.

Crime has no heart either for mercy or for courage. It is sensible alone to cruelty and fear—a short-sighted, wretched fear, which, though capable of braving, by ferocious deeds, the intangible dangers of hereafter, cringes appalled before the prospect of present retribution.

In his blind and brutal recklessness, Murrell had slain his victim, without one throb of pity, or one dread of Heaven's eternal vengeance, but when he felt the hand of the avenger fall upon his shoulder, and knew that he stood in front of an accuser, who beheld him all soiled and reeking with his crime, a deadly terror thrilled through his guilty soul, and cowering under the challenge, he shrunk down his averted head and sought to fly. But the grasp upon his shoulder was too strong, whereupon his terror changed to desperation, and jerking himself free by a violent effort, he drew his knife, jumped back, and threw himself upon his guard.

The unknown did not draw, but after regarding Murrell's posture of defence for a moment, with the utmost composure, burst into a low smothered chuckle, which showed that he was perfectly at ease.

"What the hell does all this mean? Who the devil are you?" exclaimed the assassin, still keeping his defence, but increasing in rage, as the prospects of his danger began to lessen.

The unknown laughed again in the same manner as before, and before he could follow up his glee with a reply, Murrell had leaned forward and caught a narrower glance of his outline. Then dropping his guard and putting up his knife, he peevishly exclaimed, "Why, d—n it, Harry, is it you? What the devil did you frighten a fellow so for?"

"Frighten you? Why a man of your size has got no business to be frightened at any thing," returned Crenshaw, with a repetition of his chuckle. "But what have been doing here?" continued he, becoming earnest, and pointing at the body.

"Nothing! Yes, I have, I've been making a fool of myself, by *settling* a man for five dollars and a half."

"Well, that's bad business, that's the fact! But may be you hav'nt *sounded* him completely."

"Yes, I have," answered Murrell, with a slight shudder, which would have done him professional discredit in his companion's eyes, had it been seen. "But come, let's be off."

"Are you sure you've finished him?" inquired Crenshaw, lingering, as Murrell turned away.

"Yes, quite sure," replied the assassin, impatiently, and still moving off.

"Well, I'm not!" said Crenshaw, "and therefore I'll make him safe. A good thrust is never thrown away. There—" said he, shoving his knife between the dead man's ribs; "he'll never bear witness against either of us now, I'll guarantee. There's no plan like this for disposing of witnesses of the prosecution. Dead men tell no tales, and that's a rule that beats the lawyers all hollow." Saying this, the mechanical ruffian rose from the body and hastily followed his retreating companion.

Crenshaw had arrived in town early that evening, and not finding his professional accomplice at his hotel, had set out to the various houses of bad repute in search of him. Being disappointed in his inquiries, his imagination took a shrewder guess, and he directed his course to the gaming-house. He arrived there just after Murrell had gone, and was about returning home, when he stumbled on the scene we have described. The instant he beheld the figure of a man, rising from a prostrate form, he judged him to be his partner. He was struck with this thought more readily, perhaps, because his accomplice was uppermost in his mind, and being cool and self-collected, easily assured himself of the fact, despite the darkness.

On their way to their hotel, Crenshaw gave a history of his trip, concluding his narrative by declaring that he had done nothing in the way of *speculation*, and that, so far as money was concerned, he was "*dead flat.*"

The desperate state of their finances, therefore, obliged the assassins to set themselves to work in looking up some new design; so, on the following morning, they started out to take a professional survey of the town, with a view of selecting some place for a speedy depradation.

In the course of their perambulations they walked down to the water-side, and as they were loitering about, Murrell observed the mate of a fine brig, whom he had met two or three times before, in one of the public houses that he was in the habit of frequenting. Murrell accosted his acquaintance with a cheerful salutation, and introduced his companion. A conversation ensued, which, after continuing a few minutes, was suddenly broken off by the seaman asking them on board his vessel to take a glass of wine.

The invitation was unhesitatingly accepted, and the robbers, following their nautical host to his snug cabin, were soon engaged in discussing a substantial lunch, and a bottle of the finest Santa Cruz. A pleasant hour passed away without leaving an impression of its length, and the mate kept doing his best, with true seaman-like hospitality, to make his guests unconscious of the lapse of time. At length, however, they arose to go, but just as they were about to leave the cabin, a descending figure darkened the companion-way, and for the moment interrupted their intention.

The new comer inquired for the captain, but on being informed that he would not be on board until day-break in the morning, untied a silk handkerchief, which he carried in his hand, and taking from it a small canvass bag, firmly tied and sealed, handed it to the mate, with the direction to take it under his especial charge, as it contained a sum of fourteen hundred dollars in gold, which were to be delivered according to directions already in possession of the captain. Assuring his visitor that he might rely upon the safety of the parcel, the mate took the bag and opening his state-room door, unlocked his trunk, and deposited the treasure within it.

No portion of this scene was lost to the two robbers. Exchanging glances with each other as they saw the parcel disposed of, which expressed a conjoint intention, they lingered till the stranger left the cabin, and then insisted on returning the politeness of their entertainer by requiring him to take a drink with them at a neighbouring public house.

The mate accepted the invitation and accompanied them on shore, and while drinking at the tavern, Murrell proposed that he should take a parting turn with him about town that evening.

The mate at first refused, on the ground that the vessel must be got under weigh by daybreak, when it was necessary he should be wide awake for duty; but, being pressed, yielded his objections, and made an appointment for eight o'clock in the evening. The parties then separated, with strong injunctions to each other to be upon the spot.

As soon as the robbers were left alone they arranged a plan for the robbery of the vessel, and Crenshaw, who was quite adept in the *screwman's* art, purchased some stout wire and a file, to fashion a picklock, in case the keys, in his possession, should not be adapted to his purpose.

The time of the appointment came round, and Murrell met the mate, making an excuse for his friend not coming with him, but telling him that if he did not arrive in a few minutes, they would find him in half an hour at a certain house in the quarter of the town to which they were going.

In the meantime, Crenshaw, who had procured a trusty accomplice to assist him, had proceeded to the vessel, and, as soon as the mate departed, sent his assistant on board the brig to decoy the watch on shore. The artifice succeeded, and slipping on board, as soon as the vessel was deserted, the robber soon mastered the padlock which secured the cabin-door, descended, and with equal facility unlocked the state-room door. The old fashioned sea-chest presented no obstacle to the further prosecution of his purpose, and in five minutes from the time he stepped upon the deck, he was on shore again, in possession of the prize, and with every door locked, and restored to the same order as before.

He looked in at the tavern where his assistant still held the sailor in conversation, for the purpose of giving him a signal that the work was done, and then striking up into the town, arrived at the original place of appointment before Murrell and the mate had left to seek him elsewhere. He good naturedly received the playful chiding of the seaman at his tardiness, and replying to it with a humorous excuse, the trio set out upon their evening jaunt. It is but necessary to say that the frolic was designedly prolonged till daylight by the robbers, who then released their deluded friend, that he might hurry on board and get the brig to sea.

They never heard of him again, so the probability was, that in his eagerness to make up for lost time, he never thought of the precious deposit he had placed in his chest, until he got upon the open sea.

The sum which they now had in their possession placed them in comfortable ease again, and they had the good sense to decide on bidding an immediate adieu to Mobile, that they might not leave that sum, among the rest which had been wasted on the vain and unprofitable delights of the town. They, therefore, started up the river, and taking its eastern fork, where the Mobile branches into the Alabama and Tombigbee, pursued a northern journey to Monroeville.[1] There they spent three days, during which time they purchased two strong and fleet travelling horses, and then struck for the eastern part of the State, in that mode of journeying which is best adapted to those who are seeking for adventure.

What happened to them, and what exploits they performed, in the next three months, were of too little moment to bear a record; but at the end of that time we find them both in the eastern part of Alabama, in the centre of a section which was violently agitated by the apprehension of a threatened servile insurrection. Several negroes had been detected in clandestine assemblages, and some who had been surprised and taken into custody, confessed to an organized plan for a rising on a stated day. The country was in a state of the most complete alarm. All negroes were forbidden to be seen

---

1. Monroeville is the county seat of Monroe County, Alabama, located northeast of Mobile. In later years, it was the hometown of twentieth-century writers Truman Capote and Harper Lee. Monroeville was the fictional setting for the town of Maycomb in Lee's book *To Kill A Mockingbird*.

abroad after dark, and armed patrols of anxious citizens were established in the towns where the terror was at its greatest height. What added to the horror of the design was, that a general conflagration was to be the signal for the universal butchery, and the last act of the fearful citizen, on retiring to bed, was to glance out upon the darkness, to assure himself that the sign of death had not been kindled in the sky.

Though circumscribed in their operations by the close observation which was bestowed upon all strangers during this period of general consternation, the two robbers did not fail to find opportunities for plunder, and on one occasion, while thus engaged, involuntarily brought the popular terror to its climax by accidentally setting on fire a store which they were plundering. The doubts of the most reluctant minds were then convinced of the reality of the plot, and a reward of one thousand dollars was publicly offered to any person who should catch a negro in the act of firing a dwelling, or an out house of any description whatever. As soon as Murrell saw this proclamation, it struck his subtle and atrocious mind that he might win the reward by contriving a circumstance and preparing a victim to meet its stipulations. Filled with this fell purpose, he cast his eye upon a negro slave of vicious character whom he knew to have received a severe punishment at the hands of a planter living a short distance from the town, and determined to make him the instrument as well as the victim of his diabolical design.—Contriving to meet him in a private place, he gave the simple African a bottle of rum, and informed him that he wanted him to perform a piece of service, for which, if properly accomplished, he would remunerate him largely. The negro took a liberal draught of the liquor as an evidence of his will to accept the earnest, and then attentively listened to the white man's proposition.

Murrell commenced by detailing a log catalogue of injuries which he pretended to have received at the hands of the oppreser of his listener. The eyes of the malevolent serf flashed as he listened to the artful tie of fabricated wrongs, and breaking in upon the story, he […]aved of the stripes which entitled him to an equality of hate. Affecting an astonishment and horror which inflamed the negro's mind anew, he then bluntly told him that he was desirous of satisfaction on his enemy, and that if he would help him to it, he would make him master of a sum that would suffice to buy his freedom. Actuated by the double motive of revenge and hope, and stimulated by the feverish potion he had so freely used, the wretched dupe declared himself ready to do any thing that should be demanded of him; and when Murrell gave him as his task the firing of one of the planter's barns, that very night, he agreed to the fatal proposition without a moment's hesitation.

It was already near dark at the time matters were brought to this condition, and the robber perceiving that his instrument was in the proper mood to effect his purpose, insisted on his setting out upon his enterprise at once. He then furnished him with the articles necessary for the firing, and started him off, bidding him conceal himself in the vicinity of the building to be destroyed, and not apply the match till the rising of the moon. The tempter and his victim then separated; the latter to the fulfillment of his dangerous task, and the former with the completion of the business which he had so successfully begun.

Crenshaw was awaiting the result of Murrell's interview with the negro, and as soon as he ascertained its complete success, posted off alone to a justice of the peace, and disclosed the imaginary particulars of a plot which he assumed to have detected in the most miraculous manner. He then asked for a few trusty assistants, and taking charge of the expedition by virtue of his supposed knowledge of all its parts, he set out towards the plantation which was to be the scene of the negro's exploit.

Dismounting and tethering their horses at a convenient distance from the plantation, Crenshaw and his followers crept along the hedges toward the barn which the former had indicated as the intended place of meeting for three or four conspirators. Halting within two or three hundred yards of the building, under cover of a clump of trees, they looked carefully at their weapons, and then gradually approached till they should get near enough to observe the true condition of the field.

The arrival was well timed, for just as they were within a few yards of the building, a lurid light flared through the chinks, and in the midst of a heavy roll of smoke the deluded incendiary rushed forth: not to escape, but to fall into the arms of enraged and relentless captors.

The next morning, the negro was arraigned and conjured to discover his accomplices. It was in vain he told his story of the subtle white man who had incited him to the act of fatal desperation, and protested that his plotting had no wider scope. The fabrication was esteemed so clumsy, that no one for a moment thought of seeking for the imaginary tempter, and by a universal vote the captive perished at the stake.

In three days afterwards the wretches who so coldly had contrived his doom, fingered the reward of blood, and left the place.

CHAPTER VI.

New designs of Murrell—He plans a general servile insurrection—Views of marriage—Another exploit in negro stealing—Robbery of the mail—Separation of the robbers—Exploits at horse stealing—Conviction—Sentence—Release, and commencement of the second era of his crimes.

The remainder of the proceeds of the robbery of the brig, the avails of the recent burglary, and the blood-money of the deluded negro, added together, made the robbers the joint possessors of a sum of over three thousand dollars, and contented with their new estate they resolved to turn their footsteps toward the north, and reward themselves for the exertions by a brief period of indulgence in the fascinations of the gayer and more populous cities in that quarter. Assassins though they were, they still were human to the enticements of social joys; and each, as he secretly contemplated the sum he was individually possessed of, prized it chiefly for its capacity to purchase those debasing but intoxicating pleasures, which only can be had for gold. This was Crenshaw's entire view; but Murrell's mind, though directed mainly to the same point, took a more comprehensive range. He contemplated the application of a portion of his treasure to bringing his younger brother,[1] then about sixteen, to Madison county, Tennessee, that he might make him a companion, and induct him in the mysteries of the regular profession. He also had another thought, and strange as it may seem, it was a thought of love. He remembered with as much gratitude as his vitiated nature was capable of, the unremitting attentions at his feverish bedside, of a female servant at a hotel, in Columbia, Tennessee, and in connection with the idea of sending for his brother, he determined to get married, and to establish himself permanently in Columbia county,[2] so that he might not only acquire a local respectability, but become thereafter a resident director of the movements of others, instead of continuing to take the hardships and hazard of personal adventures as before. His brother, as he had recently learned, was still in Middle Tennessee, and would be glad to accept his invitation, and he could calculate with tolerable certainty upon the consent of the mistress of his thoughts, as before leaving her he had placed her in a condition which

1. Murrell's younger brother was Jeffrey George Murrell, born in 1813. He was later described as someone "of lude habits and evil conversation" as he lived with a woman who was not his wife and they operated a "disorderly bawdy house" in Williamson County in 1828. Lal Penick, *Great Western Land Pirate*, 13–14.

2. This would be Maury County, not "Columbia county."

would make a permanent and public connection between them, a boon on his part, rather than a matter of hesitation and favor upon her. Dwelling upon the above ideas as the basis of his future intentions, his mind resolved a thousand inferior views as incidental to his intended state, the main and most important of which was, the determination that when he became established in his new neighborhood, as the reputable head of a family, to devote himself assiduously to politics, and by earning a position in the predominant party in the county, to surround himself with an influence which would protect him and his friends in case they should become openly obnoxious to the law.

It was a shrewd thought, and one which, since the period of his wise adoption of it, has been the frequent resource of many a desperate and unscrupulous rogue, in the more refined and populous sections of the country.

Thought begets thought, and the brain of Murrell, roused from the temporary torpor which had followed its previous excessive action, was not content with the settlement of one design alone, but having broken through its first confine, ranged into a wider field, and in its fervor grasped speculations, the magnitude of which, while they struck their master for an instant with surprise, appeared in the next moment to be suggested by the very energy of inspiration. The fate of the negro who had perished at the stake, and the recollection of the terror which the supposed plot among the blacks had spread far and wide throughout the section of country which he was just leaving, introduced to him the thought that was to be the leading design of his after life. This was to excite a universal insurrection throughout the whole of the slave-holding states, and to use the confederacy which he had commenced to frame, to make the rising general and simultaneous. His calculations were, that in three years he might effect secret articles with some seven or eight hundred men, who, from their locations in different portions of the varied States, might instigate the necessary servile disaffection, and finally, when it burst into the climax, take advantage of the consternation to rush upon the cities, burst open the banks, and plunder without stint. Each man was to act in the crisis as if he had no concert with the rising, or even with an accomplice, so that his conduct might only be attributed to the impulse of a base and sordid spirit, taking advantage of an hour of rapine. The general spoil was, however, to be collected together, and divided in common, as soon as a division might be safe.

Wild and impracticable as this gigantic scheme appeared to be, it was seriously adopted by Murrell, and the records of his western country, which is still fresh with his exploits, bear living testimony of the progress which he made in its consummation.

Not daring to return to Tennessee by the way they came, in consequence of the murder of the young Carolinian trader, the robbers turned west to Columbus, Mississippi, with the intention of striking the great river as its junction with the Arkansas. They did not leave Alabama, however, without another exploit. This was the stealing of a negro, on the promise of conducting him to a free State, if he would but consent to let them sell him once—in which case they promised that they would also, in addition to his freedom, give him a part of the money obtained upon the sale. The negro agreeing to the plan, they ran him into the state of Mississippi, and sold him on the first day of their arrival, for six hundred dollars. Immediately upon this, they withdrew from the town, and concealing themselves all day in a creek bottom, repaired at night, with their horses, to a spot where they had appointed to meet the African. They found him waiting with an anxiety that was not entirely unmixed with a mistrust of their return, and bidding him mount his horse instanter, the trio pushed on with desperate speed, and were soon far away from what they now considered a dangerous vicinity.

They rode nearly all the night, and after having accomplished twenty miles, hauled up at the door of a friendly speculator,* whom Murrell had been concerned with in several "jobs" in Tennessee. They were received with an overwhelming welcome, and indeed suffered from the excess of hospitality enforced upon them, by having their horses so much over fed that two of them foundered the next morning. In consequence of this mishap, they were obliged to postpone their journey for several days, instead of continuing it to the river as they had intended, after the refreshment of a single day's rest. During their detention at this place, however, their host, while on a visit to a village in the neighborhood, saw an advertisement of the stolen negro, and a minute description of the two men from whom he had been purchased.

This made affairs look unpleasant, and the robbers, as well as their host, felt that their danger was imminent. It was plain that the negro must be disposed of in some way or other, and that right speedily; and as for

* This was the common term for a professional depredator in the western country, at the time of which we write.

themselves, the night would have to be called upon to stand their friend, until they could escape into a region where the rumor of their offence was still unknown. But the first thing to be done was to get rid of the slave. With this view, therefore, they told him to prepare himself to continue his flight with them and then leading to the bank of a creek hard by, Crenshaw shot him thorough the head. This being done, they took out his entrails, and sunk his body in the bed of the stream. Returning to the house of the man, by whose advice the above act had been committed, they received from him the present of a fine grey horse, to supply the loss of one of their own, and thus provided, made their escape through the Choctow and Chickasaw nations, into Fayette county, Tennessee. There, after robbing the mail just as they met it crossing the line, they separated, in consequence of a disagreement; Murrell striking for Maury county, near the centre of the State, and Crenshaw making tracks for Memphis.

"The object of my jaunt to Columbia was defeated," said Murrell, in giving an account of this part of his history. "I went entirely to find the girl I intended to marry; but learning, on my arrival, that she had been dead and buried several months, I came directly back to Madison."

On arriving in Madison county, Murrell fell in with a young man named Carter,[3] who had for some time been a circuit preacher among the Methodists, and discovering that he was a shrewd eastern thief who had assumed religion for other purposes than the salvation of souls,

---

3. The 1830 Census for Madison County, Tennessee lists only two male Carters in the county: James Carter and John Carter. Whether one of these could be the man mentioned above is uncertain.

CRENSHAW AND MURRELL ROBBING THE MAIL.

formed a connection with him, and directed their joint attention to stealing horses and running them to the river counties for sale. They continued at this business for a considerable length of time, occasionally diversifying the pursuit, however, by making excursions to different parts of the neighboring country, for the purpose of playing the travelling preacher and of availing themselves of other depredations and amusements by that means.

"This man Carter," said Murrell, "was remarkably ingenious in the performance of every thing he undertook, and could turn off a sermon with as much ease and earnestness as if he had been regularly educated for the pulpit. It was from him I took my first lessons in divinity, and first received the notion of adopting the character of a clergyman to aid me occasionally in my speculations. Poor fellow. I lost him soon, however, for he went to New Orleans the first winter of our acquaintance, and died there of the fever."

Shortly after the departure of Carter to New Orleans, Murrell was detected in the theft [of] a splendid mare, and thrown into prison on the charge. He got bail on the day after his incarceration, and though the evidence against him was positive, and if a character that could not be questioned, he at once set himself to work to conjure means to overthrow it. He called on all his secret friends in the neighborhood with the intention of requiring from among them enough witnesses to prove an alibi, and would have inevitably been successful, had not the trial been forced on before his plans had been sufficiently arranged. As it was, he was taken by surprise, and, though he had witnesses enough and to spare, on whom he might freely call for any evidence whatever, he dared not risk the issue on their oaths for the danger of the contradictions which might arise out of their want of sufficient preparation.—The result was that he was convicted.

Being possessed of the ready means, however, he shifted the matter from court to court, through the period of a year; but finally, having run the gamut of all legal chances, the decision of the original court being sustained in every instance, he was obliged to follow the case back to the point from which it started, and undergo a sentence. The conclusion of this unfortunate speculation, therefore, was that he received a sentence to be publicly whipped, and to endure an imprisonment of three years.

The first portion of this award was a most bitter penalty for the proud convict to undergo, but comforting himself with the philosophical reflection that it was the first penalty he had ever paid, and was much less than he deserved for the tremendous unknown record that stood against him, he closed his mind to the sense of shame which should have been attendant on the degradation, and submitted to the animal infliction with the coldness of a stoic. The prison gates were then turned upon him, and for three years he did not step beyond its walls.

Though this incarceration upset all Murrell's favorite designs for the time, it did not altogether discourage them from his mind, but with a spirit which defied discouragement, and turned every thing within its reach to account, he secured an admission to the blacksmith's shop of the prison, that he might perfect himself in the business so necessary to the burglar's art. In addition to this aim he devoted his moments of respite from regular labor, to the study of the scriptures and a volume of sermons which he obtained, that he might be completely qualified, on his release, to assume the character of a divine, to the same degree of perfection as had elicited so profound an admiration from him in the case of his companion Carter. Thus we see that punishment, instead of bringing repentance to his hardened soul, only confirmed him in his wickedness, and left no impression on his mind except the necessity of additional precaution against detection in the future.

He, therefore, came out at the end of his term doubly hostile to the world, and doubly dangerous to it from the superior acuteness which had been given him by reflection.

As soon as he turned his back upon the prison walls, he set out for Memphis, where he was welcomed by a choice lot of his old companions, who greeted his reappearance by an evening revel, which was devoted entirely to the purpose of doing him honor.—His purse was stocked at once with liberal contributions from every member present, and in the encomiums which were passed upon his character and standing in the profession, he found an ample solace for all the sufferings and privations he had endured.

He had lost considerable ground, nevertheless, by his three years' seclusion from active life, and the ascendancy of fame which he had formerly possessed throughout a wide, but irregular confederacy, had passed, for the time, to other hands. It was necessary, therefore, that he should bestir himself to recover his position, and he knew that this could only be accomplished by a new series of personal exploits, which should revive the memory of his past career, and impress the fact that he was more capable of counsel and command than ever. Having resolved, therefore, to enter earnestly upon the journey-work of crime, and finding it necessary to select a special associate, he concluded to put in operation his intentions in relation to his younger brother, and thus, instead of dividing the fame of his achievements with one who might be made his rival, he would keep the charm confined entirely upon his own name. With this view, he wrote to his brother William,[4] directing him to leave his work, whatever it might be, and come to him at once; enclosing in the letter a sum of twenty dollars to enable him to comply with his request. This missive was dispatched, and in due time was affirmatively answered by the arrival of the young man himself.

After giving to the youth a few general directions, the main of which was, that he should do exactly as he told him, he purchased all the accoutrements necessary to their immediate purposes, and commenced his second era of adventures, by stealing two fine horses, and flying with him towards the Choctaw nation.

---

4. William Stith Murrell (born 1798) was the oldest child of Jeffrey and Zilpha (Andrews) Murrell. Like his younger brother, he was a convicted thief and counterfeiter. Lal Penick, *Great Western Land Pirate*, 13.

CHAPTER VII.

Arrival in the Choctaw country—Abduction of a negro family—The friendly Bayou—Embarkation—The effects of taking a cup too much—Murder of the old man—The journey's end—Sale of the captives—Life in New Orleans—Stand and deliver—The philosophy of popularity—Burglary on a Magistrate—The robbery of the young Kentuckian—Murrell's increasing fame—The effects of envy—The bloody affray.

We left Murrell and his younger brother, at the conclusion of our last chapter, skirting across the Tennessee line upon their stolen horses, and it is now our business to conduct them safely into the Choctaw country, which they had made the point of their immediate destination on setting out. Being possessed of some ready means, the brothers resolved to pause here for a time, and look about, with the intention of framing some new depredation, with which to signalize their visit to the locality, and to fill their pockets. An observing residence of four weeks was attended with the desired result; for in the course of that period the elder brother, with the superior address and fascinating eloquence for which he became so celebrated, had managed to ingratiate himself with a family of negroes, consisting of an old man and wife, and three sons, and to persuade them to consent to escape with him to Texas. The conditions by which he induced them to this agreement were, the promise that if they would work for him one year after they got to Texas, they should, at the end of that time, be set free, and be furnished with a certain sum of money to start them in the world upon their own hook.

Intoxicated with this alluring prospect, the simple old man placed himself and his family in the hands of the designing and unscrupulous robbers, who, taking advantage of the gloomy cover of a tempestuous night, set out with them for a run to the banks of the Mississippi. For two or three nights they made tolerable progress in their journey, but, while endeavouring to evade a threatened difficulty, by turning from the direct route, they got lost in the mazes of the Mississippi swamp. Here they foundered about for a length of time, involving themselves deeper and deeper in confusion at every turn, and to add to their alarm, as the geographical difficulties of their situation seemed to increase, the consumption of their entire magazine of provisions threatened them also with the fear of famine. At length, however, by one of those strokes of good luck, which would be called a providential interposition if it were directed to the relief of worthy characters, they fell upon a break in the labyrinth that let them out upon the banks of the mighty river of rivers. They were still, however, in a deplorable condition, for they had no craft to help them to the friendship of the stream, and the waters gave them no increase to their food, except the lizards, frogs, and other river vermin they could capture upon its banks.

Furiously, cursing their ill luck, Murrell ranged in a towering passion up and down the stream, and many a time did he meditate the consolation of his rage, by the immolation of the dusky captives, whose care had cost him these misfortunes. At length he found an Indian trail through the bottom, and following it closely, had the fortune to fall upon a bayou which led into the river, and which contained a large and strong canoe, securely fastened to the bank. Breaking this loose, without stopping to reason on the rights of persons and of property, they rowed the boat to the river, and it being nearly dark, all embarked, and soon found themselves descending the rushing stream to New Orleans.

In the early part of the evening they boarded a flatboat, and obtained, by purchase, such fresh provisions as they wanted, and a quantity of rum to compensate them for the fatigue and privations which they had so recently undergone. In the abundance of their restored content, the robbers allowed the inspiring cordial to make the circle of the boat, and out of consideration, as it would appear, for his position as head of the family, allowed the sable patriarch a double share. The gift proved fatal to the simple recipient, for the enemy which he put so incautiously into his mouth robbed him of the prudence which had hitherto maintained, and betrayed him into several expressions of mistrust, which showed that he had long suspected that the robbers intended to sell him and his family in New Orleans, in contravention of their solemn promises to take them into Texas.

The Murrells exchanged signs as these dangerous evidences escaped the old man's lips, and as his conduct increased in crimination and unruliness, they decided that it would not be safe to keep him with them any longer. Coming, therefore, to the fatal resolution of depriving him of life, they landed the next day by the side of an island in the river, and the elder brother, leaving William in charge of the boat, took the old fellow with him, on pretence of going round the point of the island, to seek a proper place to catch a lot of fish. Unconscious of his impending fate, the old man readily consented to the task, and the robber and his victim were soon out of sight of the boat and its crew. Murrell trudged along with the old man in an apparently pleasant humor, until he got him upon the opposite shore, when considering the place fit for the deed, and sufficiently distant from the boat to prevent the report of his pistol being heard, he fell a step or two behind, and placing the weapon to the back of the old man's head, scattered his brains in the air, and laid him dead at his feet.

There was but one measure more to take to finish the business with professional perfection, and that was to conceal the body. This was done in an instant by ripping open the belly and tumbling it inot the stream to find the bottom—never to return. Having thus finished his bloody job, the miscreant kneeled down on the bank of the river, washed his clothes, and returned to the boat. In answer to the affected surprise of his brother at his coming back alone, he replied, that the old man had tumbled into the river, while he was too far away to afford him succor, and had drowned. Adding to his account a few expressions of regret, he consoled the wife and sons with the reflection, that what was done could not be recalled, and then ordered the boat off into the stream. The old woman and the boys shudderingly suspected the truth, but conscious of the peril of avowing their suspicions, said not a word beyond the low and bitter moans which even brutality itself could not forbid them. Fortunately they were near their journey's end, and that very night landed on the western bank of the river, about fifty miles from New Orleans. Rejoicing to set foot upon the land again, they willingly followed their captors into the country, and were glad to allow themselves to be sold, without expressing a demur, for the purpose of securing a final and complete release from the dangerous ownership of their late piratical masters. The proceeds of the joint sale of the negroes amounted to nineteen hundred dollars, six hundred being allowed for each of the boys, and but one hundred for the old woman.

From the place where this latter transaction took place, the Murrells went to New Orleans, where, being tolerably supplied with funds, they both assumed the most elegant apparel, and lived with the extravagance of gentlemen of the most extensive means. Their gay habits, and the profusion with which they squandered their money, attracted the attention of the loose characters and observing speculators of the swamp, and it was not long before two of the most enterprising of the latter class, named Haines and Phelps, determined on putting the dashing brothers in a pecuniary purgation. Lying in wait till he should quit the house of a noted courtesan, into which he had been traced, these two fellows were at length rewarded for their exemplary patience, by seeing the object of their cares turn the corner in the direction of their ambush, in his road toward his hotel.

"Your money or your life," cried Haines, springing from his concealment, and thrusting a pistol into Murrell's face.

"Yes, your money or your life," added Phelps on the other side, and at the same time checking a movement of the desperate Tennessean's arm as it instinctively twitched towards the weapon on his bosom.

"Well, gentlemen," said Murrell, after a brief pause and with a quiet and complacent smile, "Since it appears from your manner that you cannot be refused, why, here's my pocket book with pleasure. It contains enough to compensate you for your pains: and I beg you to believe me when I tell you, that I am compensated for its loss by the knowledge that it will be bestowed upon men of spirit, who do credit to the profession to which I myself belong."

"What is that you say?" exclaimed Haines, with unfeigned surprise—"are you of the *cross*?"

"Behold the sign!" answered Murrell, making a slight motion of the hand.

"Enough!" said Haines. "Damn my eyes, if I ever rob a brother chip. You are free, comrade, and we have now to apologise for the inconvenience we have put you to. You must, however, lay this movement entirely to your flash rigging and your handsome jewelry. We have been watching you and the young fellow that was with you in the early part of the evening for some days, and concluded you were wealthy dandies, who might be relieved of your surplus cash, and no great harm done. But as,

I said before, since you are *of us*, here's your wallet and here's my hand." "Ah, I feel the sign again!" continued the speaker in a tone of gratification, as his palm closed with that of the negro stealer. "And now, comrade, let us know who you are."

The surprise and admiration of the highwaymen can scarcely be conceived, when Murrell acquainted them that he was the famous northern hero, whose name had long been an emulative watchword among the "River Rats," "Queersmen," "Trampers," "Smashers," "Fences," and other freebooters and speculators of the west, and in the warmth of their enthusiasm, they swore that he must repair with them to Mother Surgick's, and celebrate the fortunate event of their acquaintance in a night of joyous revelry.

Finding it impossible to refuse an invitation of his new friends, and, being introduced by them to two more of the same class, whom they found at the bagnio, they spent the night in a riotous disorder, which was quite in keeping with their characters, the place, and the event which it was designed to celebrate.

These new acquaintances proved highly beneficial to Murrell for the accomplishment of his future views. He had confined his operations heretofore, almost entirely to the upper and south-eastern country, and had consequently never extended his connections with the superior confederacies, whose nucleus and *tele du pont* were at New Orleans. This last and most necessary connection was now accomplished. Haines and Phelps were men of note among their class, and introduced the famous Tennessean to all the resident robbers in New Orleans, and likewise placed him in possession of the names and watchwords of every marauder in their clans, who lived upon the Mississippi and its tributary streams. New fields of enterprise were thus opened to him; bolder and more daring views broke upon his mind. In the enlarged scope which his vision had received, he grasped with ease the means of carrying out his ultimate designs, and, in the gratifying prospect, his ambition felt the impulse of a freshened stimulation.

To properly begin, however, he saw that his first object must be, to acquire a popularity among his new associates, and, through it, to gain the position of influence and command to which he aspired. His knowledge of the world, and particularly of the class among whom he was thrown, made him master of the secrets which lead to general favor, and which, if coupled with practical ability and personal daring, seldom fail both to win admiration and insure control. Acting, therefore, upon the shrewd deductions of a sound experience, he devoted himself to the arts that please, as assiduously as a politician. He maintained an urbanity of manners, whose smug dissimulation never curdled with a frown; the liberality of his personal expenditures were unbounded; his convivialities were generous and unaffected; and in short, he soon won the character of a most splendid fellow from all who were brought into familiar contact with him. It now but remained for him to perform some showy exploit, to give this sentiment the character of deference and admiration. He therefore projected several bold designs, which, with the assistance of his brother, he intrepidly carried into execution, and which, in addition to gaining for him ample means, also conferred upon him shining fame. One of these was a hazardous burglary upon the house of a magistrate, in the commission of which, he tied the owner to his bed, and lectured him on the philosophy of obedience, while his brother tumbled out a lot of costly silver plate before his eyes, and thrust it into a bag already bursting with other plunder. Having waited till his brother had got safely out, the elder robber backed from the room with the most polite adieus, complimenting the astounded owner, as he retired, on the improvement of his manners during the latter part of their brief interview.

Another exploit, equally daring, but evincing more address, was the robbery of a young Kentuckian of fortune, who boarded at the same hotel, and of whose superabundant cash Murrell had determined to possess himself, before the former left the city. Ingratiating himself with the young man, he at length became his companion, and led him off frequently upon evening expeditions of pleasure. During many of these jaunts and midnight returns to their hotel, Murrell might have had his unconscious friend robbed, if he had chosen; but determined to make the matter a thorough one, he wisely waited an opportunity which he could induce the youth to carry all his money about his person. At length he hit upon a scheme. He contrived a dispute between the young Kentuckian and one of his own secret associates, about a matter of fact, in relation to which, the latter was designedly allowed to have the strong position. The bait took, the controversy grew warm in proportion to the positiveness with which the accomplice maintained his untenable assumptions, and finally, as was natural in the case, the Kentuckian, out of all patience, pulled out his pocket-book, and offered to back his opinion with a bet of one hundred dollars.

"I'll not bet you *one* hundred, but I'll bet you a thousand!" said the designing disputant, with a supercilious toss of the head.

"I have not a thousand with me," said the young man.

"Well, then, you can put up a forfeit, if you haven't," coolly returned the other.

The excited youth closed with the proposal at once, and both parties selecting Murrell as stake-holder, put up fifty dollars a-side in his hands to bind a bet of one thousand, the remainder of which it was agreed should be staked that very night by eleven o'clock.

It was already nearly ten, and as the morrow was to decide the pretended wager, Murrell and the young man started off for their hotel to get the money. Obtaining the necessary amount from the landlord, in whose care the stranger had deposited his funds, they set out on their return. It is hardly necessary to say, that in their journey back they were intercepted in their lonely route by Haines, Phelps, and two more of the clan, who, being parties in the plot, robbed Murrell and his companion of every dollar, as well as everything valuable upon their persons. The Kentuckian raved like a madman at his loss; but though he cursed the whole city, and everything that was in it, in the bitterness of his heart, he did not, for a single instance, suspect his treacherous friend. On the contrary, when bidding him farewell a few days afterward, he condoled with him upon their common misfortune, and closed with an invitation to the robber to call upon him in case he ever should find himself in his neighborhood.

The manner in which this whole thing had been concocted and carried through, established Murrell's fame beyond approach as a man of superior address; and his previous achievements, with their corresponding evidences of energy and intrepidity of another order, stamped him also as a man of universal parts.

The reward for this was the general admiration and profound respect of all the rogues of the district, but this tribute found an offset in the envy of those aspiring spirits whose dark splendors he obscured, and across whose road to power his rapid progress cast a gloomy shade. Among these, a man named Drayton was the most hostile and the most embittered. A sullen scowl took possession of his face when some dashing depredation of the Tennessean was the theme of the animated secret gatherings, and while it extracted an involuntary tribute of applause from the perverted souls around him, it fell like worm-wood upon his heart, and made it shrink from the generous infection. There was a double cause for this antagonism.—Murrell had not only shoved him in the shade within the band, but had also cheated him of the wanton sunshine of his sweetheart's eyes. All this had been done by the hero without inimical design, it is true; but still it was done, and baffled ambition and disappointed love do not usually pause to analyse the justness of their wrongs, when they can find the sterner consolation of revenge.

Murrell had noticed Drayton's sullen mood toward him, but, attributing it only to a pique which could not long withstand the force of his good nature and his insidious address, passed it by without conferring up on it the slightest measure of regard. This state of things existed for some weeks, Murrell enduring, with a politic good nature, all the blunt rebuffs to his frequent friendly overtures. But the crisis was approaching, when his power of restraint was to receive its final trial. Himself, his brother, Haines and Phelps, set out one evening for a frolic in the *Swamp*, and, in the course of the night, stopped at a bagnio where they found Drayton and two others. Murrell saluted Drayton as he entered the room, but the latter did not even honor him with a recognition. The slight, though trifling, came with a double sting in consequence of the presence of the females who observed it, and Murrell, flushed with wine, half turned upon his heel to seize his enemy by the throat. Mastering his rage, however, he sat down, and, pulling a female on his lap, sought to drive the insult from his mind. The evasion was unfortunate, for no sooner had the Tennessean clasped her waist, than Drayton, who, it appears, had some previous claims to the wanton's attentions, rose from his seat, and seizing her by the arm, slung her across the room, and then stood confronting his rival with a malignant and insulting stare.

This was too much for Murrell, and springing to his feet, he discharged a blow into his antagonist's face which sent him reeling headlong to the floor. In an instant the room was in an uproar, and taking advantage of the momentary separation by the rushing of mediators in between, Murrell stripped off his coat and neck-cloth for a fight. Then, tearing into the circle like a wild beast bounding into a jungle for its prey, he grasped his enemy by the throat. A desperate struggle ensued, which at length extended to the friends of both sides, and knives being drawn in the heat of the affray, the combat soon became as bloody as it was desperate. From the time it took this change, the contest lasted but a minute, when Drayton fell before the trenchant blade of the Tennessean, fatally wounded.

Fear treads upon the heels of crime, and the instant the negro-stealer saw the measure of his vengeance was complete, he turned to fly. He rushed toward the door, but already the buzz of gethering voices was heard outside, and warned him to seek some other issue. Turning back, he dashed up stairs, and bursting into a room upon a second floor the window of which looked out upon an open lot, he threw up the sash, and putting his knife between his teeth in case he should want to overcome resistance to his escape, he lowered himself outside, and dropped to the ground. No one opposed his way, and leaping a fence in the rear, he was soon lost in the gloom of an adjoining lane.

CHAPTER VIII.

The friendly receiver—The orthodox disguise—Success as a preacher—a wolf in the fold—Natchez—Descent upon the trinkets—Vicksburg—Cincinnati—Re-unions—The southern tramp—Hymeneal views—Marriage—Resumption of a roving life—The Tipton boy—Danger on the steamboat—Lucky escape—Ingenious and daring artiface—The bloody termination of the train of crime.

Diving through the most obscure avenues of the town, Murrell at length reached an unfrequented portion of the river's bank, when, considering himself beyond the danger of immediate pursuit, he cast himself, spent and breathless, on the shore. Rising, after a momentary pause, he threw his bloody weapon into the turbid stream, and stooped down and washed from his hands and face the sanguine stains of the affray.

The conflict between himself and Drayton was a most unfortunate affair, and, viewing in any phase he might, was sure to result, more or less, disastrous to his interests. He did not dread an information from the hands of Drayton's friends, for, however bitterly they might resent their leader's overthrow, he was well aware that their professional souls would disdain a legal vengeance; but the fight had taken place in the presence of several abandoned women, who, in their eagerness to acquit themselves of any blame, would tell every detail, and not only give the name of its principal actor, but also put the officers upon his haunts. He, therefore, dared not go to his hotel, even for a change of clothes; and, added to the other evils of his predicament, he found himself with but two or three dollars in his pocket. In this dilemma he resolved, after a few moments' pause, to run half a mile further up the bank to the house of a friendly speculator, and obtain from him the necessary clothing and means to get away. The man whom he selected was just the one who was calculated, above all others, to supply his wants, for he was a receiver of stolen goods, who had obtained many a profitable "*swag*" from Murrell's hands, and his ample store of second-hand apparel was sure to furnish a ready and complete supply to his fugitive robber's wants.

Taking from this man a prim-cut coat, broad brim hat, half a dozen white neck cloths, a bible, a double-barrelled pistol, and a heavy knife, Murrell stood prepared to play the preacher or the devil, as the fluctuations of his fortune might require; and after storing them away in a small valise, and obtaining a sum of twenty dollars from the receiver, as a loan, he sat down and wrote a letter, directing his brother to meet him in the latter part of the following month at Natchez. He and his friend then started for the shore, and taking a boat, shot down the river with the current, and at midnight parted on the opposite bank—the receiver to return to the city, and the robber to set out toward the north, in the guise of a preacher of the Gospel, and with a forged certificate of probation in his pocket. Availing himself of the information he had obtained during his recent residence in New Orleans, of the haunts of the associates of the clans to which Haines and Phelps belonged, Murrell found in Ibberville[1] a friendly gang of counterfeiters, who, on a presentation of his credentials, readily admitted him to their confidence, and supplied him with a large amount of counterfeit money to aid him in his northern progress. In return, they only asked in payment for the boodle, his personal due bill, which they filed among the rest of their accounts, to await the chance when his affairs should be in a more flourishing condition. With three or four hundred dollars, mostly in spurious tens and twenties, the desperate adventurer then set out again, so as to be in Natchez at the appointed time to keep his appointment with his brother. He still kept up his character of Methodist preacher, and, during the course of his journey, delivered several sermons, and indeed lost no opportunity of ingratiating himself with the godly of each village, by a passing exhortation to sinners to seek the blessings of redeeming grace. The result of these amiable little pauses was generally the passing off of several counterfeit notes, which, in consequence of their coming from the very pouch of sanctity itself, were never mistrusted for a moment.

An instance of the ingenious manner in which he accomplished these profitable deceptions may be amiss, as

---

1. Ibberville Parish, Louisiana, located south of Baton Rogue.

an illustration of his tact. A travelling Methodist, by the name of Marvin, who had chanced to be present at one of his discourses, was so charmed with his elouquence and striking energy of manner, that he waited til he had descended from the pulpit, and, after complimenting him upon his sermon, insisted that he should accompany him to his town, and preach there on the following Sunday. Murrell readily accepted the invitation, and for the next three days the pious brethren travelled amiably together, the robber stopping now and then to make a discourse and keep up what he called the Lord's work, but really to spiritedly maintain the outlines of his assumed character. The travellers arrived at a Saturday afternoon in Marvin's town, and that worthy man, proud beyond measure of his travelling companion, started out, immediately on their arrival, among the pious notabilities of the village, and made arrangements for a prayer meeting at his house that very night. The exercises passed off with the spirit and fervor usual to such gatherings, and the preacher guest, in addition to the congratulations which were heaped upon him for his admirable conjurations, received from the stationary preacher of the place, the offer of the use of his pulpit on the following day.

The offer was accepted, and it is hardly necessary to say that the clerical marauder fully maintained, with the mass of the congregation, the impressions which he had excited among the leaders of the flock on the previous evening. After the sermon was over, the congregation flocked around the youthful wonder, with an admiration little short of idolatry, and invitations to sojourn for a few days with this one and with that, were showered upon him on all sides. He excused himself, however, by representing his engagements as imperative; that he was obliged to leave on the following (Monday) morning, and was pledged to remain with brother Marvin during his stay.

When about to start, on the following day, he pulled out his pocket-book, and, assuming an embarrassment which was natural to the situation of one who wished to be thought neither mean nor ostentatious, hinted his desire to make some pecuniary compensation for the trouble the household had been put to in his accommodation, but perceiving that Marvin seemed to be hurt at the idea, he drew forth a spurious twenty dollar note, and holding it out, with a frank and apologetic smile, remarked:

"Well, brother Marvin, I'll tell you what you can do for me. I am out of change entirely, and you can, perhaps, oblige me by breaking me a twenty dollar bill. I dislike to offer a note of that size for a night's lodging, where I am not known, for fear it may be ascribed to a desire to avoid payment altogether. The world, alas! judges all our acts invidiously, and I, therefore, always scrupulously avoid doing any thing that may, even by the remotest implication, be tortured into a questionable motive. The honor of the Lord's name is in our hands, Brother Marvin, and the spotless purity of the ministry is but second in importance to the redemption of souls."

Impressed more profoundly than ever with the refined piety of his guest, Brother Marvin was but too happy to oblige him, and running to his wife, got his keys, and commenced counting out the change. Unfortunately he could not muster but seventeen dollars and a half; but after digging his fingers in his head, for a few moments, as if he sought the balance there, he suddenly jumped up, and running out, soon obtained the remaining portion of a neighbor. Though everything was now ready for his departure, Murrell still had some further designs upon his worthy host, which required a little more delay. He did not intend, after all the trouble he had in turning from his road, and sweating through so many exhortations, to let him off at so cheap a rate as twenty dollars: so, turning on his heel, as he got on the front stoop, he cast his eyes upon a splendid mottled colt in the yard, and admiring his points, inquired of Marvin if he had raised him.

"Yes; he was foaled mine," answered the Methodist. "He is thorough bred."

"Do you wish to dispose of him, Brother Marvin?"

"Well, I raised him for that purpose; but I don't know as I can get the worth of him in this part of the country. I have never been offered more than a hundred and fifty for him; but he is worth full a hundred dollars more."

"Indeed, I think he is; and if I had the money with me, you should have no further trouble to get rid of him."

"Well, brother, that need be no hindrance to a bargain between us," said Marvin, with a jacose expression at the idea of any stronger guarantee being required. "You can take him at 'two fifty,' and when we meet at our camp meeting next month, you can hand me the amount."

Upon this, Murrell took the animal, and having warmly embraced his hospitable hots, and imprinted a respectful kiss upon the cheek of sister Marvin, sprang upon the back of his blooded purchase, and frisked up the road, more like a young brigadier upon parade, than like one of the elect.

THE LAND-PIRATE TURNED PREACHER

In a few days after this transaction, Murrell arrived in Natchez, but instead of finding his brother awaiting him, as he expected, he received a letter from the youth, acquainting him with the fact that he was then still in prison on an arrest made on account of the affray in the brothel. The letter then gave a full account of all that had transpired since the time of the elder Murrell's escape. Drayton had not died, though he remained for several days in a most dangerous situation. Haines and himself, as well as Drayton, had been taken prisoners, but Phelps and the rest of the party had escaped. Haines had been pretty badly wounded, and the writer himself confessed to a serious gash on the side. The writer concluded by expressing his complete confidence in an early release, but adjured his brother not to venture back to New Orleans just then, on any account whatever, as his share in the transaction was well known, and great efforts had been made to find him.

This was unwelcome news for the elder brother, but, making the best of the matter, he sold his colt for two hundred dollars, and sent on one-third of the amount to his imprisoned kinsman, to aid in his release. At the same time, he also made a remittance to the receiver, in payment for the clothes obtained on the night of the escape, and likewise sent a small instalment, on account, to the counterfeiting firm at Ibbersville. Having paid this religious duty to his personal engagements, he resigned himself to relaxation, doffed his prim uniform, and sought a solace for his griefs in the riotous pleasures of the town.

After a few days of extravagant indulgence, he found himself, as was to be expected, out of money, when, reproaching himself for having wasted so precious a season, he virtuously resolved to fly from the fascinations of the place. Needing funds to get away, and not being over delicate when pricked on by absolute necessity, he stole a gold watch and chain from the mistress of a house in which he had been revelling over night, and a lot of trinkets from the girl with whom had a still more intimate relation, and with the proceeds of the lot took the boat for Vicksburg. He spent a few days at this place, and after sharing in the commission and proceeds of a burglary, started on again, leaving behind him, however, a letter to be sent to his brother, directing him to repair to Cincinnati immediately upon his discharge from prison in New Orleans. From Vicksburg, Murrell went carefully through the whole Mississippi country, making personal acquaintances with all the marauders and speculators whose names and locations had been given him by Haines and Phelps in New Orleans.

He at length reached Cincinnati, where he found a large number of his old friends to welcome him, and where, in two days after his arrival, he met his brother.

Having his views now fixed with renewed earnestness, upon a grand combination of the clan, he did not suffer himself to remain long in Ohio, but with the same purpose as had actuated him during the latter portion of his recent travel up the river, he took his brother, and set out upon a grand circuit through the country. We accordingly find the dangerous kinsman making a circuit, which, starting from Lexington, Ky., embraced Richmond, Va., Charleston, S.C., Augusta, Savannah, and Milledgeville, Ga., and from thence wound back to their old stomping ground in Williamson county, Tennessee.

The particulars of this long expedition have never been elicited in a sufficiently authentic or connected form for history, but we gain a general idea of the character of the journey by the following declaration of Murrell himself, made in conversation with a supposed confederate. "In all this route, we only robbed eleven men, but I preached some d—d splendid sermons, and by that means scattered a fine lot of counterfeit paper among the pious brethren."

Though the pecuniary proceeds of this trip were but small, the elder Murrell had accomplished his leading object, of forming a personal acquaintance of every professional marauder in the southern and western country, and in impressing them with respect for his abilities.

Feeling that his position had thus acquired an additional gravity and importance, he resolved to consummate the domestic designs which he had resolved upon once before, and become stationary by marriage. His character, in Madison county, did not stand tainted with any suspicion of dishonesty, and he justly thought that if he should sit down there, as the master of a permanent domestic establishment, he would enjoy a great deal more of comfort, and acquire, even in the eyes of his clansman, more respect and consideration, than if he continued to pursue a completely roving life. These views at this time urged themselves upon him with the greater force, from the fact that he had become interested in a very pretty girl in Madison, who was a sister of one of the most influential marauders of the southern country. Writing to this man, Murrell declared his wishes, and proposed for the girl's hand. He received in answer, a letter, under an enclosure introducing him to the object of the correspondence, and urging the connection upon the female party in the most earnest terms. Thus recommended, the suitor was successful. The pair were accordingly married,[2] whereupon Murrell hired a handsome little farm of thirty acres, and established himself upon it as a respectable housekeeper. Example is catching, and the whims of a superior mind are very often the law of inferior ones. The younger Murrell took the hymeneal infection, and in the month following his elder's nuptials, went off to Tipton county, and there annexed himself and settled down in like manner.

The elder brother's honeymoon lasted for six months, when finding his money waning to an ebb, he saddled his horse, took his pistols, and started off to Tipton to see his brother. When in the neighbourhood of William's residence, he fell in with a lively negro boy, whom he drew aside and tempted to abscond from his master, on the old terms of two or three sales, a division of profits, and liberty. The simple boy, unable to reject the fascinating hope, agreed, and made an appointment with the robber at a certain place on the following night. Enquiring of his brother, then, for an assistant, he was introduced to a trusty hand, whom he sent to keep the appointment in place of himself. This man ran the negro to the Mississippi river, and from thence to Natchez, and lodging him there, according to Murrell's directions, in the hands of a trusty speculator, returned to report the result of his expedition, and to receive his reward.

2. Murrell married Elizabeth Mangham in Williamson County, Tennessee in 1829. She and her family were not from Madison County. Lal Penick, *Great Western Land Pirate*, 25. Lal Penick notes that at some point, a marriage bond for the couple signed by Murrell was stolen from the neighboring Maury County Courthouse in Columbia. *Ibid*, 25fn.

The elder brother, having by his stay in the neighborhood ascertained all the movements of the owner of the boy, set out for Natchez, with full confidence in the safety of the job. Arriving there, he took possession of the negro, and transferring him at once on board a steamboat, sailed for New Orleans. Unfortunately for the marauder, there was a man on board who knew him well, and who went privately to the captain of the boat, and informed him that the showy, well-dressed passenger with the mulatto boy, was a notorious negro stealer, adding that he had no doubt that the boy in his possession had been dishonestly obtained. The captain devoured this information eagerly, and being of an avaricious character, at once decided upon taking possession of the slave, in the hope of seeing a reward offered for him on his return to the country. He also determined to lodge the negro stealer in prison, immediately on the arrival of the boat at New Orleans.

The sagacity of Murrell, without appearing to be awake, had detected the full measure of his danger. With a practised acuteness of observation, he had observed the informer immediately after he came on board, and watching him closely from that moment, had detected all his movements with the captain, and instinctively interpreted their meaning. Taking no notice therefore of the captain's sly withdrawal of the boy from the deck to his own state-room, he sauntered about the boat with apparent indifference, and chatted with several of the passengers to avoid the appearance of having taken the alarm. The captain relied upon arresting him when he should apply for the possession of the boy, but the negro stealer was too cunning to be easily caught, for no sooner had the boat in swinging into the pier touched a corner of the wharf, than he sprang on shore and slipped away without being observed.

Before an hour had elapsed, he was in the congenial company of Haines and Phelps, who after welcoming his re-appearance among their clan, assured him that he would experience no danger in remaining on the account of the old affray. Murrell then told these worthy friends what had occurred to him upon the river, and requested Haines to go on board the boat and see what disposition was to be made with the slave. Haines easily found the captain, and soon ascertained that he intended to keep the boy on board the boat, and when he started to take him up the country with him. This was enough for Murrell, and deciding on his plan with characteristic promptness, he immediately forged a bill of sale for the negro, purporting to have been made out in Tipton county, Tennessee, in favor of the fictitious name which he had given on the steamboat. Then telling Haines to get him a good witness and have him on hand at a moment's notice, waited for the afternoon of the starting of the boat to end the matter to his satisfaction.

The day came round, when boldly going to the Mayor, the robber obtained a process against the body of the captain for unlawfully detaining his property from his possession.

The officer who had the writ arrested the captain just as he was preparing to start his boat, and brought him and the negro forthwith before his Honor. Murrell then claimed the boy, produced the bill of sale and introduced the witness, who positively swore that he was present when the negro was purchased by the plaintiff, in

Tipton, Tennessee, and that he saw him pay the money and receive the bill of sale.

The astonished captain was thunderstruck with this evidence, and to the inquiries of the mayor, was only able to reply that he had *been informed* that the plaintiff was a negro stealer. Being unable, however, to produce any proof, and having admitted that he intended to keep the slave, he was mulcted with a heavy fine and twenty days imprisonment, and the possession of the negro was given to Murrell.

Rejoicing in his triumph, the daring swindler made the most of his success, by selling the boy on the following day for eight hundred dollars. In a few nights he stole him again, and placing him in the hands of the man who had acted as the witness to the bill of sale, sent him to one of the upper parishes, where he followed in a week afterward, and again resumed possession of him. The three then travelled together, Murrell in the character of a Methodist preacher, the false witness accompanying him as his overseer, and the negro as his slave.

Under these assumed disguises, the strange trio travelled through the state and sold the boy for a third time on the Arkansas river, for five hundred dollars. Concluding, after this transaction, that the boy's face was quite worn out, Murrell stole him for the last time, and delivering him into the hands of his friend, ordered him to finish the job by taking the wretched and unsuspecting boy to a swamp and blowing his brains out. The directions were followed to the letter, and with the consignment of the mangled body to the waters of the swamp, perished all evidences of their previous train of crime.

Thus ended this expedition, and after sharing that portion of the spoil which had accrued since leaving New Orleans, Murrell bade his fellow miscreant adieu, and hastened back to Madison to receive the welcome of his long neglected wife.

CHAPTER IX.

Murrell returns to Madison and makes himself very much at home—Employs his leisure in the Study of the Law and in the secret organization of the Mystic Clan—Gets tired of mere literary and scientific Pursuits, and sets out upon the road again—The Mysterious Crime—Fortunate Escape at Muscle Shoals—The Power of Attorney—Journey to New Orleans—Flight to Texas—Visit to Yucatan—The Old Catholic and his Niece—The Fate of Crenshaw.

The profits of his last trip, amounting as they did to a round one thousand dollars, enabled the land pirate, on his return home, to feel considerably at ease. With a prudence which was the result of previous experience, he laid out one half of that sum as a part purchase of his farm, and having, with a portion of the rest, added some stock and improvements, he sat down in his domestic garrison with as much self-gratulation and contentment as if his recent acquisitions were the legitimate returns of honest industry, instead of being the harvest of a detestable train of crime and an atrocious deed of blood.

For the purpose of giving a color of integrity to his condition he employed a hired man, and shared with him the labors of the farm; but though he made this the ostensible occupation of his time, he devoted himself principally to the attentive reading of some books of law which he had recently purchased at Randolph, and to carrying on an extensive correspondence with the influential speculators who were the recognized heads of the marauding clans in the various parts of the country. The books of law he had obtained with the view of rendering himself familiar with all the rocks and quicksands that lie in the path of crime, that he might not only know how to pilot himself through the perils which environ it, but that he might also "know the ropes" of legal technicality and quibble, that would save him from danger in the last resort. The object of his correspondence was for the double purpose of keeping up his professional presence and importance in all quarters, and likewise to urge the progress of the great scheme which had been the leading object of his fiendish ambition for the previous three years.

In speaking of this portion of his career Murrell remarked: "During this period of relaxation, my great project of exciting a rebellion among the negroes of the slave-holding states returned upon my mind with double force. I had never entirely lost sight of it from the moment of its first inception; but the necessities of business, and the difficulties of so great a combination, kept postponing the object from time to time. But during the period I speak of, I had nothing to do but study and to scheme; and as I revolved the project in my mind, it appeared more and more feasible of accomplishment at every step. I not only considered it the sure road to inexhaustible wealth, but I had some injuries to avenge and some animosities to gratify, and my blood warmed with the hope of being able one day to visit the pomp of the southern and western people in my vengeance, and of seeing their towns and cities one common scene of devastation!"

Having at length completed his plans, and being tired of inaction, he resolved to set out in search of an adventure that might keep up his credit, and at the same time replenish his wasting means. While hesitating whether to take a southern or northern course, he received a letter from an acquaintance in Moulton, Alabama, offering him a share in a profitable depredation which he had in mediation, and which he assured him was safe as it was feasible. This at once decided him, and he set out southward on the following day. In due time he arrived at Moulton and performed the enterprise.—What the exact nature of it was, never has transpired, though from the mystery which its chief actor maintained upon the subject it is fair to presume that it comprehended a most atrocious deed. Suffice it, that the joint proceeds of the affair were very large, and with his share in his pocket, Murrell turned to the north, and started off for home. It appears, however, that shortly after he set out he was sharply pursued, and would have been overtaken, had he not opportunely struck the southern bank of the Tennessee river, at the head of the Muscle Shoals, and escaped by plunging his jaded steed into the stream, and swimming to the opposite bank. His pursuers, fortunately for him, were on foot, and being unable to follow for want of a boat, were forced to take the last chance for arresting his flight, by discharging their rifles at him. Escaping safely to the opposite shore, he took the road to Florence, and had the good fortune to reach the house of a friendly speculator shortly after night-fall.

Murrell remained with this friend for three or four days, and finding, at the end of that time, that the danger had pretty well blown over, bade him adieu, and on horseback again, once more turned his face towards home.

While journeying along during the first afternoon of his departure, he heard himself hailed by name from the road side, and turning in the direction of the sound, to his surprise discovered a stout, good-natured negro man, named Sam, who had been sold out of his neighbourhood, in Madison, some months before.

Drawing up his horse, and evincing pleasure at the unexpected rencontre, the negro stealer returned Sam's greeting in a friendly manner, and inquired how he liked his new master.

"Bad enough, Massa Murrell, bad enough," replied the discontented black: "work all de time, and when dere aint no work, den whip all de time. He's a hard case, Massa Murrell, he's a hard case, and dat's a fac."

"Well, now, you don't tell me so, Sam," replied the negro stealer, in a tone of pathetic surprise, and apparently half abstracted from the very contemplation of the enormity.

"Yes, Massa, I do! what I tell you is a fac," replied Sam. "Massa Eason's a mighty hard man, he is."

"Well, Sam," answered Murrell, looking fixedly at the negro, "all I've got to say is this—you know how to get away, and you know where to find *me*, and if you're content to remain where you are, and be treated like a dog, why you deserve it, that's all."

"But, Massa Murrell," answered the black, scratching his pate in great perplexity, "every body knows me in Madison, and if I should come back dere, dey would soon find out I'd run away, and den"—

"Well, then, leave all things to me. Do you only be careful to take a bag of parched corn with you, to start at night, to travel only at night, and come to me at night, and I'll look out for every thing that follows. It will not take us long to get in a free State after that, I guess!"

"Well, Massa, I'll do zackly as you say; but spozen I should beat you home?"

"There's not much danger of that, Sam, for I intend to go straight through. But if it should so happen that any thing should detain me, why tell my wife I sent you, and it'll be all right."

With this expression the conversation ended, and the parties separated.

Murrell arrived at home without any delay, and on the fourth night afterwards, the negro knocked at his door for admittance, and was promptly taken in. The negro stealer intended to make his case an experiment, in testing a portion of the law, which he had recently studied, and therefore stowed him away snugly in his house, instead of despatching him at once to some distant part of the country for sale.

As he expected, it was not long before Eason offered a reward for the slave, and advertised him as a runaway.

This was just what the robber waited for. He at once sent for his brother and a man named Forsyth, and, procuring a copy of the advertisement signed by Eason, put the negro into their hands, and started them off with the following directions:

"Boys, I'm going to put you down on a new 'pint,' and I want you to make the most of it. I have put into your hands a fine slave, and an advertisement, signed by his owner, offering a reward for his recovery. That advertisement is, I find, the same in legal virtue as a power of attorney from the ownwr, and entitles you to act for him in relation to this piece of property. It is a full commission for you to take the nigger into your possession, and if you dispose of him and put the money into your pocket, why, it is only a breach of trust instead of being stealing. The only redress the owner can get, is through a *civil* suit for damages. I want you, therefore, to put the darkee through, and sell him as often and as fast as you can. If he is recognized, or your right to him is suspected, the advertisement will be your protection; and if, after having sold him and stolen him again, you should be pursued and caught with him in your possession, your answer will be, that he has proved to be a more inveterate rogue than you thought him, and that a providential accident had enabled you to catch him for the second time. Now start, and make hay while the sun shines. Put him straight through the river counties, and run him right on to Texas, and leave him there with Hawkins. Having done this, return straight back to me, for I may have something else on hand."

Receiving these instructions with the most profound respect, the younger Murrell and his accomplice started off upon their expedition, prepared to observe their orders to the very letter. They were gone, in all, about seven weeks, when they returned with fourteen hundred dollars in cash, a draft for seven hundred more, and seven hundred dollars worth of ready-made clothing, as the proceeds of four sales. The clothing was readily turned into cash. The draft had been given in payment for the negro by Thomas Hunold, of Madison, in the state of Mississippi, upon a house in New Orleans. Shortly after Hunold had made the purchase, however, the negro suddenly disappeared, and, suspecting thereupon that he had been carried off by the very men who had sold him, he wrote to the house upon which the draft was drawn, acquainted them with his mistrust, and directing them to refuse to honor the demand. When informed of this state of things in the general report of the expedition, Murrell berated the imprudence of his two disciples, and told them, with considerable show of anger, that the merest tryo should have known enough to have got the draft cashed, before proceeding to any further operations. He, however, wound up, by softening his tone, and by saying that the draft was, nevertheless, as good as gold, for Hunold could neither prove that Sam was Eason's negro, or that they had stolen him after the sale, and, therefore, would be obliged to redeem his written obligation. He therefore directed Forsyth to at once commence a suit against Hunold for the amount.

With the money now in his possession, Murrell paid off the remainder of the mortgage on his farm, and set himself down again for another period of domestic relaxation. But this time he did not remain inactive long, for news coming to him under the signatures of Haines and Phelps, that his presence was required in New Orleans to direct the progressing operations of the mystic confederation, he was obliged to abandon home again.

He arrived in the Crescent city in due time, but as his luck would have it, he got into a bloody fracas with a body of the night patrol, during the first week of his stay, and was obliged to fly from the pursuit which it aroused, a headlong fugitive, beyond the banks of the Sabine.

Finding himself in Texas, and reflecting upon the danger of adventuring back to any portion of the southern or western country for several months, the marauder decided to push through to Mexico, to see if there was an opening in that country for speculation, and also to enquire if he could not get some friends in that quarter to aid him in the design of the negro rebellion. He went on to Matamoras, but being discouraged after a short stay in that city, he set sail for Campeachy, in Yucatan. Finding no opening there for his peculiar talents, he pushed a short way into the interior, and stopping in a village, assumed the character of a physician, and commenced practising medicine. He was able to maintain this character with tolerable success, from having read Ewel and several other elementary works on medicine during his recent stays at home, and confining his practice to the use of a few simple remedies, managed to give as much satisfaction, and to produce, perhaps, as beneficial results to his patients, as most of the more diplomatised members of the medical profession. While thus employed, he became a great favorite with an old Catholic, who adopted him as his son in the faith, and introduced him to the best families of the place, as a distinguished young physician from the United States. The intimacy resulted in

Murrell taking up his residence in the old man's house, and in his ingratiation with a niece, who had charge of the domestic government of the establishment, who was equally devout as her uncle. The supple character of the American robber moulded itself with facility to the condition of things around him, and he soon was as faultless in the observations of the Church of Rome, as he had previously been admirable in the more eccentric and violent forms of the Methodist persuasion. In what manner and how far his scrupulous sanctity availed him with the young lady, we cannot speak, but at the end of three months he got tried of his situation, and seizing an opportunity to depart with credit to his professional character, he robbed the old man's secretary of nine hundred and sixty dollars in gold, and suddenly decamped. He had not done this without making his calculations on a safe retreat, and on the day after the exploit, he was leaving the harbor of Campeachy for Tobasco.

In Tobasco he fell in with some congenial spirits, one of whom gave him tidings of his friend Crenshaw. This information did not comprise any particulars of that ruffian's recent career, beyond the fact that he had, for the last two or three years, been engaged in the slave trade, between the Brazils and the coast of Africa, and that he was supposed to be one of a party who had been overhauled in a slave brig by an English cruiser, during the previous year, and executed, under the law of nations, which regards the offence as piracy. Making no stay in Tobasco, after receiving this information, Murrell looked around for the first opportunity to return to the United States, and having obtained a vessel, set sail for New Orleans, after an absence of nearly seven months.

CHAPTER X.

The Council in Orleans—Preparations for a Grand Convention—The Road-side Murder—The New Acquaintance—The deceptive character of appearances—The Victim of Ostentation—The Speculators of the Arkansas—The Drowning Horse.

On his return to New Orleans after his visit to the Mexican Republic, Murrell gave a grand entertainment to his friends, as the precursor to that relaxation which was usual with him after an extended professional enterprise. Having continued his season of enjoyment to a limit which allowed him to calculate his remaining means in units by a single journey over his ten fingers, he held up his libidinous digression, from the same prudential motives which actuate a man, who, butting his head against a wall, resolves to go no further in that direction. He therefore ran his fingers throughfully through the remaining silver in his pocket, and resolved to renew his immediate attention to business. As he had himself been somewhat particular in his description of the transactions which took place immediately upon this determination, we will give that portion of his narrative which embraces them in his own language.

"I collected all my associates in New Orleans, at one of my friend's houses, in that city, and we sat in council upon the general interests of the clan. It was three days before we got all our plans to our notion, and then, having examined our connections in the different parts of the country, and made a fair estimate of the degree of reliance we could place upon them, we determined to undertake the rebellion at all hazards, and to only postpone the appointment of the final day, until we could ascertain the general views of the whole confederacy.— This latter object was proposed to be accomplished by a circular letter in secret characters, directing the speculators in the districts of the different States, to send each a delegate to a general convention, to be held at a rendezvous in Arkansas, which convention should devise the measures and fix the day, and then separate and return to their respective districts, to superintend the preparations necessary to the final movement. Affairs having been put in this train, and every man then present having had his share of present business assigned to him, the council broke up.

"On the following day I sold my horse to obtain present means for travel, and set out for Natchez on foot, with the intention of stealing another the first opportunity that offered. No luck turned up during the first four days, and I was growing more and more desperate as I kept getting more and more fatigued and foot-sore, and had not a fortunate chance arose, I would doubtless have been betrayed into some imprudent act of force that would have got me into trouble. On the fifth day, at the heat of noon, I retired to a shady spot on the bank of a creek, to get some water and a little rest.—While I was sitting on the trunk of a fallen tree, looking down the road in the direction I had come, a horseman hove in sight. The very moment this object caught my eye, I determined to have possession of the animal, if his rider should prove to be a traveller. My hopes turned out to be correct. I saw from his equipage, as he drew nearer, that the horseman was prepared for a long journey, and as he approached close to me, I rose from my seat, seized his rein, and drawing a rifle pistol on him, ordered him to dismount.—He obeyed without a word, and still holding the horse by the bridle, I pointed down the creek to a secluded spot, and ordered him to walk before me. He hesitated, as if unwilling to leave the hope of rescue afforded by the open road, and looked wishfully up and down to see if he could detect no traveller in sight. I understood his object, and repeated my order in a peremptory tone. He remonstrated and questioned me apprehensively as to my purpose. This time I disdained an answer, but pointed again in the direction I would have him go, and made at the same time a decisive motion with the pistol, which brought him to my obedience. We went a few hundred yards till we came to a spot well sheltered from observation, when I hitched the horse, and ordered him to undress. Finding he had no alternative but to do as I commanded him, he commenced to strip, and at length stood all undressed to his shirt and drawers. When this was done, I ordered him to turn his back to me. He then for the first time asked me if I was going to shoot him; a question which he had evidently withheld before, for fear of suggesting the danger which he dreaded. I made him no answer, but ordered him a second time to turn his back. He stretched his hands imploringly towards me, and begged for time to pray before he died. But this was not in the way of business, so I refused him the favor, and told him I never had time to address heaven for myself, and I was sure I could not find time to hear him pray. He turned from me and dropped upon his knees at this, and I shot him through the back of his head. I felt sorry for him, but I could not help it. I had been obliged to travel on foot for the previous four days, and I now relieved him of the danger of ever suffering the like. As soon as he fell, I drew my knife, and ripping his belly, took out his entrails. I then scooped up a lot of sand, stuffed it in the vacant stomach and sunk the body in the creek. I buried the entrails, and having thus removed all evidences of the deed, was free to commence searching the pockets of the clothes. I found in all four hundred and one dollars and thirty-seven cents, and a number of papers which I did not take time to examine. I then put his pocket-book and papers in his hat, filling the whole with sand, tied the mouth of it up and cast it into the creek after the body. His boots, which were brand new and fitted me exactly, did not share this fate, for I put them on, and sent my old shoes into the creek after the old hat.*

---

* Murrell did not make these brutal confessions after his captivity, but related them to a supposed accomplice who had joined the clan for the purpose of delivering him up to justice.

MURRELL SHOOTING THE TRAVELLER

"His clothes, which were new and of the finest quality, I stowed away into his best portmanteau, and then mounting as fine a horse as I ever straddled, reloaded my pistol, and resumed my journey towards Natchez, in a condition to see company.

"I reached Natchez without any new adventure, and having spent two days with the girls under the hill, left for the Choctaw nation, determined before I returned home to Madison this time, to give some one else a turn for their property. Some days passed without a chance turning up, but as I was riding along one fine morning, between Benton and Rankin, meditating upon my principal design, I was overtaken by a traveller. The stranger rode an elegant horse, and was a tall, good-looking young man, splendidly rigged off, with a heavy gold guard chain, and a profusion of jewelry, which seemed to indicate that he was eminently deserving the attention of a gentleman of my profession. I was anxious to know if he intended to travel through the Choctaw nation, and falling into conversation, soon managed to learn all I wanted to know. He proved to be very communicative. He informed me that he had been to the lower country with a drove of negroes, and having disposed of them, he was now returning home to Kentucky. I felt very grateful to my good genius when I heard this news, and laying out all my spare politeness, soon obtained his confidence, and got him to agree to accompany me through the Indian Nation. We were two splendid looking fellows, and to hear us talk of our possessions, a listener would have thought that we were both immensely rich. Observing from his conversation that he had been rather a free liver, I touched him on the subject of speculation; but he flew off in a tangent, cursed the speculators without stint, and remarked with a well feigned show of importance, that he was in a mighty bad condition to fall into the hands of such villains just then, as he had upon his person the cash that wenty negroes had sold for; adding that on that account, if on no other, he could not too strongly congratulate himself upon having the protection of my company with him through the nation. Though I had felt at times a few faint misgivings, that there was some bombast and empty ostentation about my fellow traveller, I could not but conclude that he was a noble prize. I therefore decided in favor of my own hopes and his word, and longed for the opportunity that would allow me the pleasure of counting his cash.

"The moment at length arrived. On the third day from falling in with one another, we came into one of those long stretches in the nation where there was no house for twenty miles. The country was high, hilly and broken, and selecting a place where there was no water in sight, I pretended to be afflicted with an insufferable thirst, and insisted upon dismounting and turning down a deep hollow or dale that headed near the road, to hunt some water. My companion, after regretting the delay which this digression from our road would cause us, agreed, and we turned aside from the open country. Having pursued the course of the ravine for a few hundred yards, and finding my companion in a proper position just in front of me, I drew my pistol and shot him through the head. He fell dead upon the instant, and I, equally as prompt, commenced hunting for his cash. After some effort I extracted a large pocket book from his clothes, which, from its bulky size and respectable greasiness, promised unbounded treasures. But, alas, it was my fate to prove, in this case, that appearances are sometime very deceptive, and that the pocket book was fat and greasy for nothing. The whole contents were copies of worn love songs, the forms of amatory letters of his own composition, an old play bill or two, but not a cent of cash. I began to cut his clothes with my knife and examine their lining to search for secret pockets; but my whole reward in money was twelve dollars and a half, in change, and no more. 'As this is rather a small show for twenty negroes,' said I to myself, 'I'll see what your watch and jewelry are worth.' But these, (with the exception of the chain, which was gold) I found to be in keeping with the contents of his pockets; the watch being nothing but a brass and gilt affair, that did not run, and his breastpin, tinsel. The man was an imposter, and had deceived me. I felt no regret for him, for he only lost a worthless life by his own foolish lies, and I had got the worst of the bargain by being obliged to commit a dangerous act for an inadequate object. I turned away from the conceited coxcomb with the reflection that the sooner all such fools were dead the better. I left him to rot where he laid, and took his horse and swapped him the next day for four Indian ponies, which I sold in my route to the Mississippi river. I sought a directly westward track to get out of the trail of pursuit, as well as to find a market for my ponies.

"On arriving at the Mississippi I went directly across and followed the stream on the other side till I came to the mouth of the Arkansas. There I made a visit to two or three old friends, one of whom hailed my arrival as an opportune assistance towards the accomplishment of a job he had in hand.—That very morning an honest neighbor had found a fine horse standing on the steep edge of the Mississippi river, looking up at the high bank without being able to surmount it. The animal had probably fallen off some boat and swam to the shore, and was patiently waiting till some human friend should appear to rescue him from his position.—There was but one way to save him, and the man hitting upon it, dug away the bank and led him up. The horse, of course, was his prize, unless the owner should appear. The speculator who communicated these facts to me, told me that he had examined the horse completely, and had taken all his flesh marks, with the view of sending the account to some member of the clan, who not being known in the neighborhood, could come forward and claim the animal as the owner. He preferred giving me the chance, as a small testimony of his respect and consideration. I took the description, and conning it over for a few minutes, set out towards the finder's house. I knocked at the door, and asked the man if he had found a horse of such a description—describing the animal he had rescued in every particular. The man answered in the affirmative, and produced the horse, whereupon I pretended to recognise him at once and claimed him as my property. There were no objections made, and giving the poor fellow five dollars for his trouble, I took the horse away with me. I have swam the Mississippi twice upon that horse."

After the above affair, Murrell at once set out for Madison county, and without any further adventure arrived at home after the absence of a year.

CHAPTER XI.

Murrell's Social Position in Madison—His Depradations in the neighborhood—Abduction of Long's negroes—The Ambush—Detection—Trial—Indignation of the Citizens at the prospect of his Escape—The formation of a company to lynch him—Murrell fortifies his house and places himself in a position of armed defiance—The result.

Being now in very comfortable ease from the proceeds of the last bloody expedition, Murrell might well have afforded a very protracted period of domestic ease. His uneasy nature, however, would not allow him to remain quiet long, and while he was not occupied in conducting his nefarious correspondence he was continually contriving minor depredations upon the inhabitants of the surrounding country. These enterprises he would generally place under the direction and management of his brother; but now and then he would toss one to a needy speculator who might be passing through the region, on the condition of a certain per centage of the spoils.

The number of losses from the different plantations in the surrounding country at length began to excite serious alarm, and in the fruitlessness of the repeated efforts to detect the secret instruments of the disaffection, each man felt inclined to suspect every neighbor who stood in a less intimate relation than a bosom friend. In its journey among others, suspicion at length rested upon Murrell. His frequent journeys from home, his popularity among the slaves, and his strange mode of life, occasioned vague speculations in the minds of many persons, and the fact that strange men had been seen to arrive at his dwelling at night, and to leave before the break of day, gave color and encouragement to the most injurious rumors. He was not long in ascertaining this state of things, for such of his friends as were situated in society and were supposed to be unblemished men, gathered all the particulars of the rumor, and acquainted him with its location and extent. As soon as he surveyed the whole condition of things he would boldly meet the danger, in whatever quarter it lay, and by a series of well-managed manuvers or explanations turn the prejudice into friendship and confidence. When he failed in this, however, he addressed himself to the compensations of revenge, and the secret destruction of his enemy's property or character would be the sequel of his hate. In a pursuit of this latter kind Murrell had never-tiring perseverance, and many a thriving man sunk under the influence of his great managing power. He lived in his neighborhood, therefore, respected by some, suspected by others, but in consequence of the mystery which hung about his character, rather avoided by all.

Though the actual work of his casual contrivances was generally done by other hands, Murrell did not remain altogether at home. The progress of his great design was gradually cementing the speculators of all the country into one general confederacy, and the rendezvous having been pitched in a deep and tangled wood, a few miles from the Arkansas shore, he would now and then set out from home to preside at council. He had not proceeded far in his organization before he found it necessary to divide his clan into two classes, the first of which were to be designated as the "Grand Council," and the second as the "Strykers." The Grand Council was a directing and controlling body, to be composed either of the acknowledged leaders of local gangs, or of men whose individual intelligence and personal deeds were to be the claim for this distinction. The "Strykers" were the workies or the industrii of the profession, and were not to be made confidants of the whole of the grand schemes of the main body. They were sprinkled all over the country, and who would obey the direction of any superior mind without questioning the motive or object of the act. "For a few dollars," said Murrell," we can get any number of this class to run a negro or a horse to some safe place where we can get possession of them without danger, and never trusting them with any plans until we see the period for their execution near at hand, we, of course never run any risk from their imprudence.—These fellows are exceedingly useful. Indeed they are the very hands with which we must work; but as they have not all of them got heads, it would be bad judgment to let them into the whole of our designs."

While these arrangements were going on Murrell still kept up his desultory depredations, and just previous to an intended visit to the rendezvous in Arkansas, cast his eyes upon the negroes of a Mr. Long, in the neighborhood, and determined to speculate upon them by seducing them from their master. Having bent his attention to this object, he was not long in producing an impression, and in a short time succeeded in decoying away three of the negroes, and in concealing them in a wood at no great distance from his home. He intended to have them run away that very night, but contrary to his expectations, he was obliged to keep them concealed for a considerable length of time, through an accident which overthrew his plans for their immediate removal, and he was also obliged, while they were thus situated, to convey them food at great risks of detection. The negroes had been secreted for several days, when one of them, who coveted some clothing which he had left at home, emerged from his concealment and started back to his master's plantation to obtain possession of the articles. Fortunately, the overseer of the establishment happened to discover him, and, after a short chase and the crack of a gun, succeeded in frightening the fellow to a stand still. Finding himself fairly caught, and being interrogated upon pain of the severest punishment, the slave at length revealed the whole story of his abduction, exposed the agency of Murrell, and indicated the place where the other fugitives were kept concealed.

This was the first actual confirmation of the suspicions which had so long hung over Murrell, and while Mr.

Long and his friends rejoiced at the prospect of unveiling the scoundrel, and visiting him with his deserts, they knew that they could not even yet succeed in detecting him, unless they proceeded with the greatest caution. They therefore determined to select a sufficient company, and, surrounding the spot where the negroes lay concealed, gradually close in upon the rogue while he was in the very act of his dishonest and felonious communication.—As soon as this plan was fully decided upon, the party set out. They were led by the captured slave, who cautiously conducted Mr. Long and his oversser in advance of their friends, so that they might overhear, as well as observe, every thing that took place. When they had arrived at a proper distance, the negro, by direction, then left his master and joined his two awaiting brethren, receiving, at the time, the positive command, not to communicate to them the least alarm.

Unsuspicious of this ambush, Murrell, at the dusk of evening entered the wood with a basket on his arm, and, advancing in the midst of the negroes, commenced delivering out their fare. While thus engaged, the slave who had been captured, put several questions to the negro stealer, according to the previous directions of his master, to induce replies which might be useful in evidence against him. This ruse having been attended with the desired effect, and Mr. Long, conceiving he had heard sufficient for his purpose, gave the signal, the party closed in, and took the negro stealer prisoner. Though taken all unawares, Murrell had sufficient control of himself not to evince the least alarm; but immediately turning the matter to the best account that the circumstances admitted of, turned to Mr. Long and congratulated him on the recovery of his property, and with an admirable plausibility stated that he had discovered the negroes but a little while before, and had been feeding them, and bolstering them with false promises, for the sole purpose of obtaining an opportunity to give information of the place of their concealment. This story, so ingeniously contrived and bravely ventured, might have been successful had Mr. Long not been convinced by what he had seen and heard that it was merely trumped up for the occasion. As it was he paid no heed to it, but seizing the offender, marched him in custody out of the wood and lodged him in prison.

The rumors which had so long been floating about the country in relation to Murrell now became tangible, and every body believed implicitly in his guilt. Indeed, all the then recent abductions in the country were attributed to him or to his agency. To the surprise of every body, however, he got bail on the second day after his commitment, but so dark were appearances against him, that it was universally predicted that he would not appear upon the day of trial. The community of Madison, however, did not know their man. They made calculations upon him going to the penitentiary if he appeared, but he soon ascertained that his offence did not extend beyond the penalty of a fine. Relying, therefore, upon the resources of his band to sustain him if he should be mulcted in damages, he resolved to show a bold attitude, and employed a very eminent lawyer to defend him.

On the trial day the Court room was crowded, and the excitement was immense, but in the midst of the agitation which surrounded him, the land pirate displayed an equanimity that refused to be disturbed. On the investigation of the case, the crime charged against him, according to his calculations, could only be proved to be *negro harboring*, instead of *negro stealing*, and consequently he could not be punished by damages and costs. This point having been settled by the court in his favor, a verdict was rendered against him for several hundred dollars, with the condition attached that he should become Long's slave for five years, if his property was not found adequate to the fine. Though abundantly able to pay the mulct, the land pirate resolved not to yield quietly to a verdict so dangerous to his position, so he made an appeal to the Supreme Court, and took ground against the constitutionality of the law in relation to negro harboring.

The unexpected escape of Murrell from the penitentiary struck every body with astonishment, and perceiving, by the course the matter had taken, that he was likely to escape punishment altogether, a number of the most indignant citizens formed a company for the purpose of giving him a visitation of popular vengeance, or in other words, of Lynching him unless he left the place. This voluntary band was called "Captain Slick's Company," and its leader advertised for all honest men to meet on a given day at a certain school-house in the neighborhood, to take means to expel the common enemy. This movement, though formidable in its character and appearance, instead of exciting alarm in the negro stealer's bosom, only aroused a feeling of resentment, and a determination to resist it to the last. He saw the strength of his position, he felt for once in his life the novel confidence of having the law on his side, and he rejoiced at an opportunity of being able to wreak his vengeance and gratify his inhuman thirst for blood without any legal risk.

The day which had been selected for the operation of Captain Slick's company upon the land pirate, had been purposely set at a period sufficiently distant from the fulmination of the advertisement to give him an opportunity to quit the country if he would.—This was a fortunate circumstance for the robber, for it afforded him time to appeal to his resources. Applying himself with desperate energy to the crisis, he dispatched missions in every direction, calling back the numerous members of the band who had secretly swarmed to the vicinity to be present at his trial, and demanding their aid in his extremity. His brother was charged with the gathering of these forces, as well as with providing ammunition and other materials of defence. While he was thus engaged outside, the hero of the drama himself was busily occupied within, in putting his strong log-house in a perfect state of defence, in cutting port-holes, erecting barricades, digging traps, and contriving safe positions for the discharge of fire-arms upon the expected assailants. All this was very well so far as it went, but he evinced still higher qualities of generalship by detailing two or three of his most capable professional associates to join the insurgent band, and to give him notice of all their proceedings. By this means he made himself acquainted with all "Captain Slick's" designs. The very rules which governed the movements of the insurgent company were put into his possession, and he was enabled to treasure up the names of those whom he considered most entitled to his future vengeance. On the day set for the armed assault, his little castle and outbuildings were in a perfect state of defence. Eighteen desperate and daring men were the defenders of the main building; two heavy brass blunderbusses grinned from a barn behind the house, which commanded the road, and every point of the works gave the same appearance of complete defensive preparation. Captain Slick's company started on their errand, but before it had arrived at the turning of the road commanded by the blunderbusses, they received a hint of the preparations which had been made to receive them. As soon as the formidable dangers of the enterprise became fully known, and had made their due impression, the secret friends of Murrell in the company, openly withdrew from the ranks, and declared that they would no longer be partners to the quixotic enterprise of attempting to vindicate the errors of the law at the price of bloodshed, and at the expense of their own lives. "If the law was so weak," said they, "that bad men must escape, why the proper place to fight the battle was in the Legislature, or at the ballot-boxes, and not against armed men who fought in defence of an unlawful assault." The example of defection thus boldly set was not long in spreading itself throughout the whole startled company, and in a few minutes the band which had marched up so bravely, and with such ostentatious indignation, were glad to take shelter from the threatened danger under the cover of prudential considerations and respect for human life— in other words, in consideration for their skins. Thus dissolved this danger, and the land pirate and his virtuous company, in lieu of the enjoyment of the expected strife, shed gallons of red wine, and made the walls of their stronghold tremble with their boisterous wassail.

There was nothing now left for Murrell, in relation to this business, but to prove the danger of interference with his course to all who had been most active against him.

This he succeeded in doing most effectually within the few weeks immediately succeeding the threatened siege, and every man who had taken any share in the transactions, felt, in some shape or other, the sharp effects of the robber's secret vengeance.

Among the men whom Murrell had selected out as the principal objects of his vengeance, was a family of the name of Henning,[1] which resided about two miles from him, and the principal members of which consisted of an old preacher and his two sons. These people had been the earliest in the country to suspect his course of life; and subsequent to his apprehension on the charge of stealing Long's negroes, they had been among the most eager to insist upon his explusion from the neighborhood. Murrell had lost no portion of their operations against him from first to last, and it may, therefore, be readily supposed that he determined that his revengeful visitations should be in proportion to the provocation. Just, however, as he had decided to commence the business of the offset by the abduction of two of the preacher's negroes, he found it necessary to set out for the grand rendezvous in the Arkansas valley, to attend the meeting of his gang, the date of which, though long before prescribed, had, in consequence of the recent stirring circumstances, came upon him almost by surprise.

---

1. John Henning is also described as "Parson John Henning" and may have been a Methodist preacher. Perhaps Henning and his son Richard testified against him or were among Slick's Company who attempted to apprehend and lynch Murrell. Lal Penick, *Great Western Land Pirate*, 34.

CHAPTER XII.

The Grand Council of the Arkansas—Reports of Committees—Contributions to the Treasury—Character of the members of the gathering—Murrell Addresses the Band—Developes his plan for the Rising—His insidious incitements to Revenge—Suggestions for an oath—His Correspondence with a celebrated Abolition Lecturer on the subject of the Rising—Produces the last letter of the lecturer containing his view of the Plan and its results.

Elevated above the rest, and with an influential satellite on either hand, the robber chieftain sat in the midst of the Grand Council of the Arkansas, and gravely administered the duties of the chair. Having received and passed upon the list of chief directors, a number of committees reported in turn; one answering for the manner in which the disposal of certain mystic circulars had been distributed; another handling in a set of regulations which had been framed for some specific safeguard, declared to be necessary at a previous gathering; and another, on finance, reporting the state of the treasury, and the character and the amount of the contributions which had been turned into the strong box of the brotherhood by the different local gangs. While the chairman of the last committee was engaged in reading his report, he was frequently interrupted by murmurs of applause, at some district, more fortunate than those which had preceded it, stood accredited for a superior sum.

"Bravely done for Alabama! Bravely done for Andrew Boyd! Who says Talladega county aint been up and doing?" were the exclamations that ran through the assemblage; and when some extraordinary sum, the result of some remarkable exploit, would challenge an especial acknowledgment of admiration, a cheer would involuntarily burst forth, the echo of which might reach the ears of the most distant of the "strykers," who stood picketed at various points about the council-hut, for the distance of a mile. Murrell looked round with an expression of satisfaction as he saw the enthusiasm of his band, and as his eye travelled over the nefarious assemblage, he also felt a swelling sentiment of pride as he noted among its members, men, who not only held prominent positions in society, but who were the incumbents of honorable and lucrative State and County offices. It was on the judgment, standing and resources of such men as these, that the robber chieftain felt the strongest reliance for the eventual success of all his plans. On them, and on their social positions, he could rely for a description of assistance which could not be contributed by an other hands. If any point in the grand design should miscarry, and an inkling of the danger that was afoot leak out to the public ear, these men could crush it at once by ridiculing the report as groundless, and thus the alarm would perish in its birth. They were the strong pillars of his mystic mansion, and, in addition to their importance as practical auxiliaries, their adhesion was calculated to be truly gratifying to the conceit of the young leader.

After the formal proceedings had been disposed of, Murrell, who had been warmed by the enthusiastic demonstrations which had broken from all sides during the report of the finance committee, rose and commenced a speech in which he developed all the features of his plan. The method and amount of this address were preserved in the memory of one who was present, and its relations were subsequently confirmed by Murrell himself.

"Comrades, the grand object that we have in contemplation, and which calls us here tonight, is well known to you all. You already understand the frame-work of the design, and the only thing that now seems to be necessary, is that we should settle on the particulars. We of course must manage to have the rising commence every where at the same hour, so that each community will be paralyzed at the same time. Our power is very well distributed, and there is scarcely a locality but owns an overawing clan.—To each of these must be consigned the care of its immediate vicinity, and the time between now and the appointed day must be employed in strengthening the bands. Of this, however, I have spoken before, but I cannot too often impress upon you the necessity of extreme caution in making proselytes, and especially in developing your plans to the negroes themselves. Though you own experience and judgment will direct you how to deal with a negro, it may not be out of place for me to tell you how I myself proceed in such cases. I do not by an means go to every negro I see and tell him that his brethren throughout the States intend to rebel upon a certain night; but I look carefully around upon the large farms for the most vicious and daring, and after having carefully felt my way, commence poisoning their minds by telling them how monstrously they are mistreated; that they are entitled to their freedom as much as their masters, and that, as all the wealth of the country is the proceeds of black people's labor, that the black people have a right before God, to resume it when they will. That it is theirs by the best right which mean can have to property, and that those who stand between them and their own in the hour of their rage, must take the consequences of a just revenge. I then sting them with their own degraded condition, which their laborious toil has conferred upon the ingratitude of others. When I have got as far as this, I generally consider that I have aroused enough energy in their usually torpid minds to make them capable of ambition. I then tell them that all Europe has abandoned slavery; that the West Indies are made free, and that they got their freedom by rebelling a few times, and slaughtering a few thousand white tyrants who had whipped them to the revenge, and that it was but for them to follow the example of these brilliant and daring spirits, to obtain the same freedom, and invest themselves with the same privileges and power. That, in short, it rests entirely with themselves to agree together and say whether they will be equal with the whites, marry white women, and with their luxuries, share also their pomp and state. If with all this inducement and encouragement, they still hesitate in doubt of their own power, I then boldly avow that I am an emissary from one of the free States, the whole of which, as well as England, I tell them are in favor of the movement, and would not raise a finger if the negroes were to butcher every white man in the slaveholding States.

"I have never found this management to fail, and I can already count some two or three hundred blacks, in different parts of the country, whose minds I have thus prepared for the naming of the fatal day. That day, however, must not be committed to them, until they are duly sworn to secrecy, by the same oath and terrifying proceedings as are used among ourselves at the initiation of a new member. If this cannot be performed, in all cases and at all times, a horrific picture can be painted, representing the infernal deity who is to deal with them if they betray their trust; and they can be safely sworn on that. The main part of the form of our own oath will do, and if that don't bind their superstitious souls, then there is no force in terror.

"After we have sworn one of them, we must then instruct him to hold the same language to his fellow-slaves that was first held to him. He is to convince them of the great injustice of their being held in bondage, and, in addition to arousing their revenge, must excite their basest appetites for lust and rapine. Revenge, however, must be the great point to urge, and they must not be allowed to forget a single stripe that they ever received. The leading negroes, if carefully selected, can have frequent gatherings of their fellow-bondsmen, and they must be supplied with money to pay for plenty of drink, for that will not only be sure to call them together, but will make them more apt to the business in view. At these preliminary gatherings, nothing should be said of the settled purpose of rebellion. But when the night itself comes, then there should be an extra quantity of drink on hand, and after the party become sufficiently inflamed, the black emissaries can boldly declare that there is but one way to end their miseries, and that way is, rebellion and revenge. That all the negroes in American were to rebel on that night; that there were some distinguished white men from the north and from foreign countries, who were nigh at hand to help them, and who were so resolved to emancipate the slaves, that, for the sake of posterity, they would rather cut down any negro who should refuse to lend his aid, than see the struggle fail. The leaders of the local clans could then be introduced among the blacks, and, after giving the black hounds a fraternal grasp of the hand, and a pledge of eternal friendship, in a glass of rum, should deal out the weapons, and give the signal for the havoc. The infuriated negroes will rush in for carnage and for slaughter, and our detachments must fire the towns and rob the banks and richest shops, during the confusion and dismay!"

Having worked himself up to this climax, the speaker paused for a moment, as if lost in the contemplation of the terrific picture which his overheated imagination had conjured up, and his audience, relieved from the spell of his eloquence, broke out in a general tribute of applause. When they had subsided, the speaker, as if challenged by an afterthought, continued,—

"It is true, that in many places in the slave States, the ratio of negro population is unequal and inferior in numbers to the whites; but those places must be among the earliest care of the committees, and our force must be so appointed as to save them from being overpowered. In those places, we must have our most capable leaders and our most resolute men. Their business, with a choice reserve of blacks, will be to huddle the population together in their defence, and then to keep them in check, while the rest are heaping ruin upon revenge in every quarter.

"The necessary arrangements for all these extensive operations will even yet require considerable time and considerable money. I have great satisfaction in contemplating the present condition of our finances and other resources, and it affords me great pleasure also to inform you that I have prospects, from certain quarters, of the most flattering nature in relation to future aid and in the way of funds.

"In conducting my correspondence on this subject, I sounded a celebrated English anti-slavery lecturer, who is now agitating abolition in the Eastern States, and succeeded in opening a correspondence, the result of which has been to assure me of the aid of extensive means and other assistance from that quarter as soon as it may be demanded. This correspondence has been conducted with extreme caution, and I could only get a definite reply by despatching a confidential agent to confer with this man in person. I will now communicate to you one of his letters, as an evidence of the spirit in which we may hope to be met from that quarter, reserving only the name of the writer, in obedience of the solemn pledge which I gave him at the outset of our correspondence. You will not fail to appreciate the binding character of this obligation of secrecy, inasmuch as the man may be considered in the light of your sworn accomplice." Murrell then drew a letter from his bosom, from which he read as follows:

"Boston, March 18th, 1834.

"MY DEAR SIR,—

"Your favor of the 4th has come to hand, and its contents have been carefully observed. I think you can count upon the aid you demand with tolerable certainty by the time you name. I approve of your arrangements, and can perceive abundant justification for your views.

"Could the blacks effect a general concert of action against their tyrants, and let loose the arm of destruction among them and their property, so that the judgments of God might be visibly seen and felt, it would reach the flinty heart of the tyrant. We can do much at the East by working on the sympathy of the people; but when we remonstrate with a Southern tyrant, he counts the cost of his annual income, and haughtily hurls it in our teeth, and tells us that the Old and New Testaments both teach him that Slavery is right. We must teach the tyrant in another way. His interest must be affected before he will repent. We can prepare the feelings of most of the Northern and Eastern people for the final consummation of the great work, by lecturing. Interest is the great cement that binds the few Northerners who are friendly to Southern tyrants; and if their cities, with all the merchandize in the country, were destroyed, and their banks plundered of all the specie, thousands of Eastern capitalists would suffer great loss, and would henceforth consider a slave country an unsafe place to make investments, and thousands would leave the country. The state of affairs would naturally diminish the value of slave property and disgust even the tyrant with the policy of slavery, while the country would be thus in a state of anarchy and poverty. Their banking institutions and credit sunk into disrepute with the commercial world, it would be an easy matter to effect the total abolition of slavery.

"Desperate cases require desperate remedies.

"And suppose the blacks should refuse to serve their tyrants any longer, what right would the general government have to interfere with the internal disputes of a State respecting her State laws? The blacks would not be rebelling against the general government, neither would they be invaders, but Americans, and citizens of a State refusing obedience to a State law and power that are, before God, utterly null and void, being an audacious usurpation of his Divine prerogative, a daring infringement on the law of nature, and a presumptuous transgression of the holy commandments, which should be abrogated by the Christian world. Would not the general government have more right to interfere in behalf of the injured and oppressed than that of the tyrants and oppressors? The United States' troops would be finely employed in the Southern plantations forcing obedience to the unjust laws of a few tyrants and man-stealers.

"The Southerners are great men for *State rights*, and in a case like the above we would give them an opportunity to exercise their sovereign functions. Make slavery unpopular with a majority of the people of the United States, and Southern tyrants will find a poor comforter in the general government."

"These, my friends, are the sentiments of a man distinguished for his influence and talents, and they may afford you a tolerable idea of the impression which our movements will make upon a great portion of the North. I do not say this with the idea that any of us will be weak enough to make calculations on applause; I only present the fact that we may make count upon impunity from the sympathetic torpidity of an extensive quarter of the country." ****

With these remarks, Murrell folded the letter carefully up again, put it back into his bosom, and with a slight inclination of his head to indicate that he had done, sat down amid the most lively demonstrations of applause.

CHAPTER XIII.

The Band fix upon the day for the Rising—The Terrible Mysteries of Induction—The Chamber of Horror—Death and the Dead—The Revel—Exodus of the Marauders—Murrell returns Home—Abduction of Henning's negroes—Introduction of Murrell's Evil Genius—Virgil A. Stewart devotes himself to the task of following Murrell and delivering him up to Justice—He sets out on the Expedition—The Beginning of the End.

After the chief had resumed his seat, the mechanical progress of the business again went on, and the debate commenced in relation to the day which should be set for the rising. This occupied a great share of the subsequent deliberations of the evening, and finally was decided, after having drawn out expressions of opinion from every member present, in favor of the 5th of December, 1835. This gave them eighteen months for final preparation, and the great point having thus been unanimously settled, there remained nothing left for the night, but the admission of some new members who were detained in an adjoining building by a company of "strykers," to await the order of business which would allow their applications to be entertained by the council.

As soon as the 5th of December, 1835, had been settled upon by the band as the day of the general insurrection, there was no business left but the admission of new members, and, as a feast was to crown the deliberations of the evening, the members of the Grand Council looked around, with considerable anxiety, toward those of their number who had proposed the names of applicants at a previous meeting, to be revouched for, and introduced at this. The time having arrived for their introduction, Murrell rung a bell to make an inquiry from a sort of sergeant-at-arms, whether every preparation had been made for the usual mysteries of induction; and being answered in the affirmative, he gave the signal for the new men to be ushered in.—As soon as the direction was given, five aspirants for the honors of the order, were introduced by their several vouchers and arrayed before the tribunal of the chief, to listen to a short general address on the importance of the obligations they were about to assume, and the perils attendant upon the betrayal of any of their trusts. This being through, the name of the first in order was called. Upon his standing forth, a man, dressed in a sombre and peculiar uniform, and holding a drawn sword in his hand suddenly issued from the folds of a heavy black curtain behind the chieftain's chair, and, taking the hand of the neophyte, disappeared with him through the aperture by which he came. From the council-hall the bewildered aspiraint, after being led through several tortuous passages, was thrust into a dark and cavernous apartment, the jet black walls and gloomy atmosphere of which were only sufficiently relieved by a misty sort of light to betray the horrid spectacle what was designed to make a fearful impression on his mind forever. Looking round for an instant, and finding he was left alone, he exercised a natural curiosity in seeking to piece the gloom that pressed in upon him on all sides. By degrees, the heavy shadows yielded to the perseverance of his vision, and then, with a terror that started all his joints, he beheld before his eyes a bier, bearing a ghastly corpse, trickled out in all the livery of the grave, with its pale and sunken cheeks triced in a napkin, and its hands folded solemnly across its breast. Behind, and standing immediately over this appalling sight, was seen a skeleton, with its fleshless arm up-raised, and poising a spear, which was aimed directly at his heart. Shuddering at this awful spectacle, the terrified beholder almost cowered to the earth, but before his startled mind could recover from the first impression, the silence was broken by a deep and impressive voice which appeared to issue from the corpse, and which commenced the recapitulation of an oath as horrifying in its terms as the details of the scene. The ceremony ended by a solemn abjuration to swear by kissing the body, which being done, the door of the apartment opened, and the awe-stricken and unnerved victim of the scene was led out again by his mysterious conductor.*

In this way the five ambitious aspirants, who had applied for admission to the band, were made members of

---

* The body on the bier was represented by a live robber who was dressed out for the occasion, but whose condition was concealed by artful preparation, assisted by the imperfect light.

the brotherhood, after which a general feast wound up the proceedings of the evening.

The second morning after the meeting, saw Murrell across his horse, with his head turned in a northerly direction. He had bidden a warm good-bye to most of the members of the band, and had he not been pressed by some commanding interests at home, would have consulted the policy of remaining yet another day to perform the courtesies of the last adieu. He was a skillful observer of human nature, and knew the value of the final impression; but upon thinking over all the triumphant characteristics of the gathering, he came to the conclusion that he could afford a partial compromise with a point of judgment, and venture a trifling infraction of his theory. He travelled alone. Yes, this powerful chief started off without a single attendant. Friendship did not cling to his side, and not even an admiring "Stryker" could be seen hovering about his trail, to watch over his safety, or to gaze upon his greatness. But crime can hold no state in the face of Heaven's light. The sun either drives it into hiding holes, or condemns it to desolation. Every rogue of the Grand Council of the Arkansas was in much the same condition as his chief, and if he were not skulking off entirely by himself, he, at any rate, was not trusting himself with more than a single companion. The chief's safety, however, admitted of no such risks; so his security, on an occasion of so much importance as this general dispersion, was consulted by absolute desertion. He arrived at home in time for the business which inspired his haste, and after its performance immediately resumed the direction of the complicated secret machinery which was necessary to the proper maintenance of all the unseen, but not less numerous and important details of a plot so gigantic as the one which occupied his bad heart and scheming brain.

Occasional intervals of leisure would direct his attention to trifling speculations, and in the course of the two months succeeding his return from the Council, he pointed out a negro a-piece to three several Strykers, who dropped in to see him at various times, each of whom faithfully ran off with the slave, according to direction, and as faithfully returned the leader his share of the avails. It was not long before the neighbourhood began to buzz again at these repetitions of an offence, which, it was hoped, was at an end, and attention again turned to Murrell as the perpetrator. Suspicion had rested on him before, and it turned itself naturally back to him again. Many thought him innocent, however, and at the instance of his secret friends, believed that Long had persecuted him; while others, arguing with a more accurate judgment, insisted that the scene in the woods, where he had been detected with the negroes, was only capable of a construction in favor of his guilt. Among those who held the latter opinion were the old preacher, Henning, and his eldest son; and as they had been the most active against him, during his original difficulty, and in the episode of Captain Slick's company of "Regulators," Murrell was reminded of the obligations of hatred he was under in that quarter. He was, therefore, determined to give these two pursuers a serious pecuniary blow, and, as the readiest means of effecting it, he decided upon the abduction of two of their finest negroes. With the intention of putting this immediately in force, he wrote, in the latter part of December (1834), to one of his most trusty men in the Arkansas, and directed him to come immediately on to him, in Madison, on a matter of importance. As soon as he dispatched this letter, he devoted himself to the task of preparing the slaves for the desertion of their master. He found this a more difficult effort than he had at first imagined. The negroes had been well treated; one of them was a great favorite with his master, and both had been impressed with a profound prejudice against the negro stealer. But though these were checks, they were not insurmountable obstructions to his hopes, and the insidious and smooth-tongued white man soon conquered their simple power of resistance. On the night of the 18th January, but three weeks after his first attempt at their seduction, he was enabled to deliver them into the hands of the Arkansas Stryker, and despatch them with one of his fleetest horses to share the labor with the stout steed that the Stryker had brought with him. Having accomplished this feat triumphantly, he considered himself half acquitted of his obligation of revenge.

As soon as the Hennings discovered their loss, they at once attributed it to the agency of their malevolent and dangerous enemy, Murrell, but having no evidence by which to trace it to his door, they were obligated to conceal an open expression of their suspicions and seek to ascertain something which might lead to his detection, by some secret management. With this view, they set a shrewd neighbor to work among the residents of Murrell's more immediate vicinity, who, devoting himself assiduously to his task, soon contrived a chance interview between his own and the robber's wife. This was well conceived, and resulted in the partial satisfaction of drawing from the thoughtless gossip of the latter, the important fact that her husband intended to leave for Randolph, a town on the Mississippi river, on the 26th. This information was immediately conveyed to the Hennings, who, on receiving it, determined to watch Murrell's movements, and have him followed, under the impression that his object was to proceed to the place where the negroes were concealed.

Here was a grand point lost by the negro-stealer, without his being conscious of it; but he had an offset in the imprudence of the possessors of the secret, who by communicating it to others, did not leave him long at his mercy. The Hennings, unwilling to trust entirely to their own judgments in what they considered a very important matter, consulted with some friends as to the future course of proceedings. It happened that among these, was one of their own most respectable and esteemed acquaintances, who also possessed the double advantage of standing equally high as a member of the grand council of the Arkansas, and consequently owned superior obligations to Murrell. By this man, Murrell learned not only that the old preacher suspected him, but also learned that they had kept spies around his house ever since the night after the abduction of the negroes, and received from them in conclusion the information, that they intended to follow his trail when he left for Randolph. The young leader smiled at the design, and was prompt in his decision, not to alter the resolution of starting at the designated time. He only considered one measure necessary, and that was one of bravado and effrontery. He did not choose this course merely because it gratified his hostile feelings, but because he thought it really more precautionary than a timid or evasive policy. He therefore sat down in a day or two afterwards, which delay he only submitted to on account of the friend who gave him the information, and wrote to Richard Henning, the old man's son, the following letter:—

Denmark, January 23, 1835.

"Sir:—I have been told that you accuse me of being concerned in stealing you own and your father's negroes, and I have been told also, that you have thought proper to vapor about what you would do with me if you could be sure of having me on equal terms. I say I have been told these things, and I wish to reply if they be true, that I can whip you from the point of a dagger to the anchor of a ship. But, sir, if I have been misinformed by malicious persons who wish to do you a discredit, I trust you will receive this letter as a message of friendship.— I am about leaving for Randolph, and shall be pleased to have your company on any terms you may choose, or to satisfy you, if it is necessary, that my intentions and business are honest.

"Yours according to the truth or falsify of the rumors.
"JOHN A. MURRELL."
"RICHARD HENNING."

This letter was despatched by a trusty carrier, and was delivered into young Henning's own hand. No answer came, but Murrell did not expect any. He only wished to be satisfied that it reached its destination, for he felt certain that its tenor would have the effect of deterring pursuit. He made his calculation on the ground, that young Henning would naturally conclude, that a man who would thus boldy invite scrutiny, would hardly betray himself by any incautious act.

But there was a danger brewing of which Murrell had made no calculation, and which, fortunately for society, he received no notice of. This was the unheralded arrival in Madison of a young man, about twenty-five years of age, named Virgil A. Stewart. He was a native of Georgia, but at the age of twenty-one had migrated to Madison county, with the avails of an early partnership which enabled him to purchase himself a handsome farm within a few miles of Jackson. While at this place he became acquainted with the Hennings. He did not remain long in Madison, however, for selling his farm in 1832, he turned in the direction of the Choctaw purchase, and there entered into business with a man by the name of Clanton.[1] This latter connection lasted till the close of 1834, when we find him returning to Madison County, at the above period, and on the night of the 28th of January, 1835, paying a visit to his old friends, the Hennings. This man was destined to be the evil genius to Murrell—the opposing influence which, after circling round his fate for a period of years, was doomed to find the contract which should end in his destruction.

The Hennings, after the usual greetings of an unexpected meeting were over, informed their young friend of the whole affair of the abduction of the negroes, and communicated to him their suspicions of Murrell, and their belief that his intended departure for Randolph on the 26th was the commencement of a journey to the place where the negroes were kept concealed. After some

---

1. Matthew Clanton, a merchant and farmer with whom Stewart had dealings in Mississippi.

reflection and deliberate consideration of the letter to the preacher's son, Stewart came to the same conclusion, and then, with a generosity natural to his years, offered to contribute his services to any measures that might tend to fasten the guilt upon the perpetrator, or that might be required to drive him from the country. Mr. Henning soon satisfied Stewart that the latter could not be effected by any but legal means, if even by that, and then having confidence in the frank offer of his young friend, proposed that as he had represented himself free from any pressing engagements for a time, he should accompany his son Richard in pursuit of Murrell when he left for Randolph. Fired with indignation at the perpetrator of such villanies as stood reputed to the negro stealer, Stewart readily acceded to his proposal, but when the old man with a natural sense of justice hinted a remuneration for his time, he warmly rejected the offer, and declared that the gratification of being instrumental in bringing such an offender to justice, was more than a compensation for all the exertions he could bestow upon the object. Inspired with these feelings, and with a sincere desire to serve his old friend, Stewart took leave of Mr. Henning on the night of the 25th to proceed to the house of a Dr. Evans, at Denmark, where he was to meet young Henning by appointment at an early hour on the following morning.

In the mean time, Murrell, who was entirely unconscious of these gathering dangers (Stewart having had the caution to insist on the perfect secrecy of his expedition,) made more than his usual preparations for his journey. He thrust his best pistols in his bosom and armed himself with his truest knife, and then, having given full directions as to certain matters that were to transpire in his household previous to his return, he saddled his best horse while the stars were yet winking in the sky.

Honesty was not less awake then knavery, however, and when the first peep of dawn saw the well appointed robber wave an adieu to his wife who watched him from the gate, it also found his Evil Genius pacing up and down beside his horse at Denmark, impatient to fall upon his trail and stamping fretfully about at the strange delay of his expected companion. Time kept slipping away without any sign of young Henning's appearance, until at length finding that the delay had extended to the measure of four hours, Stewart concluded his friend had been taken ill, and determined to undertake the expedition alone. He therefore mounted his horse at ten o'clock, and leaving Denmark, proceeded towards the turnpike at Estanaula, over the Hatchee river.[2] This was about seven miles distant, and being the only crossing in the winter season, he could safely calculate upon either intercepting, or gaining intelligence of the object of his pursuit.

The weather was unusually cold, and the hard frozen road, cut by recent travelling into heavy ruts, was also stiff and sharp with a glaze of sleet that presented equal impediments to his comfort and his speed. While he was slowly progressing over this perplexed and painful route, the peculiar dangers of his enterprise, made greater by the absence of any weapon but a single pistol and the failure of young Henning, rose in succession in his mind to deter him from his expedition; but he had

---

2. Estanaula, Tennessee was located on the northeast bank of the Harchie River in southwest Haywood County.

taken his resolve, and his determination was superior to any arguments of fear.

When he reached the toll house at Estanaula, he inquired of the keeper if Murrell had gone by, and on receiving a reply in the negative, he further inquired, "if he might not have passed the gate during the night without his knowledge." Just as the gatekeeper was about to reply to the last interrogatory, his eye caught a glimpse of an object coming down the road, and after leaning forward a moment to satisfy himself, he drew back and nodded his head in the direction of his sight with the remark of "Yonder comes Murrell now."

CHAPTER XIV.

Meeting between Stewart and Murrell on the turnpike—Dialogue between the marauder and his pursuer—The theory of crime—Murrell's admiration of his new acquaintance—His disguised description of the character of his clan and their leader—Roadside stories—Poplar Creek—Night—Arrival at the house of one of the "Strykers."

Stewart had seen Murrell but once in his life, and then at such a distance that he would not have been able to recognize him on this occasion, had it not have been for the direction of the man at the gate. He therefore drew carelessly to one side of the road, as if maintaining his conversation with the toll-gatherer, though his real purpose was to get a good look at the terrible marauder, whose fate he was about so boldly to measure with his own.

Murrell rode quickly up, and after taking a sharp and rapid glance at the horseman, dropped his fare in the toll-gatherer's hand, and continued on his way without looking back. Stewart then renewed his conversation with the gate-keeper, and upon being assured that there was no mistake, that the person who had just passed was Murrell, and no person else, he paid his toll and proceeded after him. Studying the gait of the robber's horse, the pursuer measured his own speed so as to lay exactly on his trail, though he would occasionally drop behind, and entirely out of sight, for the purpose of preventing Murrell from having any suspicion of his intention. In this way the two travellers proceeded on their route for the period of two hours. The day was bitter cold, and the rude winds swept the road and lashed their faces without mercy. There were no objects in sight but themselves. Both man and beast were housed, and, save their presence, desolation reigned supreme. The meditations of Stewart were anything but pleasing. The grim and cheerless aspect of the landscape, the keen and searching blast, and the figure of the terrible marauder, rising and settling over the undulations of the perspective, seemed to flit before him as gloomy warnings against his enterprise. In despite of himself, he relapsed into sad and discouraging reflections, and allowed himself to dwell suppositively upon the dangers he was provoking. While thus wrapt in a maze of conflicting thoughts, his horse, as if taking advantage of the absence of his master, insensibly increased his pace, until he had doubled the cautious gait to which he had been previously restrained. In this way a quarter of an hour elapsed, when, on mounting the culmination of a long stretch of ascent, which, during that time, had shut out the view beyond, Stewart was suddenly aroused from his reverie by finding himself hard upon the robber's heels. He had the mortification to observe, moreover, that the object of his pursuit had noticed his approach, and was taking a long stare at him, which showed that he considered his movements were entitled to a special interest. Matters had now arrived at a crisis, and Stewart found himself forced to change his policy. He accordingly promptly decided on the only course left him, and, as is customary with daring and decisive minds, adapted the accident to his purposes, with an alacrity which seemed as if he hailed it as a stroke of fortune. He restrained his first desire to draw a check upon his neglected rein, and, touching the heedless animal lightly with his spur, trotted briskly up to Murrell's side. Bowing respectfully as he reined in company with the marauder, he accosted him with, "Very disagreeable travelling, sir."

Murrell turned half round in his saddle at the salute, and, after a sharp scrutiny of the stranger, softened into suavity, and with an equal degree of politeness, replied, "Extremely disagreeable, sir."

"I think we shall have snow before night."

"It will snow nothing but flints, then. A flake of snow would freeze to death in such an atmosphere as this;" said the robber, drawing his coat collar up about his ears.

"I believe you're about right," returned Stewart, shrugging himself within his coat. "Well, the travelling and the weather are not more disagreeable than my business."

"Indeed! Pray what can your business be, that you can compare it to travelling on such a road, and in such a day as this?"

"Horse hunting, sir."

"Ah, horse hunting, eh! Well, this is disagreeable, indeed—disagreeable, indeed! Where did your horse stray from?"

"From Yallabusha river, in the Choctaw purchase."

"Where is he striking for?"

"I can't decide. I am told that he was owned before I purchased him, by a man in this part of the country, somewhere; but it is uncertain if he has strayed back or no—a sort of cross-and-pile chance, any how."

"How far down will you go?"

"Well, I don't know exactly. The roads are so bad and the weather so extremely cold, that I am becoming very tired of so uncertain a business. I am tired, too, of travelling by myself. How far down will *you* go on this road?"

The robber did not appear to notice this skilful evasion, and the return of the question against himself, but answered without hesitation. "I go down about eighteen miles, to the house of a friend. I am anxious to get there to-night, but it will be very late travelling in such cold weather; so we are both pretty badly off. But, perhaps, instead of being strayed, your horse is stolen?"

"No, I guess not," returned Stewart, slowly; "I guess not; but I had much rather some gay fellow had snaked him off, than he should be straying at the mercy of such housing, only as he can find in weather like this."

As this expression fell from Stewart, the land pirate turned full him with a steady and inquiring gaze, but finding no professional reply, he contended himself with a slight but gratified smile at the liberal philosophy of his companion, and continued—

"Are you acquainted in this part of the country?"

"No, I am an entire stranger about here."

MEETING BETWEEN STEWART AND MURRELL

"Where are you from?"

"I was born in the state of Georgia, and was brought up there; but I moved to the Choctaw Purchase some nine or ten months ago."

"Well, how do you like that country?"

"Why, I must say I like it very well, all things considered."

"Is there much stealing going on there?"

"Well, no, I can't say there is very much, considering the wild state of things there, and that we are pretty much savages and forerunners mixed up together. You know how all new countries are generally first settled."

"Excuse me for interrupting you, sir," said the robber abruptly, as if challenged by a sudden idea; "but I'll tell you who you put me in mind of, every time you speak—I suppose you don't know him though—I mean John A. Murrell, who resides in Madison, within a mile or two of Denmark. You must have *heard* of him at any rate."

"Murrell—Murrell—well, no, I can't say that I have," said Stewart, repeating the name with admirable dubiousness—"Murrell—Murrell—yet it appears to me I *have* heard that name before, too."

Completely imposed upon by his companion's superior dissimulation and presence of mind, the wily robber now abandoned his former guarded manner, and entered into a more free and general conversation. With the natural mistrust of one who knows that he deserves to be detected, he had feared at first that he might be in company with one of Henning' spies, or, at any rate, with a person who was acquainted with his character; but having satisfactorily applied a test, which he thought that no man who really knew him could endure, without eliciting some alteration of countenance, he felt that he had no further precaution to assume. The information, moreover, that Mr. Stewart was from Georgia, and had resided in the Purchase but a few months, was an additional assurance that he could know but little, if anything, of his character or career.

Observing the marauder's satisfied ease of mind, Stewart, on the other hand, experienced a great relief in his apprehensions, and he felt convinced that he had but to sustain the impression he had already made, to insure ultimate success. Bearing in mind that Murrell had expressed an intention to visit a friend, he at once determined on accompanying him despite the weather, for he was strongly inclined to believe that Mr. Henning's negroes were at the house of that friend, awaiting the arrival of his fellow traveller.

As the horsemen proceeded, the conversation took a variety of turns, but Murrell, as if he took a great pleasure in hearing the liberal views of his companion, would continually revert to the subject of "speculation," and dwell with delight upon the deeds of the marauders. This was his common plan of drawing out those whom he desired to convert, and as he had already conceived the idea of making the young stranger a proselyte, we shall be enabled to obtain in the course of their dialogue (faithfully preserved by Stewart) his system of seduction.

"This country," said he, "is about being overrun by a company of rogues, who are so numerous that nothing can be done with them. They operate with impunity, and seize what they list, and if the losers are bold enough to suspect or to accuse any of their members, the rest pounce upon a further portion of the sufferer's property, as a warning to submit with a good grace to exactions in future. This system of retaliatory visitation has been so invariable, that many of the plundered have already found that it is the wisest plan to be on good terms with the band, and wink at an ordinary depredation. The movements of this banditti are directed by two young men from Middle Tennessee, who have moved down to Madison County, and are now resident there. They are both shrewd and daring fellows, and the eldest, in addition to his other accomplishments, is one of the best judges of law in the United States. His judgment directs all the enterprises of any moment, and he generally so guards his own offences, that the law slips away from him like rain from a duck's back."

"Well, sir," said Stewart, "they must be remarkably capable men, and for my part I do not see but their abilities are as creditably employed as are the talents of many who are accounted the pillars of society. In this world every man must take care of himself. Some do it by siding with the majority, and by helping to enforce set-laws, while they violate higher moral obligations themselves, without scruple; a smaller portion despise hypocrisy, and set themselves in open opposition to the rest. It is a mere difference of opinion, which makes one party lock the other up when they get them in their power, and which makes the other party retaliate by plundering or killing the first, whenever they get a chance. It's a game. Luck changes from side to side, and it occasions me no grief when I see the weaker party now and then get the upper hand. I believe, sir, in respect for the law, when the law takes care of all alike, but when war is open between classes of society, I say let the hardest fend off. That's my doctrine, sir, and I don't care who knows it."

"Just so," said the robber, his face suffused with pleasure at the congenial eloquence of his companion. "Just so, sir. That's my doctrine too, and you have expressed my sentiments on the subject much better than I could myself. Now, I have no doubt that these two brothers are as honorable among their associates as any men on earth. That is as much as any member of the other portion of society can say of himself, and a great deal more than most of them can. It is true they are perfect devils to their enemies, but power is always terrible to any thing which conflicts with its will. I don't care whether it is in the pulpit, or in the hands of a court of law."

"Your philosophy is correct, sir, and you might have added, that that power is doubly obnoxious when comes coupled with a hypocritical pretence of affection for the object of its vengeance. How old is the elder brother that you speak of?"

"He is about thirty, I suppose, but his stirring course of life has given him the experience of fifty years. He has experienced some reverses of fortune, but some of which are an off-set to his successes. The citizens of Madison once attempted to storm him from the county, but he would not endure the movement; so he passed the secret signal to the most trusty of his clan, and soon found himself surrounded by enough and to spare of daring and undaunted spirits.—He fortified his dwelling like a castle of war, and throwing himself on his legal rights, to live where he pleased, in this free country, stood ready to maintain them with a posse comitatus of his own. The "regulators" marched up towards his dwelling for the purpose of sacking it and hanging its owner to the next tree, but when they saw the muzzles of five or six brass pieces peeping at them down the road, and ready to rake them into eternity, they took thought upon the matter, and asked one of their number, who had been a justice of the peace, if it would be according to law to take the building, any how. The justice told them that they would render themselves liable if they should provoke extensive bloodshed by proceeding to take it *vi et armis* in the face of a determined opposition; whereupon they concluded to abandon the attempt like good citizens, and show their respect for the laws, by dispersing and going home. Ah, sir, society will seldom venture to trifle with the powerful, but it will tread upon a beggar and disdain to calculate the wrong."

"What a wonderful man you tell me of."

"He is indeed a wonderful man, but he is most wonderful in his determined WILL. After all, that is the greatest quality of man, sir, for it goes to its purpose when genius forgets it, and it accomplished every thing, when mere genius can accomplish nothing. It is found in a brave man's bosom, and it is worth half the qualities of the head.—The man I tell you of never forgets his purpose, and those who have provoked him have learned too late the force of that unswerving will. All who have ever sought to persecute and drive him, have got sick of it, and are trying to make fair weather, and I am told that some tremendous plans which he has nursed for years, are now on the point of consummation."

As Murrell was carried away by enthusiasm of the character he was describing, Stewart was secretly rejoicing over the discovery of the weak point in his character; and having found that with all his shrewdness and penetration the robber possessed an overweening self-conceit, that was directly accessible to the grossest flattery, he felt that he had gained an advantage which was in itself an offset to a hundred obstacles that presented themselves before.

"Why, sir," remarked he at the conclusion of the robber's last expression, "such a man as you describe, is a genius of a most extraordinary character, and needs but circumstances and opportunity, to make him an Alexander or a Napoleon. He possesses the highest kind of greatness—a greatness that does not grow out of birth or conventional position, but one that springs from the force of his own mental powers."

"He is equal to Hare, the renowned highwayman,[1] who spread such terror through the South and East at the commencement of the present century," said Murrell, "and that," added he, "I consider as the highest kind of praise."

Mr. Stewart and his companion had now reached the valley of Poplar Creek. It was late in the afternoon. The sun was just sinking behind the hills of the west, but its descent was unseen, except in the reflection of the light that gilded the icy fringes of the numerous poplars that stood in grim batallions around their pathway.

"This is a beautiful scene," said Murrell, "it continues throughout the valley of this creek; but when we have passed beyond, a good road will conduct us direct to the house of my friend."

1. Joseph Thompson Hare was a Pennsylvania-born robber who with his gang terrorized travelers along the Natchez Trace between Nashville, Tennessee and Natchez, Mississippi in the early 1800s.

While they were yet in the valley and admiring the abundant growth of young poplars in every direction, the shadows of the evening closed upon them. Both travellers appeared to feel the influence of the darkness, and benumbed with cold and tired of talking, each declined his head and gave himself up to his reflections.—To Stewart, all that he had see and heard now seemed to take the air of mystery. He conned over the terrible deeds of blood in which his companion had dilated during an afternoon with a fiendish luxury of description, and at times he could scarcely realize that all that had passed within the last few hours was not the portion of a dream. A thousand images of terror flitted before his imagination, and as the wind swept by, now wildly screaming in his ear, now wailing wofully among the swinging trees, he felt half inclined to believe that the unseen spirits which preside over the destinies of men were struggling for the decision of his fate. His apprehensions were not the offspring of timidity. Caution alone, pointed out a hundred perils. There might be danger in the house of Murrell's friend, and there, his existence and his expedition might find from the hands of the pair, a bloody sequestration.

While indulging in these gloomy thoughts he and his companion had left the valley several hundred yards behind, when coming suddenly upon an old log burning by the road side, the robber drew up and proposed they should dismount and warm themselves.

"You appear very cold, my young friend," said Murrell to his companion, as they were seated by the fire— "Here, take a pull at this flask and eat this piece of cake. It will revive you up a little. I fear you are frosted. Ah, I see you can't stand it like me. I have undergone enough hardships to kill a horse. Take some more: take another drop, I tell you—it won't hurt you, don't be afraid of it. There, that'll do—now I'll guarantee you'll feel like a stallion in five minutes."

"I am deeply obliged to your kindness, sir; I think it will revive me. I did not know I was so extremely cold."

"Ah, you ought never to start out unprepared. Now, for my part, I would as soon think of setting out without a bridle as without a flask and a bite. I travel a considerable, and my old woman never neglects to have these things on hand for me. Ah, the fire feels good, and we may as well enjoy it for a few minutes. It will be pitch dark yet for half an hour, then the fair queen of night will favor us with her silver beams, and light us to a more hospitable lodging. Have you ever travelled much by moonlight?"

"Not much, sir."

"Then you have not the same love for her beams as a veteran in the mysteries. Here, take another pull at the flask, and I will tell you an adventure I once had with a party of Camanches on the Arkansas river."

Before the robber had finished his story, the icy branches of the surrounding trees began to sparkle with refracted light, and when he had concluded, the risen moon poured a full stream upon the surface of the road, and reminded him it was time to resume their saddles.

They rode briskly on with renovated spirits. Stewart increasingly in his caution as he approached nearer and nearer to the seat of danger, and managing all the while to keep slightly in the rear of the marauder, so as to maintain a watch upon his movements. At length Murrell noticed that his companion lagged, but not attributing it to an ulterior motive, exclaimed—

"Come, come, my friend, ride up, the night is cold, and we have still far to go. Let us therefore get over the ground as fast as possible.—Come up, and I will tell you of another feat of this elder brother of whom I have been speaking."

The robber then went on to detail several of the exploits which have been related in their regular order in the course of this history—concluding with a description of the manner in which he obtained the sorrel colt from Marvin the methodist, on pretence of being a broken preacher. There, however, he broke off, and looking round at the landmarks of the scene, exclaimed—

"Well, sir, we are now within three miles of my old friends; ride up, and we will soon be there. By the by, will you go down as far as Randolph? Your horse may have got down in that quarter."

"I think it's likely I will, sir; and if I were not scarce of funds, I would continue my journey over to Arkansas, so long as I am so near it. I have heard much of that country, and I think the land and the people would suit me."

"I would be very glad if you would go over with me," said the robber. "I will supply you if you get out, and will show you the country as long as you want to stay. I have a thousand friends there, and it need cost us nothing if we should stay six months. If you'll say the word, I'll guarantee you shall go where you can come away with a better horse than the one you're now hunting for. A man with as keen an eye as yours, should never spend his time in looking after a lost horse."

This concluding remark was uttered with a significance of tone and with a pointedness of gaze, that expressed a world of insidious meaning, but Stewart parried it with admirable skill, and without appearing to observe its aim, simply thanked the robber for his offer and his compliment, and gave a half promise to accept the invitation on the morrow.

"Well, then, we'll see in the morning, as you say. But here is my old friend's. Come, alight, every thing is quiet."

While awaiting an answer to their summons, Stewart slipped open two buttons of his over coat, and thrust his hand into his bosom to feel that his solitary pistol is placed ready to be drawn at a moment's need. After the lapse of an minute the robber repeated his rap, when the shuffling of a pair of slippered feet gave information that an inmate of the mansion was approaching to give them entrance. A watch-word passed, the lock turned, and holding his night clothes close against the entrance of the sharp and penetrating air with one hand, and the edge of the door with the other, a stout old man about sixty years of age, let them in.

Recognizing his leader after a moment's scrutiny, the old stryker, for such he was, gave Murrell a cheerful greeting, and the latter, replying to his courtesy in the same tone, introduced Stewart as a recent friend.

Stewart glanced hastily around the apartment, in apprehension of being seen and recognized by the parson's negroes, whom he believed to be on the premises; but observing no object to justify his alarm, he yielded to his fatigue and sat down by the fire. Murrell and the old man drew to another portion of the apartment and engaged in a low conversation. Seeing this, Stewart took the circumstance as an excuse, and requested to be shown to his room. The request was granted with alacrity, and taking a parting drink with his fellow traveller, and exchanging a "good night," he followed his host up stairs. Fastening his bed-room door securely, and laying his pistol under his pillow, he went to bed, when, after a few anxious conjectures as to what course he should pursue in the morning, to avoid the recognition of the negroes if he should chance to meet them, he sunk under the agitating thought, and fell asleep.

CHAPTER XV.

Reconnoitering—An Equal Start—Exchanges of Courtesy—
Approach to Wesley—Apprehensions of Stewart—Ingenious
Extrication—A Friend in Need—The Repast in the Thicket—Murrell
Discloses himself to his Fellow Traveller—Exchange of Pledges—
Plans and Prospects for the Future—Revelations of the Past—
A Hard Ride—The Banks of the Mississippi.

After a night of tolerable ease, Mr. Stewart rose at an early hour in the morning, and faithful to his purpose, took advantage of the first light of dawn to stroll over the premises in search of Mr. Henning's negroes. He hoped by this course to provide against the danger of an accidental meeting with the slaves, by warning them not to recognize him in the presence of Murrell. There was some risk in this, for the negroes might be considered in the light of willing fugitives; but he felt convinced that he could in a very short conversation assure them of the fate in store for them at the hands of their new friends. A half hour industriously spent, convinced him, however, that the runaways were not there, and returning to the house he found Murrell abroad, and giving directions to the landlord to prepare their horses. As costing the pair with a cheerful salute, Stewart made particular inquiries of the host after his stray horse, for the purpose of giving color to his story, and ended by leaving a pretended description of the animal, with strict directions for its detention until his return, in case it should stray to the neighborhood. He then followed Murrell's example and threw himself across his horse, and bidding the host adieu, trotted off with his companion at a brisk pace over the frozen road.

"Well, my young friend," said the robber after they had got fairly side by side, "what say you of the trip to Arkansas this morning?"

"I have not fairly made up my mind even yet, whether to go or not. How far is the next town in this direction?"

"We come to the village of Wesley,[1] in Haywood county, next. I should say it's about six miles."

"Well, I'll decide between this and that; but I incline to think I'll go."

"Go, why yes, certainly you'll go! If you don't you're a fool, that's all I have got to say. I can show you some of the handsomest girls you ever saw, if you do. I'm in town when I get there."

"You talk right towards me," replied Stewart, in the slang suited to the subject. "Nothing suits me better than pretty girls."

1. Wesley, Tennessee was three miles from the Hatchie River and 31 miles from Randolph.

"Why, now you begin to come up," exclaimed the robber. "I knew I was not mistaken in you; and you'll see that you'll not be much mistaken in *me*. I'll put you right among 'em. But let me see, I've never thought to ask you your name!"

"No: our conversation has been so interesting since we fell in together, that neither of us have thought of it yet. I'm not over particular about names anyhow, but Adam Hues suits me very well for the present."

The secret point which was evident in the studied tone of this remark, drew from Murrell a quick responsive glance to show that it was fully understood, and his first impulse appeared to be to answer by opening his confidence, but he seemed to be checked by an after thought, and after delivering himself of a short cough, replied:—

"My name is Merrill, and I can only say, Mr. Hues, that I like you, because you're the right kind of man, and if you'll go with me where I want you to go, I'll put you in the way of something handsome. But I won't over-urge you. I'll give you the chance—you want to decide yourself; and in the mean time, while we're between this and the village, I'll tell you another feat of that elder brother we were talking about yesterday."

Murrell here related the adventure with the Tipton boy, who after being sold and abducted five or six successive times, was murdered in the swamps of the Arkansas.

At the conclusion of this horrid take the travellers found themselves within half a mile of Wesley. Stewart, who had acquaintances in the neighborhood, began to feel considerable anxiety lest his friends should recognize him, and thus subvert his plans. It at length occurred to him that the pretended looseness of one of his horse's shoes might furnish an excuse for a separation, which would enable him to take the necessary precautions. Accordingly, as they entered the village, he contrived to get Murrell to point out the tavern where he intended to stop and get breakfast. Having secured this point, he appeared suddenly to bethink himself of something, and desired his conductor to drive on and order their meal, while he turned aside to a blacksmith's shop.

Not suspecting, any ruse, the robber bade him make haste, as they had no time to lose; and then rode briskly to the tavern.

Fortunately for Stewart, immediately after Murrell had parted from him, he saw a gentleman named Colonel William H. Bayliss, with whom he was well acquainted, passing along the road. Attracting his attention, he beckoned him aside, out of sight of the tavern, and rapidly made him acquainted with his situation, and the whole condition of affairs. He then impressed upon Bayliss the necessity of his not being recognised while in Murrell's company, and directed him to go at once to the tavern, and if he found any of his acquaintances there to put them on their guard. "I shall follow you immediately," concluded he, "and after I once get in, I want you to watch the door and see that no one else enters to interfere with my arrangements. I shall not detain you long, for we shall merely stay for a hurried breakfast, for I intend to accept his offer to accompany him to Arkansas. I have entered into the business with the intention to succeed, and I will not give it up till I have tracked the villain to his den."

Bayliss then inquired of Stewart if he was properly armed, and finding that the young man had but a single pistol in his possession, he insisted upon his turning into the blacksmith shop until he ran to the house and obtained him another. Stewart followed his advice, and receiving the weapon from the hands of his friend, after the delay of a few minutes, had the satisfaction of seeing him make the best of his way to the tavern. He followed in a few minutes. On entering the bar-room he noticed two of his friends sitting by the stove, but observed by their perfect inattention to his presence, that Colonel Bayliss had faithfully followed his directions. Calling him by the name of Hues, Murrell then invited Stewart to take a drink, which being done, they adjourned to a back room and got their breakfast. In the course of the meal, Stewart informed his fellow traveller that he had concluded to accept this friendly invitation to accompany him to Arkansas, and received in return an approbation of his resolution. In half an hour after their arrival at the inn, the travellers were once more upon the road, heading for Randolph, on the Mississippi river. Stewart expected, now that he had virtually made himself a disciple or follower of the marauder, that as soon as they should leave the house, he then would unbosom himself, and define their future position to each other; but he had not yet sounded the profound depth of the villain's character, and did not credit him sufficiently for prudence in supposing he would place him in possession of a tremendous secret, without first having him completely in his power, and without also testing his sentiments on "speculation" still further. Murrell, therefore, for the first half hour, occupied himself with indifferent subjects, and then, but as if without design, returned again to the feats of the marauders. Three hours were thus occupied, during which Stewart kept increasing the confidence of the robber by expressing his unqualified admiration of the most desperate and bloody deeds of the celebrated elder brother.

"I do not wonder," said he, at the conclusion of one of Murrell's most glowing descriptions, "that this man is a terror to his enemies; neither am I astonished that he should wield such unlimited control over his clan. Such talents and capabilities as he possesses are destined to exercise a wide influence, and joined to his qualities of character, make him truly deserving of the adoration of his followers. I must confess that all I have heard of him commands my admiration, and that I should be proud to consider him my friend."

The warmth and earnestness of this apostrophe seemed to bring the victim of conceit to a sudden determination, and making a remark that the sharp air had already made him both hungry and dry, proposed to turn aside from the road to select a spot for a repast from the cold lunch in his portmanteau. Stewart readily agreed; but when they had gone about a hundred yards into the woods, he felt a sentiment of uneasiness, and enquired the object of leaving the road so far.

"Why, to tell you the truth, Hues," said Murrell, making a partial pause. "I am a particular friend of the young men of whom I have been speaking, as you might have guessed, and as they have recently stolen three negroes in Madison from an old preacher and his son, I should not be surprised if the owners should follow me under the impression that I might have something to do with the business. Indeed Dick Henning, the young man, threatened he would trail me, but though I could settle him and all his party, single handed, as fast as they could come, I do not choose to be taken unawares."

"Well, they shall not do that while I am about," said Stewart, in a spirited manner. "You can count on me to the last, if there's fifty of them!"

"Ah, that's spoken like a staunch man and a true friend. We'll go a little further to the left, and I think we'll soon find a spot to our mind."

The companions pursued their devious way some hundreds of yards further, in an oblique direction, when, coming to an old log, in the centre of a dense jungle, Murrell reined up his horse, and commenced preparations for their repast. After they were fairly seated, and Stewart had taken a preparatory draught, at the solicitation of his entertainer, the robber, taking his lips from the flask, and looking steadily and meaningly into the young man's face, remarked—

"Mr. Hues, I think you're a liberal-minded man."

"I am gratified at your good opinion, sir."

"I think, Mr. Hues, between ourselves, that I can put you in a *leetle* better business than trading with barefooted Indians."

"I have no doubt you can, sir."

"You say you never heard of these devils, the Murrells, up in Madison county, in this State?"

"It strikes me I have heard their names, but I am an entire stranger to their persons, and know nothing of their history."

"Well, sir," said the robber, while his form dilated with conscious pride as he spoke, "they are the two young men of whom you have heard me say so much, and I—I, sir, am that elder brother."

"You!" exclaimed Stewart, rising as if impelled by an involuntary admiration, and taking off his hat, in reverential homage. "You, sir! Is it possible, then, that I have the pleasure of standing in the presence of that wonderful genius!"

"Genius or not, you stand in the presence of John A. Murrell, the chieftain and leader of a nobler clan of valiant and lordly bandits than ever rallied under one command. A clan, not composed of a lot of ignorant ruffians, who skulk in mountain fastnesses, and only know enough to plunge down and cut a throat, but a clan consisting of the knowing and fighting men of the age. A band of men of mind, who with every thing against them, have won places in the state, and are regarded, in many instances, as the very pillars of the society which they undermine. A band that stretches through a half million of square miles, and strikes terror into five millions of people. Yes, sir, I am John A. Murrell, the land pirate."

"Excuse me, sir," said Stewart, really struck with the enthusiasm and the dignity of the robber chief, "but you have almost deprived me of the power of speech. I was not prepared for such a surprise. I can scarcely conceive I am awake. I can scarcely hope that you will take me under your patronage and protection. I can—"

"I will do everything for those I like and whom I think worthy of my friendship," returned the robber with dignity. "I have studied you closely, and I think I know you. I have tested you a hundred times when you did not suspect my object, and I feel satisfied that I am not mistaken in your character. I am willing that you should be my friend, and I do not fear you if you should choose to be my enemy. Your own sense will tell you that treachery is the most dangerous curse you can pursue, for if, after the disclosures I have made, you should feel disposed to seek my injury, your wisest course would be to draw your knife at once, and seize the only equal chance you'll ever have turn aside the consequences of my revenge. You'd be hunted like a rat, sir; yes, sir, and caught and smothered out of life, without ever having another opportunity to cross a blade in self defence, if you should betray this confidence."

"If I could contemplate treachery to so noble a character, sir, I would be deserving of the worst consequences you describe. I am only anxious of becoming your disciple."

"I do not mistrust you; I believe you to be sincere, and as an evidence of it, I will admit you to my band, and personally give you all the instructions you require. You have fine abilities, and shall belong to the Grand Council of my clan. But come, we have got through with our meal, and now let us gather up the fragments and talk the rest of the matter over as we go along. I have much to say to you."

When they had struck the road again, Murrell resumed:—

"I am now going to the place where I sent the old Methodist's negroes to await me. The time is already past for me to meet the person who has charge of them, and for fear I may miss him, I shall have to insist upon your travelling all night. My delay was occasioned by the suspicions of the owner, and the threats of Dick Henning to follow me. When I heard this, I sent him a letter which I think cooled the fever of his desire for pursuit. But, sir, I can take Dick Henning by my side, and steal and make sale of every negro that he and his father own, and he shall know nothing of the transaction."

"That would be a masterly manœuvre, indeed. I should like to know the process."

"I will explain it by-and-by. It was never my intention to disturb or depredate upon my immediate neighbours until they had commenced the war. These people have persecuted me, and they may now look out for breakers. Their long prayers and Methodist coats shall be no protection against my sworn vengeance."

The conversation of Murrell now turned upon his future prospects of plunder, in which he took pains to impress upon his listener his superior powers of management and the wisdom of his plans. Advancing by degrees, he broke to him his scheme of the negro rebellion, and having warmed with his subject, revealed all the projected operations, which stood recorded on the mystic journals of the mysterious Grand Council. Stewart, in the meanwhile, listened with a breathless and a patient attention, not unmixed with admiration and horror.

"The art of making proselytes," said Murrell, during this conversation, "is very easily accomplished. There is no animal so easy to study as a man. You must commence in this way: Begin to tell some act of villany, and notice the answers and countenance of your listener, as you go on with your story. If you discover him to lean a little, you advance: but if he receded, withdraw, and commence some other subject. If you have carried the matter a little too far, and excited his suspicions while sounding him, make light of the whole affair, and pass it off as a joke."

They rode and talked thus till a late hour of the night, when Stewart finding himself suffering very much from cold, and withal extremely jaded with fatigue, insisted on seeking lodgings. Murrell consented, though he had never once complained, nor seemed to feel the keen cutting wind that proved so unmercifully upon the frame of his less hardened companion. They accordingly obtained quarters at the first house on the road.

At daybreak, the next morning, they were again upon the road, Murrell urging speed, and expressing a determination to reach Arkansas that night. They pressed forward, therefore, at a pace that admitted of but little conversation, but when their steeds had become tolerably worn and lagged for rest, the robber commenced a history of his life. The day was spent in this manner, and when the shades of twilight blotted out the features of their path, the land pirate had not yet concluded the train of his adventures.

Towards the close of the day their progress was considerably interrupted and delayed by the high waters of the Mississippi, which had overflowed the low country adjacent to its right bank, and rendered the ordinary track impassable. This state of things obliged them to change their course, and direct it higher up, so as to strike Chickasaw Bluff, above the plantation of a Mr. Shelby, and from that point to continue down the immediate bank of the river, till they reached a spot which was used as the private crossing place of the clan. As they were crossing Mr. Shelby's plantation, Murrell, by way of displaying his tact to his young friend, entered into a conversation with some of his negroes at work on the bank of the river, and soon succeeded in exciting their discontent to a pitch which extracted from the promise to accompany him to a free state whenever he should call for them.*

When they had progressed about four miles below Mr. Shelby's, they found their way so much embarrassed by the recent overflow, that they were obliged to forego any further efforts to advance, and therefore took lodgings at the house of a Mr. John Champion for the night. They had not been long in the company of Mr. Champion before Murrell commenced sounding that gentleman on the subject of "speculation," by relating the same stories of the marauders with which he had at first amused his fellow traveller. The landlord, however, did not become so readily enamored of the character of the elder brother as the seducer hoped, and after a while, from lack of encouragement, he desisted from the effort, and declared himself ready for bed. Both travellers were then shown to the same chamber, and, soon after lying down, the robber sunk to sleep.

The agitation of Stewart's mind, however, denied him the privilege of so ready a repose. He was on the point of launching himself among a band of fiends, and separating himself from all human aid, and he debated whether he could not at once deliver up the sleeping wretch, and thus spare himself all further peril and privation. But a difficulty presented itself. The world might be incredulous of his story, and he had as yet no sufficient evidence to defeat their doubts. All that he had at present was only hearsay, and his mere personal oath might not be considered as sufficient to substantiate an account of

---

* These minor circumstances are not ommited, as they form points in the testimony of Stewart, on Murrell's trial.

transactions so unusual, and so much above the common order of human crime. He knew the difficulties of legal proof; he foresaw the storm of slander which the organized gang would bring about his ears, and he shrewdly decided that he would have to produce the strongest kind of testimony to carry his point. He therefore boldly resolved to maintain his resolution of crossing to Arkansas, and of beholding with his own eyes the gloomy haunts and sanguinary doings of the ruffians of the morass.

This struggle over, his mind subsided from its strife, and he sank to sleep. Thus ended the third day between the pursuer and the pursued.

CHAPTER XVI.

Watchfulness—A Dark Morning—A Confidant—Commencement of a Foot-tramp trough the Swamp—The Missing Gloves—Arrival at Mr. Erwin's—Disappointment--Employment of the Delay—Storm on the Mississippi—Land Ho!--The Arkansas Shore—Familiar Ground—The Journey's End—The Hut of the Grand Council.

The dawn had not disturbed the shadows of the chamber where the travellers laid, when Stewart found himself awake. He had slept sound during the brief period of his repose, but charged with the weightiest cares, he broke from his heavy lethargy as through he had merely undergone a change of thought and had not slept at all. The robber still laid plunged in a profound repose. As Stewart rubbed his eyes, scarcely more than a moment appeared to have passed since the period of his unconsciousness, and the young adventurer resumed his thoughts at the point where he had resigned them to his dreams. His last resolve had been to stake everything upon tracking the marauder to his den. His next purpose was to take such measures as should reduce his personal risk; or in case the worst should happen, as might avenge his fall and make his death the means of insuring that destruction of the horrible banditti which his life might be scarified to accomplish. In the deep earnestness of his purpose, he had almost lost sight of the original object of the expedition, and the merely contingent hope of finding Mr. Henning's negroes had now comparatively little weight in shaping his determination, or strengthening his devotion.

During the conversation between Murrell and Mr. Champion, on the previous evening, Stewart had watched the landlord closely, and formed an opinion in his favor. He felt convinced from the repugnant horror which the latter had evinced at the robber's recital of various tales of rapine, that he might trust him with his confidence and claim his aid.—As soon as he had arrived at this conclusion, he prepared to act upon it by descending to the landlord's room, but ere he was fairly out of bed, his purpose was defeated, by a sudden pause in the robber's heavy breathing, followed by a slight rustle, and a half drowsy challenge of

"Hues—are you awake?"

"Yes: I was just going to take my watch to the window to see how late it is?"

"The window'll do you no good. It's blacker than the hinges of hell outside.—You'll have to open it and feel the face. Hold on a minute. I'll try mine. I'll tell you in half second how late it is. By the Lord, it's a quarter of six," added he, suddenly, after a moment's pause. "We must be up and off. It'll be daybreak before we can get dressed." Saying this, the robber sprang out upon the floor.

This defeat of his first purpose was ominous, but Stewart did not suffer himself to be discouraged by it. He possesses one of those resolute minds that are only confirmed by disappointment. He dressed himself with alacrity, and on descending with his companion found Mr. Champion astir, with their breakfast half prepared. While at their meal, Murrell learned from their host, that the country was so bad below, that they could not well proceed any further on horseback. That about three miles further down, they would come up to the house of a Mr. Erwin, who could furnish them with a skiff to cross the river; or in the event of disappointment there, they might get one at the Rev. Mr. Hargus's, a little further on. Upon learning this state of things, Murrell determined to leave their horses with Mr. Champion and work their passage through the swamp on foot.

They had proceeded but a few hundred yards from the house in accordance with this resolution, when Stewart, bent upon his purpose of gaining private speech with Mr. Champion, excused himself to his companion till he ran back for his gloves, which he had stupidly, as he said, left lying upon his landlord's table.

Expressing dissatisfaction at the oversight, Murrell bade him lose no time in coming back, and then sat down upon a log by the road side to peevishly await the young man's return.

When he reached the house, Stewart rapidly unfolded to Mr. Champion the nature of his expedition, and was gratified to learn by the mode of the landlord's response, that he had not mistaken his character. Mr. Champion readily entered into Stewart's plans, and handing him an additional pistol and a small pocket flask of powder, assured him of the assistance of a guard of fifty men at any time within six hours of a demand. Recommending the young adventurer then to make a similar confidant of Mr. Erwin and Mr. Hargus, he bade him hurry back to his awaiting companion, to save appearances and to prevent suspicion.

Stewart found Murrell where he left him, somewhat chafed at his delay, but still evincing no mistrust at its object. They were soon again upon their journey, and after two hours of extreme difficulty and toil, in crossing the sloughs in the morass, they succeeded in reaching Mr. Erwin's.

There, however, they were doomed to a serious disappointment, for Mr. Erwin's skiff had been loaned to a neighbor two miles lower down, whose residence could not be reached in consequence of a recent lake that had intervened since the overflow, to prevent the ordinary means of intercourse. They were compelled, therefore, to stop at this house to await the chance of some trading boat or other craft upon the river itself, which they might engage to ferry them across to the Arkansas, or to take them lower down.

This chance did not occur till the following afternoon. During the stay at Mr. Erwin's house, Murrell represented himself as a negro trader, and took an opportunity to make a contract to furnish Mr. Erwin with three negro men, to be delivered within three weeks, at the rate of six hundred dollars each. Stewart, on the other hand, occupied himself in making written memorandums of all that had transpired since his start, for future reference and guidance. He likewise succeeded in snatching an opportunity to hold a similar conversation with Mr. Erwin, as he had had with their landlord of the night before, and to bid him to be upon his guard against his dangerous guest.

On the afternoon of the 30th January a small trading boast stopped at Mr. Erwin's wood-yard, on board of which the wayfarers managed to secure a passage as far down as Mr. Hargus's landing; but then could not induce the skipper to take them across the river, on account of the lateness of the hour, and the roughness of the weather. It was within a half hour of nightfall when the trading boat landed them at the designated point, when they discharged their skipper, and sent him on his way. On applying to Mr. Hargus, and informing him that they had been referred to his assistance by his neighbors Champion and Erwin, the Parson readily afforded them what he stated to be his only conveyance. This was an old and shackly canoe, which, from long disuse, was very frail and sadly in need of repair. This circumstance, though an apparent obstacle to their expedition, was of substantial service to Stewart; for while Murrell, with his ready talent, was busily engaged in caulking the canoe, the former obtained an interview with Mr. Hargus, and, by telling him his situation, added another link to the communication and defences of his rear. It was long after nightfall before the robber had finished his nautical task, and it was, therefore, adjudged prudent by both the travellers to postpone the crossing till the morning. They accordingly took lodgings with Mr. Hargus for the night.

On the following morning the two travellers were early at the landing, making arrangements for launching their boat; but a dark warning in the southwest announced a gathering storm, and suggested to them the prudence of delay. A brief time proved to them that they had not misinterpreted the warning of the skies, for they had scarcely regained the house when a tornado smote the face of the waters, with a violence which seemed to make the gigantic stream jump fairly from its bed, and roar at the assault. The wind was followed by a driving snow which added a new element of confusion to the previous terrors of the scene.

"We have had a narrow escape!" said Stewart, with a shudder, looking back into the striving sky as they reached the door.

"All hell appears to be combined against me," muttered Murrell, as the only comment to his fellow-adventurer's remark.

"God be praised, my friends!" exclaimed the parson, opening the door for their entrance— "God be praised that you did not start before. The first stroke of that tempest would have smote you to the bottom, and have scattered your boat before it like a handful of match sticks."

"Our escape is, indeed, providential, sir," returned Murrell, with well-assumed solemnity.—"We are indebted to heaven alone for the preservation of our lives."

The storm continued throughout the day, and the following morning found the river still raging at the wind, and the snow still falling in heavy quantities. Murrell's impatience, however, would endure no longer check and after having gone out of door some half a dozen times in the course of an hour for the sole purpose of easing his heart by cursing at the wind, he insisted upon daring the fury of the storm. As Stewart regarded this resolution as a sort of challenge of his daring, and feeling himself really not inferior in courage to the robber, he made no opposition, and communicated to his host their determination to depart. Perceiving that no arguments could turn them from their purpose, and feeling a deep interest in the safety of the young traveller, since he had been made acquainted with the self-sacrificing generosity of his enterprise, Mr. Hargus was indeed to grant a favor which he had before withheld, and spared them the stronger and more substantial boat which his business required for constant use, and the possession of which he had till this moment concealed.

Staggering through the heavy drifts of snow, the companions reached the beach, and with their stalwart shoulders soon succeeded in thrusting their little vessel into the stream.—The tempest was indeed fearful. The river was one sheet of turgid foam, and, as the agitated surface pitched them aloft to launch them down terrific slopes, or sunk in huge hollows from their adventurous bows, it seemed as if outlaying all its might and cunning to drive or suck them into its revengeful depths. The densely falling snow bound them in a dim and narrow hemisphere which shut out the adjacent shore, and deprived of any land-marks, they had nothing left them for their guides but the rushing current and the howling wind. Straining at their oars, and struggling for their lives, the daring voyagers never lost a stroke, and after an hour and a half of almost superhuman effort succeeded in striking the western shore, opposite the mouth of Old river where it joins the Mississippi, at the Chickasaw Bend.

MURRELL AND STEWART CROSSING THE MISSISSIPPI

Drawing a long breath, after he had sprung upon the shore, Murrell gazed for a moment fiercely back into the stream, and then bursting into a volley of the highest oaths, exclaimed,—

"Damn and set fire to that canting old hound. He came within an ace of sinking us both in that cockle-shell of a canoe, for fear we'd go to hell in his best boat! Damn and set fire to him, I say! There," said he, raising his foot and placing it firmly upon the bows of the dancing boat, "there's the first instalment of my revenge upon his cold-blooded meanness!" and the indignant robber shot the vessel back into the current and had the satisfaction of seeing it spin swiftly out of sight. A long draught a-piece from the flask, refreshed them both, and then Murrell led the way from the shore in a northwesterly direction.

Their progress was painful and difficult. The swamp, always perplexed by a thick growth of cane, was now additionally encumbered by capricious drifts of snow and capacious reservoirs of water. When they had labored through this painful foot-ground for half an hour, they suddenly emerged from a thicket upon the borders of an extensive lake, which, swollen by the freshet, had escaped its usual bounds and stretched among the surrounding timber beyond the bounds of sight. The marauder, however, was upon familiar ground, and continuing a short distance along the upper shore, soon discerned, on the right, a large bayou, on the edge of which stood a cabin which he recognized as the residence of a friend. A brief greeting passed at the threshold, a short stay by the crackling fire on the hearth followed, and then the energetic robber demanded of the inmates a boat to cross the lake, that he might continue on at once.

He was instantly obeyed, and the owner of the hut, himself, rowed the twain across. Leaving the boat, they continued their northwesterly direction along the borders of the overflow until they spied a small open hut in the distance, which from the volume of smoke that curled away from its chimney, gave token that it was tenanted by those who had a regard for, at least, one of the comforts of their life. Murrell made directly for the object with a quickened step, but still preserved the thoughtful silence which had taken possession of him since they left the borders of the lake.

As they neared the point of their immediate destination, Stewart felt his earlier apprehensions revive, and fearing that he was now upon the point of being suddenly confronted with the Henning negroes, almost shrunk back as he approached the door. It was too late, however, either to flinch or to retreat: so keeping but a step behind the more enterprising advance of his companion, he cocked two of his pistols for the worst, and muffled his face as much as possible with his handkerchief to conceal his features upon his first entrance. His precautions proved unnecessary, and finding no accustomed features in the faces of the three white men and two negroes who were grouped together around the fire, he recovered his confidence and assumed an air of cheerful unconcern. One of the white men, whom Murrell accosted by the name of Rainhart, seemed to claim the robber's chief attention, and after running through several rapid inquiries as to the condition of the band, the chieftain bade the group, "good day." Still wending westward they crossed three more sheets of water, on the nearest bank of each of which, however, they found skiffs conveniently awaiting them.

On the further side of the last bayou there stood a wretched cabin, which they entered with the same unceremoniousness as they had the previous two. A man, his wife, and two children, who sat in drowsy and almost torpid silence by the fire, were the inmates of this gloomy habitation. The chieftain recognised them all with an air of careless familiarity, that bespoke them old acquaintances. A brief private conversation ensued between him and the man, and the travellers pushed on again. An hour's journey over another sheet of water, and a short but toilsome struggle through another strip of cane, brought them in sight of a rude temporary camp, constructed of boards, which also gave an evidence of habitation by its cloud of smoke. On entering this latter novel, they found only three filthy looking negroes, huddled by the fire. Stopping but to inquire what had become of their master, Murrell proceeded on, and in a few minutes more plunged again amid a search of cane. After they had progressed a few hundred yards through a reedy jungle, the robber suddenly paused, and pointing through the morass to a large cotton-wood tree that rose far above the surrounding growth, remarked—

"Hues, do you see that lofty cotton-wood that towers so majestically above all the other trees?"

"I do."

"That tree stands in the center of the 'Garden of Eden,' and it tells us that we have now but a quarter of a mile to travel to the grand rendezvous of the Arkansas, the head quarters of the noblest clan that ever flourished in the world!"

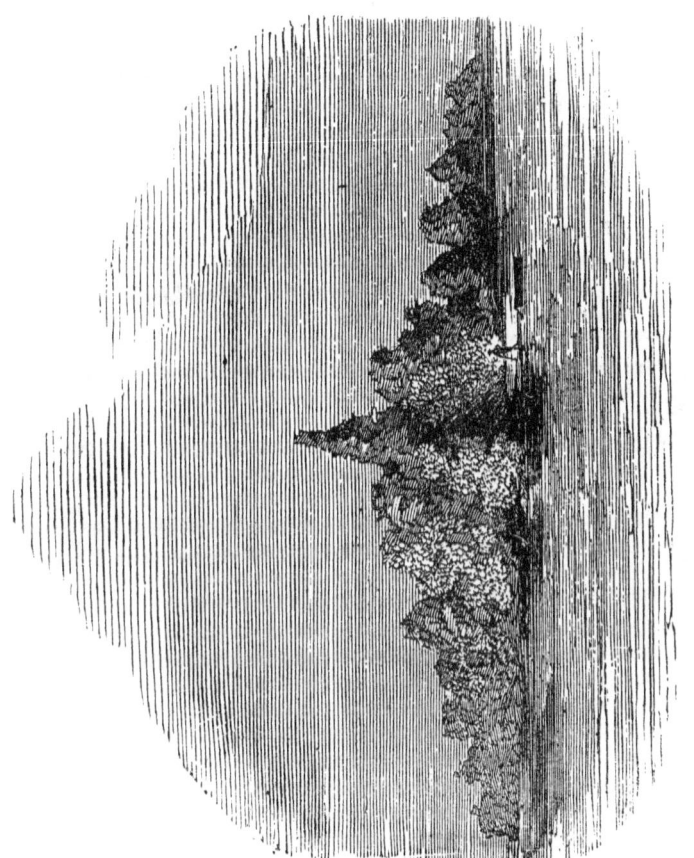

MURRELL'S ISLAND; OR, THE MARAUDER'S PARADISE

This was said with great dignity, and as he concluded, the chieftain strode rapidly onward, with a step so vigorous that Stewart found it difficult to keep the measure of his pace. When they were fairly out of the brake, they stood on the borders of a lake which bore a little island in its midst. On this, stood the cotton-wood tree to which his guide had previously directed his attention. They jumped into a canoe which lay ready for their use, and made toward it. The island was covered with a thick matting of cane and a growth of lofty trees, interlocked below with a heavy crop of bushy under-wood, which gave it a dense and wild appearance. They landed on a near point of the island, and leaving the boat, proceeded up its banks. Winding through an ingeniously devious labyrinth, they proceeded deeper and deeper into the maze, until arriving at its centre, they came full upon a large and substantial log cabin.

Their journey was ended. They stood before the Grand Council-house of the Mystic Confederacy—the head quarters of the terrible robbers of the morass.

CHAPTER XVII.

The interior of the Hut—Welcome of the Councillors—The Rebuff—Introduction of Stewart—The Address—The Preliminary Introduction—Honors in Perspective—Calculations on Business—The Treacherous Overseer—Stewart Contrives an Excuse to Leave the Morass for Home—Murrell Assents upon a Condition—Freedom—Preparations for Muzzling the Tiger.

On entering the council house, Murrell and Stewart found eleven rough, ill-dressed and ill-favored looking men, sitting round a large oaken table. Most of them had pipes in their mouths; and a huge jug in the centre of the board, with a number of small tin cases divided among the audience, showed that though the tenants of a wilderness, the inmates were by no means devoted to an ascetic life. The apartment was unusually large, and its furniture, although simple, strong and unostentatious, was of an excellence seldom seen in the cabins of the far west. The walls were ornamented with four battle pictures, and the mantlepiece bore the old fashioned plaster figures of the virgin and her son. A huge fire roared and crackled in the chimney place, and on the smooth clay hearth lay stretched in torpid luxury, a rugged looking hound, of the most formidable looking size and character.

As soon as the chieftain made his appearance, the circle of his henchmen arose, and with the warmest expressions welcomed his arrival. Stewart was for the time entirely unnoticed, and rejoicing at the chance thus afforded for the concealment of his embarrassment, he sidled up to the fire and became a silent spectator of the enthusiastic party.

"Well, boys, well," said Murrell, dropping from each side of him the last two hands which made the greeting around the circle complete. "How do things go? Any thing new or wonderful turned up of late?"

"Well, no," replied one who answered to the name of Sperlock, "every thing has went on smooth and straight. Dodridge and Barney brought in six horses and two woolheads day before yesterday."

"Well, what has been done in the way of 'bogus' and 'queer'?"

"The operations have been slack," returned Sperlock, "but there has $10,000 gone down the river a few days ago. But that puts me in mind of your last business. What prevented you from being here day before yesterday, to meet the Striker who had your negroes in charge?"

Murrell here explained the suspicion of the Hennings, and the storm which cost him two days' delay, and inquired what had become of the slaves.

"They arrived here eight days ago," said a man, whose name Stewart afterwards learned to be Haines. "They were very badly frosted, and as they were spoiling on our hands, we judged it best to push them into market, and make as early sale as possible. They were put on a trading boat, along with three others, under the charge of Corbin and Sims, and we gave them the ten thousand, so as they could drive a double trade. I'm afraid your two niggers will not fetch much in their present condition."

"And I'm afraid that you entrusted too much to the drivers, and that the money will spoil all. Ten thousand is too much to trust in the hands of strykers, or to comparatively inexperienced men, at one time. I do not speak on account of the value of the property, but for fear they may compromise much greater interests by some act of indiscretion. But never mind; now that it is done, we must hope for the best."

As Murrell concluded his sentence, a sharp growl from the direction of the fireplace turned attention towards Stewart. The young man while pretending a careless inattention to what was going on, had stooped to pat the dog; but the animal had resisted the overture with a threatening snarl that bespoke the viciousness of his nature and the rudeness of his breeding. The incident served the purpose, however, of reminding the chieftain of the duty he owed to his travelling companion, and breaking from the conversation, he introduced him to the circle with many flattering encomiums on the qualities of courage, liberality, and intelligence, which he had evinced during their recent acquaintance. So high a voucher as this of course secured for its object a warm and enthusiastic reception, and thus welcomed, Stewart felt it necessary to make a due reply. He accordingly returned the complimentary reception with a brief address, in which he very ingeniously reiterated the sentiments he had previously expressed to the leader of the band, and also introduced an argument to justify the system of out-law life, to which he was apparently about to devote himself.

The address drew forth a burst of applause, and as a tribute to his unusual merit and capacity, Sperlock proposed that they should give him the two degrees without the usual test. He therefore received the sign of the stryker on the spot, and was promised the investure of Grand Councillor on the day after the morrow.

When the interest of this little circumstance had subsided, the conversation again became of a general nature, and the inquiries of the chief as to the number of proselytes which had recently been made by each member of the cause, as to how many names stood on the records as candidates for admission, &c., placed Stewart in possession of the most important secrets of the band. He now felt convinced, that with the chance which he would have of catching Murrell in his guilt when he attempted to fulfill his contract by supplying stolen negroes to Mr. Erwin, he might safely return to Tennessee with an assurance that his adventures would be brought to a successful conclusion. He could gain nothing more against Murrell by staying where he was, for he already had enough, and the gathering of the clan, two days thence, might bring in some member who would recognize him. There was, therefore, every thing to risk and nothing to gain. He also dreaded that he might be obliged to undergo some disgusting ordeal, and assume some horrid oath as the preliminary conditions to the high honor to be conferred on him at the grand meeting of the day but one. In addition to these reasons for starting, he felt a natural uneasiness at being fastened to such uncongenial company, as well as a natural fear that his life might fall a sacrifice to some accident. In connection with this last thought, it was but little consolation to him to know, that according to directions left with Mr. Champion, if Murrell should return before him, and alone, he would be taken into custody and charged with his murder.

A few minutes spent in these cogitations set him to contriving some excuse for his departure; and a few minutes more decided him on representing that during his journey he had sustained a loss of valuable papers, which he might have left at either of the three last places at which they had stopped on the eastern bank of the river. Fixed in his intent, he cheerfully accepted the invitation of the chief when he had finished his talk, to accompany him in a visit to one or two friends on the banks of the river. At this signal, the assembly, which had been in debate at the time of their arrival, dispersed, each to his own residence; for many of them owned huts, which they had erected about on points of high land contiguous to the morass, under pretence of keeping wood-yards to accommodate the Mississippi boatmen, though really on account of their privacy and convenience to the operations of the clan.

The object of Murrell's present jaunt was to the house of the Jehu Barney, who received a complimentary notice a while before from Sperlock, for his recent exploits in horse and negro stealing. In their road, they passed four negroes near a small hut, cutting wood, whom Murrell pointed to as recent prizes, making the remark at the same time, that he had now some fifty-five, counting the three he had promised Erwin, all sold, though he admitted he as yet had only thirty-two towards the contract.

They at length arrived at the cabin of Barney, and as it was near sunset, and there was no prospect of finding more agreeable quarters for the night, they concluded to remain. Barney was a man of remarkably affable manners, and made his guests right welcome. During the evening, conversation turned on various topics, and Stewart, who had already learned the value of being a listener in a region where every sound was dangerous to public safety, added not a little to his stock of information, in relation to the past doings and future plans of his friends of the morass.

Pretending to doze upon his chair, to give Barney a confidence independent of the assurance of his chief, he heard Murrell open to the former the difficulties of meeting the demands which he now had on his hands for negroes.

"Yes, and the difficulty is greater than you think, for I myself have five engaged," said Barney.

"Well, there's fourteen of the first fifty-five can stand over to the next month," said Murrell, thoughtfully; "Erwin's three we will leave six that we lack."

"Eleven, you mean; you have forgotten my five."

"Yes, yes, that is true. Well, let me see. Ah! now," said he, raising his head, as if struck with a sudden thought, "if Nolan should only be prompt in his business, the calculations would be made."

"Who do you mean, your wife's brother, who is overseer to Henderson's estate in Alabama?"

"Yes; Henderson is spending the winter at the North, and Nolan has promised to slip six of his likeliest negroes into the hands of a trusty friend of ours, who is to go with in ten miles of the plantation, and wait there in a two horse carry-all. Nolan is to give an apparent cause for the flight of the slaves, by raising a charge of insurrection against them the day previous to their abduction, so their disappearance will look plausible to the boss when he comes home. When they are once got into the waggon, the curtains are to be tied down and fodder thrown over them, and while they are driven towards us, Nolan is to be beating the woods with the neighbors, and leading pursuit in an opposite direction. This arrangement was to have been undertaken early in January, and it is most time we should hear something of it."

"Well, that still leaves five," said Barney, whose admiration did not appear to be the least excited by the ingenious plan which he had just heard developed.

"Well, that five," said Murrell, "I shall have to get from my own country, and I shall have to go straight back to do it, too. But come, let's go to bed. Hallo, Hues, old fellow, are you asleep?" and the yawning robber rose and shook the young man by the arm.

Stewart roused up with well-assumed reluctance, and after stretching himself once or twice, followed the heavy step of the equally weary robber chieftain. It is hardly necessary to say, that after the perils and extreme fatigues of the day, both fell readily asleep.

Early in the morning, which was now the 1st of February, Stewart made known to Murrell his pretended loss of valuable papers, and the necessity of an immediate return to the houses where they had stopped along the opposite bank, in search for them. Murrell appeared much chagrined at this resolve, but upon being informed that the documents alluded to were the notes of others, held only as collateral security, articles of copartnership on which his claim rested for the settlement of a previously extensive business, and other matters of that sort, he admitted the pressing nature of the case though he still sought to persuade his young friend to remain, at least until the next day to be present at the Grand Council.

Stewart, however, put off all these importunites by dwelling upon the magnitude of his loss and the danger of delay, and Murrell at length gave in, and agreed to absolve him from his obligations to remain, in case he would wait a day for him at Mr. Erwin's on the other side. "I find," said he, "that I shall be obliged to hurry back to Madison, and now that Henning's niggers are sent down the river and disposed of, there is nothing to keep me here but the Council day."

Stewart readily agreed to this condition, whereupon the robber, accompanying him to the beach, ordered a Stryker to row him across in a skiff. The chieftain watched the young man till he saw him safely landed on the opposite shore, and then turned thoughtfully from the bank. The direst enemy he had in life, had slipped from his hands, and he had unconsciously accelerated his own fate by the aid which he had furnished to his escape.

When Stewart struck the eastern side of the river, and saw the Stryker re-embarked upon the stream, he felt as if he had undergone a new enfranchisement. The perils which had surrounded him, and the tremendous responsibilities which he had assumed for his friend, had afflicted him with a heavy and continual care. He now, however, felt free again in body and mind, and after the first expression of gratitude to the Power which had protected him, he set about contriving how he should finish his expedition in the best manner for society. He first ran over the category of the murders which Murrell had ascribed to the "elder brother," but from the imperfection of their details, arising out of the fact of their having been related in an assumed character, soon became convinced that the hope to substantiate them was distant and indefinite.

In relation to the crime of robbery, that of Nolan, the Alabama overseer, was doubtless too far advanced to arrest. But the contract with Mr Erwin, would enable him to catch the villain in the act, and insure his arrest and prompt and speedy punishment, and at the same time, or before any of the band could learn the apprehension of their chief, an armed party might cross suddenly to the Arkansas swamp, under the cover of the night, and surprise the resident marauders in their dens, capture their stolen booty as evidences against them, and then burn their cabins to the ground, as a first instalment of the vengeance due to their inhuman deeds.

The idea was well conceived. It remains for us to see how it was carried out.

CHAPTER XVIII.

Return of Murrell to the eastern bank—Arrangement for the sale of the Negroes—Separation--Arrival in Madison—A Midnight Consultation—The Community in a ferment—Gathering of the Regulators—The March—The Negro Spy—The Argument of a Bowie Knife—The Forewarning—The Tiger in the Toils—The Tiger at bay—The Accuser—The Spring of the Tiger—The Beast in Bonds.

On arriving at the house of Mr. Erwin, Stewart was welcomed by that gentleman with expressions of the liveliest congratulation on his safe deliverance from the hands of the marauders, and was next assailed with a volley of inquiries as to what had taken place since his departure. Mindful of the importance of his mission, the young man contended himself with general replies, and finally got released from further importunity, by promising a full detail of all that had transpired when the business had been properly consummated. He then communicated to Mr. Erwin his ideas in relation to encouraging Murrell's contract for the three negroes, and his desire that the land pirate's arrest should finally take place at his house, mentioning that Murrell would be there on the morrow, and that the time could be fixed for the delivery of the slaves, and the consequent winding up of the whole affair.

Mr. Erwin, not only readily agreed to this arrangement, but appeared to think that he was specially favored by being assigned a part so strikingly instrumental in a great public service. He agreed to fulfill his portion of the task with the utmost fidelity, and also to have a strong guard in secret readiness to perform whatever additional service might be required.

Towards the close of the following afternoon, the robber chieftain was seen entering through the gate, and in the next moment was met and welcomed at the door of the house, by his travelling companion and the host, in a most cheerful and flattering manner.

"Well, as I find you in the first stopping place, I suppose you recovered your papers?" said the robber, taking Stewart's hand.

"Oh, yes, Mr. Erwin had found them for me, and was kindly keeping them in charge till my return."

"Well, I'm glad to hear it; and I'm glad to see that you waited for me according to promise," returned Murrell, releasing the young man's hand with an impression of the private signal.

"I share your satisfaction in finding you true to your promise also," said Stewart, returning the sign, "I must say, however, that you hav'nt much more than kept your word, for the day is on its last legs."

"More need that we should hurry forward then. I guess we can get to Champion's tonight, and once on horseback, we—"

"But I shall put my veto upon that," said Mr. Erwin, pleasantly. "I am going to claim the privilege of giving both of you a good supper and good treatment to-night, and then you can start fair in the morning. Besides, Mr. Murrell, you'll recollect we've a little business between us."

"Ah, yes, sir, you remind me of a thing, which, though I had not forgotten, had, indeed, slipped my mind for the moment. I will accept your courtesy, sir, if the proposal is likewise agreeable to my friend."

This settled the arrangement for the night, and Mr. Erwin and the robber, as soon as they had got comfortably seated, commenced upon the subject of their contract. The day for the delivery of the negroes was set, and the plan for the arrest having thus taken an actual shape, nothing further was left to be done for the time.

Early in the morning, Murrell and Stewart were on their way to Champion's, where, staying but long enough to mount and settle with the owner, they pushed on for Madison county. Their arrangement was to part at Wesley, Murrell to continue on to his home in Madison, while Stewart was to make a hasty trip to the Choctaw Nation, finish up his business, and hurry back to Madison. He was then to put himself completely at the chief's control.

The two companions travelled together the whole of that day, pursuing nearly the same road back which they had followed in their previous journey south. Murrell occupied time as usual with stories of his exploits, while

Stewart, by apparently incidental questions, managed to obtain confirming points to the information which he had gained before. He learnt that the Henning negroes had been put through the Choctaw Pass to the Yazoo market, and he also gained the names of several of the most prominent of the clans in the various states. These items he would secure as they turned up from time to time, by marking them down on his nails, on the leather of his saddle or bridle, &c., until his memorandums filled all the space within the reach of his hand.

Night fell before they arrived at Wesley, and they lodged together for the last time. In the morning, now February 5th, they were on the road again at their usual early hour.

There remained now but two miles between them and Wesley, which was to be the place of separation. Murrell evinced much concern, and expressed himself very unwilling that they should part from each other at all, offering the hospitalities of his home, and urging many reasons for their continuing together. But Stewart remained immoveable. He represented his business an imperative, and at length made the chieftain completely willing that he should go his journey, on condition of a quick return.

The travellers did not enter Wesley together, but just before arriving at the village, Stewart took his leave, and turned down a road that branched off to the left hand. When he had pursued his course a few yards, he hauled up under cover of a clump of trees, and watched the form of the robber as he trotted briskly along the direct northern road. The rapid figure was soon out of sight, and then the pursuer turned in his path, and regained the road which he had only left for the purpose of blinding his companion.

Stewart rode directly on to Wesley, knowing that Murrell would make no stop. Arriving in the village, he proceeded at once to the house of Colonel Bayliss, who had done him such staunch service at the tavern on his previous visit. He found the Colonel in, and delivering him back to the fire-arm which he had furnished him, gave a brief general detail of what had recently transpired. He then proceeded on for Madison, taking a route different from the one which he knew Murrell to have decided on for himself.

It was not until the following night at twelve o'clock, that the worn and jaded traveller arrived at the residence of Mr. Henning, for whom he had undergone so much fatigue, and for whom he had braved so many perils. His arrival was well-timed, for it was unknown, and the last twelve miles having been performed in the dark, left no danger of his presence transpiring on the following day to challenge the speculations of the curious.

A family council was at once called, and in the midst of the wondering circle Stewart sat and related his adventures. He wound up by disclosing his plan for the arrest, and then, having the satisfaction of hearing all his views certified by the endorsement of his listeners, he yielded to their advice that he should retire immediately to bed, and be invigorated for a fresh consultation in the morning.

When Stewart arose in the morning, he was a little surprised at finding himself introduced to several prominent residents of the neighborhood, with whom Mr. Henning informed him, he had thought proper to consult.

Though he felt displeased at this course, it was too late to disapprove of it, and as the secret could not be withdrawn from their bosoms, he submitted with good grace to the necessities of the case, and gave his opinion of the best course to detect the robber and secure his punishment. The majority, however, did not agree with him, but were for arresting the villain at once.

Stewart urged that the punishment of the man now depended, as matters stood, upon his solitary evidence. There would be a temptation, therefore, for the marauders to assassinate him, as his death would destroy the case and place the chieftain out of danger. He also urged that a detection at Erwin's, would bring another case against the marauder, as well as add as many witnesses as they chose to take with them to the spot.

This prudent counsel gained no favor. Burning with rage at the atrocities which were still fresh upon their ears, the excited citizens were incapable of entertaining ideas of delay. They replied to Stewart that his testimony was as much as would be necessary, and as to his assassination, *they* would take care to prevent that. They did not care about another case against Murrell; they had enough to begin with, and they believed, moreover, that they would not catch him at Mr. Erwin's at all, for now that the matter had gone so far, the villain might gain information that something was going on, and not keep his appointment. Again, he might not be bale to keep his contract from other circumstances, and even if he were, that he would be just as likely to send a person in his stead with the negroes, and thus give them the slip and laugh in their faces after all, "No, no," said one of them, who enforced these views more earnestly than the rest, "he is now in our power, and we will make sure of him. We will never entrust so dangerous and fearful an enemy beyond our reach again!"

One of the above arguments made a forcible impression upon Stewart's mind. Though it did not conflict with his original views, it fell with strong effect upon the present state of things. The secret was out, and there was great fear, indeed, that Murrell would get wind of what was going on if the climax was delayed. This would render his position truly dangerous, and if he should attempt to visit the marauder in the interim, might subject him to his extremest vengeance. He, therefore, acquiesced in resolutions which, had the matter remained in the condition in which he brought it to the house, he would have denounced as intemperate and hasty.

The consultation lasted for about two hours, and in the course of it a great number of new persons were introduced. This added fuel to the flame, and it was at length decided, upon its being ascertained that Murrell had arrived at home the previous day, that a body of armed guards should be selected to visit his house that very evening, and take him into custody. This being settled, Stewart claimed to be one of the band.

The day ran round, and when the gathering darkness had crowded the reluctant twilight fairly below the horizon, forty armed men stood in a solitary spot, apart from the dwelling, awaiting the word to march upon the monster, who, but half a mile thence, was serenely enjoying the comforts of his home, unsuspicious of the slightest danger. The word was given, and the avenging body moved slowly on, deeply impressed with the importance of their expedition.

There were spies abroad, however, for a negro slave whom Murrell always kept upon his farm happened to be abroad, and to strike within ear-shot of the tramp. The wondering African drew near the unusual sound, and perceiving its cause, at once connected the formidable movement with danger to his master. He fled with all speed to give the alarm. His course was direct across the fields, and the protecting genius of the robber appeared once more to have stepped in to save him from the fate which he deserved. The negro neared the house, and saw the lights twinkling through the closed shutters, while the guards, or "regulators," were still ten minutes distance off. He had laid his hand upon an outer fence, with the intention of bounding over it, but ere he sprang he was grasped in the arms of a stalwart man and dashed to the ground. He uttered a cry, but in the next moment a knee was on his breast and a bowie knife glittered before his eyes. Danger makes the most ignorant of creatures wise, and the negro, as he saw the impending weapon gleam, made as rapid decision between expediency and duty as ever was performed by the most shrewd and supple politician. He behaved himself like a philosopher, and submitted to be bound and gagged with as much resignation as a Hindoo delivers him self up to the devouring embraces of the Ganges.

"The regulators are not the fools you took 'em for, you black vagabond!" said the guard complacently, as he rolled the negro beside the fence and resumed his gun.

Murrell heard the cry of the slave, and started from the table where he had been reading, seized his knife and flung open the back door. He peered for a moment into the absolute and unmitigated gloom, but hearing no recurrence of the sound, stepped back and closed the door. He appeared to be concerned, however, for he did not lay down his knife, but consigned it to its usual place upon his person. He then sat down again, and resumed the occupation which had been so strangely broken off.

But a few moments more elapsed, when a sharp rap was heard at the door. He directed his wife to open it, and then arose to receive the visitor.

The bolt was drawn and the latched raised, and a dozen armed men poured into the room. The robber fell back that he might not be surrounded, but as he reached the wall, the sound of voices in the rear of the building, told him that he was completely and hopelessly cut off. His heart sunk for a moment, but regaining his composure, as soon as he found no double hope was left to distract him, he looked with a moderate surprise upon the stern faces that surrounded him, and mildly asked their leader to what he owed this rude and unexpected visit.

"We came here to ask questions, not to answer them!" said the leader sternly.

"But you are in my house, and courtesy gives me the first privilege."

"You are in the hands of the law, and that does not require any forms but those of justice!"

"How, and for what am I in the hands of the law?"

"You are in the hands of the law because I now proclaim you, in the name of the People of Madison, to be under arrest; and you will be held to answer a solemn charge preferred against you by a citizen of this county, for stealing two of his negro slaves; that's the why!"

"Indeed!" said the robber, drawing himself up with a complacent and contemptuous smile—"and this is your

ARREST OF MURRELL.

charge and this is your procedure! Gentlemen, Mr. Henning is a weak and misguided old man, and you are on an unprofitable errand. I shall not resist your process, because my innocence will establish itself without an effort; but I give every man present, and all concerned in this movement, to understand, that I shall seek redress by law for this false arrest and all its subsequent detention. I have long been the object of a small conspiracy in this county, but this time I will grapple with it and send it to the wall!"

The earnest eloquence and dashing bearing of the robber, was not without its effect, and there were those among the listeners, who felt shuttering doubt whether the whole movement on the part of the Hennings, was not precipitate and unwarranted. The captain, however, did not participate in this feeling to an extent, though he was slightly staggered by the cool audacity of the robber's declarations.

"That is all very well, Mr. Murrell," said he; "that's all very well, but will you be good enough to inform me who travelled with you on your recent journey to Arkansas?"

"Well," said Murrell, "as you answered my question first, and as I have no reason to conceal any thing connected with my life, I will answer you in turn. The young person who went with me to Arkansas, was a young man named Hues."

"Did you ever see him before that journey."

"Never," answered Murrell, becoming puzzled at the course of the inquiry. "I saw him for the first time at the bridge at Estanaula, on the 26th of last month."

"Well, here is that man!" said the officer, beckoning Stewart in through the half open door, and leading him into the centre of the room. "Here is that man, and he now confronts you as an accuser!"

Had the spectres of all whom he had sent to untimely graves, have risen before him to claim a combined and instant vengeance for their wrongs, the countenance of the arch-demon could not have experienced a more sudden and appalling change. The terror appeared to have smitten his very marrow, and his strong frame trembled as if an invisible hand shook it with the force of a paralysis. A faintness bleached his cheek, and for a moment his drooping eyes have danger of a swoon. But the robber had a strong will, and a desperate effort summoned back his strength. The faintness left his lips. His stature raised and nerved itself afresh, and the ashy witness which had stolen a momentary empire over his cheek, gave place to the flush of rage. Hope, too, sparkled in his eye. The door stood open. Two of three good blows, and an active bound might clear the circle and place liberty within the chances of a dark night and open field. Revenge also lent its exhilaration to the charge. Before him stood the traitor who deserved the first vengeance of his knife, and the thought of burying its trenchant blade into his skull, inspired him with a sort of savage ecstasy, that seemed like joy. His resolve was taken, and the approaching mischief gave its warnings in his dilated form and flashing eye, and as he drew his blade quickly for a sudden blow, his arm was caught behind, and in the next instant he was pinioned on the floor. Stewart spoke no word and took no part in the affray, but when he saw the wretch firmly secured, he went quietly and sadly home in company with a brace of friends.

The reflections of Murrell on his road to prison must have been most mortifying. The idea of having unbosomed himself in all the confidence of fancied friendship and security, to one who was merely playing the part of the spy and an accuser—of seeing himself out-generaled by a youth whom he imagined he had captivated by the splendor of his great abilities—afflicted him with shame, and wounded his self-opinion with a levelling blow. It was the second lesson in his life of the folly and danger of conceit. The first he had taken in the wood, near Nashville, from an experienced preceptor. The last he received, and it might be a fatal one, at the hands of a juvenile corrector. Though he could have devoured his very heart with rage, he maintained a sullen demeanor on his way to prison, and only asked two questions to indicate the point and focus of his thoughts.

"Who is this man Hues?" said he, in a tone that was intended only for the ear addressed.

"He is a stranger in this county," said the guard, wilfully misleading him.

"Has he any acquaintances about here?"

"None, that I have heard of."

"He had better remain a stranger," muttered the robber, through his set teeth; "for I have friends here, and, as there's a God above, I'd rather be in my condition than in his."

CHAPTER XIX.

The first night of captivity—Calculations–A gleam of light—A legal point—The robber's wife—The convict alphabet—The mission—The two couriers—Arrival of the sheriff—Departure for Jackson—The evil genius—The march—Signs of trouble—The pistol shot—The severed bands—Frustration of the attempt at rescue—Arrival of Jackson—A gloomy revelation—The examination.

The crowd moved slowly on, with the captive robber in their midst, but no further words were changed with the sullen hero of the scene than were noticed at the conclusion of the last chapter. The destination of the regulators was to a tavern about half a mile distant from the scene of the arrest. There they intended to consign Murrell to the keeping of a special guard till morning, when he was to be removed to Jackson, the capital of the county, for regular examination and commitment to the prison of that place.

When the posse had entered the tavern, the pinioned robber was assigned a seat upon a bench, and a rope connected with the lashings of his arms was fastened to a staple in the wall behind. Twelve picked men were then charged with the defence of the place, and with the safe keeping of the prisoner, till his custody could be transferred to the legitimate detention of the sheriff of the county on the morrow.

Though affecting a contemptuous indifference to the rude measures of his captors, and to the gossip which passed between them, the mind of the marauder was keenly alive to every word that passed. No expression escaped the sifting of his thought, and every precautionary direction that fell upon his ear, suggested a counteracting plan. In the intervals of silence, when his observation was allowed a respite, his subtle brain flew with an electric speed over all the vast net-work which his wily enemy had been weaving about him for the previous eleven days, and in its hot excursions it sounded with a vigorous sharpness, the strength of every mesh that seemed tenuous or tactile. Its flight was hopeless for a time, but at length it felt a thread which promised to snap under a well-directed force, and to frustrate the whole elaborate fabric of his foes.

He had heard one of the guards inadvertently remark that the Hennings were under heavy obligations to the young man who had tracked him to the swamp, and he heard another say, that Hues was poor. These two expressions put together, as afterwards appeared, gave him his point, and that point was the hope that Stewart had been labouring for reward.

MURRELL IN CUSTODY OF THE REGULATORS.

The brightest thoughts are struck from the deepest gloom, as the most dazzling exhalations burst from a mephitic atmosphere. Murrell described the conception of this hope as one of the most complete and enlivening transitions from despair to a state of exulting confidence, he had 'ever known. From the manner in which he afterwards adapted it to his purposes, his inward soliloquy at the time of its conception, may be supposed to have run somewhat thus:

"So, Master Hues, you set out at the request of the old man, Henning, did you? and to recover his slaves, eh? And you are poor, too ! Well, all that is very good, very good! Poor men cannot work for rich ones for nothing, and you could not have undertaken this long and weary enterprise without promise of reward. Let me but establish that fact, my fine fellow, and your testimony isn't worth a damn! You are an interested witness, sir, and your testimony is inadmissible. Here are several respectable and substantial gentlemen from Arkansas, who declare that you admitted in their presence, that if you succeeded in trapping and convicting me, you was to be well paid for it. There is no soul present who can impeach their testimony, sir, and your hopes of gain dependent on the result a this trial, incapacitates you as a witness. The court decides to reject you. The rule is well settled in all the books, and you must stand aside, sir.

"Ah, you are pretty smart for your years, Mr. Hues, but you are, nevertheless, a shade too young."

When Murrell might have been supposed to have arrived at the conclusion of this inward peroration, his attention was drawn to a direction which was given by the leader of the regulators to one of the band, to ride to Jackson and acquaint the sheriff with what had passed, that he might be present in the morning to' give sanction to the removal of the prisoner. This order appeared to suggest a sudden idea to the robber, for on the instant he started up and looked eagerly around the circle as if to find some friendly face, but he peered in vain, for none of his adherents had yet come in. When about giving up the task he espied his wife on the outer edge of the throng, with her knuckles doubled in her eyes, shedding tears in affectionate abundance, and giving other evidences of grief equally appropriate to the occasion. He beckoned her toward him with a motion of his head, but before she had made her way half through the press, her progress was checked and she was informed that no person could hold communication with the prisoner.

"We ask no favors, sir! We ask no favors!" exclaimed Murrell sharply, breaking silence for the first time. "It was no thought of mine to afflict your sensibilities with a domestic scene. Jane, you had better go home. This is no place for you."[1]

But Jane did not go home, for she received a secret sign from her lord and master which contained a counter-direction. She therefore, only drew herself from the centre of the crowd, and then after sobbing a moment on its edge, sidled round until she got against the wall behind her husband. Her object was to get in a position where she could observe his fingers. These could communicate in full what was forbidden in his tongue, for he had served a term in the penitentiary some years before,

1. The name of Murrell's wife was not Jane, but Elizabeth (Mangrum) Murrell.

and there had learned the deaf and dumb alphabet, so common among convicts in all State prisons.—Murrell was a master or these digital signs, and, with a view of adapting them to certain domestic exigences, had learned them to his wife after his discharge. He had found them of frequent and substantial service in the presence of third parties and suspected guests, and he was now about to adopt their singular advantages to the most desperate emergency of his life.

The wife of the robber soon gathered from the rapid movements of his hand a full communication of his most urgent and immediate wishes. Withdrawing slyly from the room when his orders were complete, she slowly crept away from the vicinity of the tavern. Having at length made the distance safe, she looked cautiously around to see that, no spy observed her, and then flew with the speed of an Atalanta to the dwelling of one Watkins, a prominent member of the clan.

We are not in possession of the burden of her message, but the result explains its purport. In ten minutes after her arrival at Watkins' house, that worthy gentleman flung himself across his horse and was dashing southward with an eager speed.

At the same moment, and not a quarter of a mile distant, a courier turned his steed in an opposite direction with a message for the sheriff of Madison.[2] Thus worked and counter-worked the schemes of the captors and the captive.

The wife of Murrell had not finished her behest with seeing Watkins off, but called at another cabin, and left her story with its owner, who then took up her task, and

2. The sheriff of Madison County was Mathias Deberry (1788–1839).

devoted himself to rousing all the friends of the chief throughout the night. On her way home the female emissary did not neglect to stop at the tavern where her husband was held in bonds, for the purpose of consigning his mind to ease by signifying that her mission had been faithfully performed. Having done this she went wearily home, and Murrell, freed from any further cares for the night, leaned back against the wall and resigned himself to sleep.

With the morning came the sheriff, Mr. Deberry, from Jackson, with some half a dozen men, to take possession of the prisoner, and with the morning also came a number of anxious faces clustering around and in the tavern, and pressing close upon the accused. The excitement and the indignation of the assemblage at the stories which connected themselves with the arrest, appeared to be extremely high, but strange to say, the robber seemed to derive an exhilaration from its very violence. He seemed cheerful, bold, and confident, and when he was summoned to arise and proceed with the Sheriff, he started up with alacrity, and proclaimed himself anxious to advance at once, As he stepped into the air his eye met Stewart's, who sat waiting on his horse to follow in the retinue of justice. The betrayed marauder made a dead halt as this hateful vision once more crossed his path. He evinced no special emotion, however, but gazed steadily for a few moments into the young man's eye, as if studying his soul. Without any further evidence of hate, or scorn, or passion, he then passed coldly on.

The Sheriff's posse was not considered large enough by the citizens of the place to make the custody of the marauder safe, and numerous citizens, therefore, flinging their muskets across their shoulders, volunteered to strengthen the guard. There were many of these volunteers—indeed, more than the Sheriff chose to see, but the right of the citizens to follow on was a matter which he could not control, and to which he was therefore quietly obliged to submit. He did once ask a very respectable looking gentleman near him, if the fidelity of all the crowd could be relied on, but receiving the answer that Murrell had not a friend ten miles around, he quieted the slight uneasiness which had once or twice previously disturbed his mind.

When about half way to their destination, the road became densely bordered by a heavy growth of trees, which grew upon sudden undulations extremely favorable to concealment. While passing through this portion of the route, a pistol shot was suddenly heard from the right side, and upon the sound, Stewart found his bridle shot in two. A number of the guards instantly plunged off in the direction of the report, the wildest confusion ensued, and for the moment, the prisoner seemed to be entirely forgotten. The golden chance was not lost by Murrell's friends, for taking advantage of the temporary distraction, five or six of the crowd swerved suddenly upon the prisoner, and thrust him quickly to the left side. The result of this movement would inevitably have been a rescue, had not Mr. Debery, with professional acuteness, became suddenly impressed with a suspicion that the pistol shot and movement of the crowd, were portions of concerted plan. Upon the thought he ordered the men back, and wheeling round, encircled the prisoner with his own chosen force just as he was disappearing in the copse.

"We saw a negro diving away into the thicket," said one of the guards, as he returned into the road. "It must have been he who fired the pistol."

"And while you was seeing that, we came very near losing the prisoner," said the Sheriff angrily. "There are traitors in the crowd! An attempt has been made for a rescue."

"You're right, Sheriff, you're right," cried another guard, "for look here, the lashings of his hands are nearly cut through, and only hold by two or three strands."

"Then take my handkerchief and bind them anew," said the Sheriff. "Close around him, and suffer no person to approach within ten feet."

"There are traitors and suspicious persons amongst us!" exclaimed several of the crowd, and the exclamation fell loudest of all from the lips of Murrell's men. Their ruse had failed, and not having succeeded in rescuing their leader, they now found dissimulation necessary to protect themselves. They, therefore, went in front of their captive chief, and taunting him with the futile effort that had been made, reviled him in the grossest terms.

Murrell paid no apparent heed to any of these movements, save by a slight smile which was intended to express his complete indifference to all that was going on.

On arriving in Jackson the prisoner was first conducted to a tavern, and was there detained in custody till a court could he called. The novelty of the arrival aroused the curiosity of the whole town, and throngs who had got the leading features of the story, flocked out to see the renowned robber and his no less famous conqueror. Stewart stood near the prisoner, but by this time, in obedience to his directions, all who knew him addressed him by the name of Hues. Deeming it however no longer of importance to continue this disguise, he requested his friends to call him by his proper name.

The astonishment and confusion of Murrell at this unexpected revelation can scarcely be described; it was the severest blow he had ever received, and dissipated the main of his recent hopes in a breath.

Instead of having to wrestle with an opponent who was a poor and obscure stranger, whose character he might whistle down with an ordinary effort, or whose life he might quench with tolerable impunity, he found he had to deal with a man who was in the midst of his friends, and whose cause and reputation would be tenaciously defended by numerous staunch and influential supporters.

In his testimony before the committing court, Mr. Stewart confined himself to such facts as related to the abduction and subsequent disposal of Mr. Henning's slaves. The deep laid and sanguinary plan for the negro rising, he deemed it prudent to withhold for a while, for fear that its strange and almost incredible atrocity would stagger the belief, and cast a doubt upon his whole relation. This omission puzzled Murrell more than all the rest, and when the accuser got through with his testimony, he appeared to experience a great relief.

Upon the testimony of Stewart, Murrell was then fully committed to await his trial at the approaching May term.

CHAPTER XX.

The Messenger of Evil Tidings—Consternation in the Morass—
Scattering of the elements—Murrell's Secret Circular—The Yazoo
Pass—The Separation—Corroboration—The Return to Madison—
Slander and detraction—The Chafing of the Tiger—The Secret
Proceedings of the Council—Plans of Rescue and Assassination.

Having now secured his first object by Murrell's arrest, Mr. Stewart, with every new moment of reflection, became impressed with the necessity of obtaining evidence to corroborate the confessions of the accused, and to strengthen his own statements. This he considered not only important to the matter in issue, but necessary, also, to the protection of his private reputation and veracity.

Murrell had told him, among other things, that Mr. Henning's negroes had been sent in charge of the subordinate agents of his clan, down the Mississippi to the Yazoo Pass, where, if a market offered, they were to be sold. Hoping to find the captives there, he determined to proceed at once to that part of the country, accompanied by a son of Mr. Henning, for the purpose of overtaking and reclaiming them.

In coming to this conclusion, Mr. Stewart found himself obliged to neglect important interests of his own, which now called him to the Choctaw purchase. He had left his property and business in the hands of a man named Mathew Clanton, who though perfectly substantial and in good repute, was not capable of making certain investments, which at that time promised sudden and heavy profits. Setting aside the calculations of trade, however, in the devouring excitement which had taken possession of his mind. Stewart waited upon young Henning, and stating his determination, Henning immediately agreed to the proposal, and on the following morning the two young men set out together for Manchester, Mississippi.

We must not forget Watkins, the courier, who, receiving the message from Murrell's wife on the night of the arrest, had mounted his horse and started in the direction of the Arkansas rendezvous. Swiftly and faithfully did the marauder ride in despite the cutting wind that kept stinging him for his sharp progress; and the morning found him pausing only for the refreshment of a hasty meal, and the aid of a fresh horse. He then sped on again.

In brief time he arrived at the Mississippi bank, crossed the river, passed rapidly from hut to hut on the Arkansas shore, scattering his bad news as he went until he at

WATKINS ACQUAINTING THE MARAUDERS WITH THE CAPTURE OF THEIR CHIEF.

length arrived at the cabin on the island. A few blows from his riding whip dealt the mystic signal on the door, and bursting in as soon as it was opened, he communicated his thrilling information in a breath to a council of some dozen men, who were debating on business at the time.

The news of Watkins created the greatest consternation among the inmates of the hut, and for the first few moments all was terror and confusion. A thousand questions were asked for the few answers that could be given, and several plans of precaution, of vengeance, and of assistance, were proposed on the spot. The first measures that seemed necessary, however, were ones of precaution, and dispatching Watkins back with assurances that measures of assistance would be immediately devised, the marauders commenced demolishing the council hut. Before the night of the day on which they received the news, it was levelled with the ground. The logs were made into a raft, shoved into the lake, and towed into an obscure cove. The furniture was distributed among the various cabins scattered about the morass; on the empty site were hastily planted several small cedars, and then the whole arena was strewed over with a thick carpet of dead leaves, in a manner that completely concealed the fresh and broken ground. There was a small clearing, but no evidence of a habitation: and when a band of regulators visited the spot some weeks afterwards, they were disappointed in finding any traces of the celebrated council hut. The main marauders slipped away, and the rest distributed themselves like rats among the mean cabins of the morass, relying for safety upon their apparent poverty and insignificance.

The Barney's, Loyd's, and Tucker's, and some others of the most *respectable* and prominent, who had woodyards on the river, held their ground, and continued in ostensible legitimate business. But the agitation was intense. Secret meetings were held every night. Emissaries were despatched north and south to spread the disastrous news, and plan after plan was proposed for the rescue of the chief.

In the meantime, the imprisoned robber was himself contriving schemes to circumvent the steps which had been taken against him. His wife was admitted to see him after his first day's confinement, and to her he confided his plans and communicated his directions. On learning the departure of Stewart and young Henning, the robber issued secret orders to have the character of the former blasted by the most injurious rumors during his absence, and he also furnished his retainers with an accurate description of his person, that he might be cut off by violence and his mouth in that way effectually closed. No money or exertions were to be spared to accomplish these objects, and arrangements were also to be put in train at once, to break the accuser's testimony down, by legal imputation.

To this end he concocted and addressed a circular letter to his chief men in Arkansas and on the river, directing them to have witnesses prepared fur the day of trial, to swear that Stewart and himself stopped at their houses on the celebrated jaunt in question and that while there, Stewart had informed them that he was tracking the prisoner on suspicion of his having stolen some negroes in Madison, Tennessee, and that if he succeeded in convicting him he was to have a large reward. The witnesses were further to say, that the story of Stewart on the occasion referred to, was rambling and inconsistent, and that from the manner in which it was communicated they had placed but little reliance upon its truth. This testimony it was calculated would be a complete offset to the evidence of Champion, Erwin, and Hargus, who it was to be assumed had been deceived, and it was expected that the respectable appearance of the witnesses would make a favorable impression upon the jury.

The following is a copy of the circular letter above alluded to. It was subsequently found on Murrell's person in a manner to be hereafter explained. The first portion or certificate, is apparently designed for signatures, and to guide his lawyers in the summoning of witnesses, and the postscript develops a series of directions under the artful guise of foregone facts.

CERTIFICATE.

"This day personally appeared before us, &c., Jehu Barney, James Tucker, Thomas Dark, Joseph Dark, Wm. Loyd, &c., &c., who, being sworn in due form of law, do depose and say that they were present and saw ___

___Stewart of Yellow Busha, in the evening of the first day of February last, in company with John Murrell, at the house of said Jehu Barney, over the Mississippi river; and that he the said Stewart, informed us that he was in pursuit of John Murrell for stealing two negro men from preacher Henning, and his son Richard, in Madison County near Denmark; and that he had told Murrell his name was Hues, and he wished us to call him Hues in Murrell's hearing. We also recollect to have heard him, the said Stewart, say distinctly that *he was to get five hundred dollars for finding said negroes and causing said Murrell to be convicted for stealing them.* Said Stewart did not say who was to give him this reward, but he stated that he held the obligation of several rich men for that amount."

Signed, "____ _____

The above is a *copy* given to me, by one who heard him make the admission therein contained in your presence. You will therefore please send me the names of all that *will* testify to these facts in writing, and also send me the names of all and every man that will certify these witnesses to be men of truth.

J:††‡‡ MURRELL.

P. S. But above all things, arrest him, (the said witness) *for passing the six twenty dollar bills.* You will have to go out in Yellow Busha, Yellow Busha County, near the *centre*, for him. Undoubtedly this matter will be worthy your attention, for if it be one, two, or three hundred dollars, the gentleman to whom he passed (100) it, can present it before a Magistrate and take a judgment for the amount, and his provision store &c., is worth that much money. I shall conclude with a claim on you tor your strictest attention. My distressed wife will probably call on you, and if she does, you may answer all her *requests* without reserve. Yours, &c.

J:††‡‡ MURRELL."

The above document is admirably ingenious in all its parts, and while it appears only to advise in relation to the management of an existing state of things, it lays down a specific, intricate and methodical system of arrangements for future action and guidance. Every point seems cared for. Stewart's interviews with Champion, Erwin and Col. Bayliss, which Murrell heard of for the first time in the testimony before the committing court, had suggested to his subtle mind the multiplication of witnesses upon that point, who, by adding to, or detracting a little from the story, would throw the whole into inextricable confusion. The idea was a shrewd one, for if Stewart had opened his bosom to strangers on one side of the river, it was reasonable for the jury to suppose he had done so on the other side, and more especially that he had done so upon that side where he would most need succor. It was a thought which stuck at the root of the case, and that took in the scope of all his danger.— Great ingenuity is also shown in the careful omission of the names of the persons whose obligations Stewart is charged with having held for the five hundred dollars reward, for the omission put it out of the latter's power to prove the negative, as he could get no witnesses to rebut the elusive allegation.

The postscript is the most artful and insidious of all. It presents a plot, perfect and complete in all its parts, the aim of which was plainly to enable the villains to get Stewart in their custody on an infamous charge, and thus enable them. while pretending to carry him to Arkansas for trial, to despatch him on the way.

Delivering a copy of this subtle document to his wife,[*] Murrell bade her attend to its safe despatch remarking that if it reached its destination speedily, and was faithfully carried out, he had nothing to fear; but adding that he was in hopes of breaking the d—d prison and of taking a hand in a portion of the business himself before the time came round for trial.

On their way south the two young men stopped at Stewart's neighborhood in the Choctaw Purchase. While there they called at the house of Clanton and a man named Wm. Vess, both of whom had property of Stewart's in their charge, and who, up to that hour, had always been regarded by him as friends and honest men. Clanton was rich and of high standing in the place but Vess was poor, yet nevertheless of equal respectability. Stewart acquainted Clanton with his mission, and told him of Murrell's arrest. Clanton, on hearing the latter piece of news, evinced a surprise and concern that would have excited Stewart's suspicions had they been betrayed by a stranger: but attributing the shadow only to uneasiness for safety, Stewart assured him that he would

---

[*] The following is a copy of the certificate which is attached to the above letter of Murrell, to attest its correctness. They are both taken from the records of the Madison County Circuit Court.—

"*State of Tennessee, Madison County.*

I Henry W. McCorry, Clerk of the Circuit Court of Madison County aforesaid, certify that the foregoing is a true and perfect copy, in word and letter, of the instrument of writing filed in my office, and read in evidence against John A. Murrell, upon his trial for negro-stealing at the July term of our said court, 1834.

"In testimony whereof I have hereunto subscribed my name and affixed my private seal (there being no public seal of office) at office in Jackson, the 29th of September, A.D. 1835.

[Sealed.] "H W McCorry"

keep carefully upon his guard, and not incur danger by travelling at night.

On the next day the young men proceeded on their way to Manchester, but after searching around the vicinity for five or six days, they were informed by a boatman, of whom they made inquiry, that at the time the boat they sought for was to have been at the pass, no boats could enter it. He added that it was therefore probable that its conductors had turned off and gone further down the river.

Taking the theory of the boatman to be correct, the young men concluded to waste no further time in searching about the neighborhood, and Stewart proposed that they should separate—Henning to pursue his inquiries in the direction of Vicksburgh, and himself to proceed to Madison County, Mississippi, to see if he could find the Mr. Hunold spoken of by Murrell, to whom Eason's negro had been sold. Stewart had no difficulty in finding Mr. Hunold, who proved to be the wealthy and respectable planter that the land-pirate had represented him. He explained his mission, and received from Mr. Hunold the certificate of the truth of the story of the stolen negro which we have already described. This was a strong piece of corroboration for Stewart, and feeling amply paid for his visit, he set out on his return to Tennessee.

On his road back he found that the arrest of Murrell was generally known throughout the country, but he was also frequently reminded of the dangers he had incurred, and of the arduous and unthankful task he had assumed, by the disparaging rumors in relation to himself, which constantly met his ears. All affected to rejoice in the capture of the ruffian whose bands had so long been a pest and terror to the country, but very many sneered at the captor, and insinuated that he was merely a treacherous and dissatisfied associate, who through hate, envy, or some still baser motive, had betrayed his chief. It was not difficult for Stewart to ascribe these rumors to their proper source, nor to understand their aim, and he therefore did not suffer them to either alarm or discourage him from his purpose. He pursued his course to Madison, reported his mission, and lodged the corroborative certificate of Hunold in trusty hands for use at the proper time. He found in Madison the same spirit of detraction and abuse that he had discovered at points along the road. As the most of this, however, was confined to a certain class of people of no influence or standing, he did not affect to notice it, but he grappled with two or three slanders, which came from people whose apparent position gave their assertions influence, and exposed their utterers to public shame. The contest was unequal, but still he did not despair. His enemies were numerous and active, but he presented no penetrable point to all their insidious assaults, and the consciousness of the justness of his motives made him insensible to fear.

On the first of April, Stewart left Madison for home, with the intention of settling up his affairs, that he might leave the country as soon as the trial was over. Being impressed at the time of starting with the peculiar dangers which beset him, he exacted from his friends a promise that in the event any thing should transpire to make it dangerous tor him to attend the trial (which had been set down for July,) they would transmit him intelligence at once, that he might adopt such measures for his safety as the exigencies of the case should demand. Keeping secret even from his best friends the time of his departure, he selected a favorable moment, and set out for home by a circuitous route and under an assumed name.

The friends of Murrell had not been idle during the recent stay of Stewart in Madison. The chief chafed at his imprisonment, and while he upbraided his followers with inertness and neglect in suffering Stewart to go and come from one end of the country at pleasure and unharmed, he also rebuked them for not releasing him from his irksome detention by force. These complaints lent new vigor to the debates of the councillors of the morass, and adopting a policy more bold than the mere dissemination of slanderous rumors, they organised a chosen band of picked men to gather at Jackson on a certain night and take possession of a man who should undertake to proceed to Yellow Busha in the Purchase, and assassinate the enemy who had given them so much trouble. Both of these measures were acted upon and arranged at the same meeting, and the charge of the latter and most important of the two, fell to a desperado named Aker. Rejoicing in the chance that had conferred the bloody expedition upon him, this ruffian prepared himself for the atrocious task with the utmost relish and alacrity, and it is somewhat singular that on that very day (the first day of April) on which Stewart set out for home, Aker commenced his journey to the same place to encounter him and take his life.

CHAPTER XXI.

Stewart's History and Connections in the Purchase—Stewart's Return Home—The Dead Alive—Suspicious Characters—Symptoms of Danger—The Midnight Assault—Reception of an Assassin—The Regulators—Lynch Law—Arrival of Aker the Assassin—Emissary of the Grand Council—Accidental Interview between him and Stewart—The Price of Blood.

We left Stewart at the conclusion of the last chapter, on the point of setting out for home, after a protracted stay of several weeks in Madison, and we must now anticipate his arrival in the Purchase, by a brief attention to characters of that neighborhood, to whom we have heretofore only granted an incidental notice.

We allude to Matthew Clanton and Wm. Vess. The first of these men was of considerable importance in the neighborhood, and was the possessor of considerable property. He was shrewd, artful and designing, and was, therefore, as dangerous as he was affable. Vess, on the other hand, was a man of weak mind and indolent habits, and barely supported himself by occasional jobs as a journeyman carpenter, and some trifling assistance which he received now and then from Clanton. Of Clanton there was little known. He had come to the Purchase about four years previous to the date of which we write, and opened a country store. In the course of time the fact developed itself that he was rich, but whether he had been possessed of wealth when he first arrived, whether he had acquired it by his retail trade, or whether he was indebted for it to some secret financial speculation with the strangers who visited him from time to time, was never ascertained. At any rate he was recognized as a substantial, and therefore as a *respectable* man, and in this light Stewart was told to regard him when introduced to him on his first expedition to the Choctaw country in 1833. Stewart took with him to the Choctaw country at that time the avails of a handsome farm which he had disposed of, in Madison, for the purpose of investing it in articles for Indian traffic. With a large sum in his possession, and an evident tact for business, in a growing country, he was a very desirable associate for business; and Clanton, perceiving his value, proposed a connection with him. Stewart, however, having already invested most of his ready funds in articles for Indian trading, postponed a decision on the offer until he had brought his experimental barters to a close. An intimacy was thus formed between himself and Clanton, which continued till the fall, when the latter requested him to take charge of his business during an intended visit to Tennessee, Stewart agreed, and thus a still more intimate connection was formed, though it still did not take the shape of actual partnership. In January, 1834, Clanton returned, when Stewart still rejected the offers of copartnership, resigned the store to its owner, and received from him an eligible building lot as a reward for his attentions to his interests during his absence. It became necessary on Clanton's return, that Stewart should remove his own goods, which had been accumulating in the premises, to some other place of storage, and he was advised by the former to take them to the house of Vess, who, he observed, was a clever fellow, and would also board him, while he was building a house for himself, a proceeding which Stewart had now decided on. This advice was followed, and during his stay in the Purchase, Mr. Stewart became a regular member of Vess's family. In due time, his building was erected; but about the time of its completion, some business interests induced him to make the visit to Madison County, which resulted in his expedition against Murrell. The details of that expedition have already been faithfully detailed, but in developing the power and extensive associations of the marauder, the thread of the narrative did not admit of interruption, for the purpose of alluding to Matthew Clanton as one of his secret adherents. Such, however, appears to have been the fact, and in it we find a solution of the extreme concern evinced by Clanton, when informed by Stewart during the visit with young Henning, that he had trailed and trapped Murrell. As soon as Stewart had disappeared on that occasion, Clanton communicated the information he had received to his associates. His news, though not fresh to the council, revealed a most important fact—a fact that one of their party had the confidence of the common enemy, and might thereby insure his ruin. Clanton was peculiarly calculated to be of use in that way, tor his business dealings with Stewart would afford an opportunity for a plausible imputation of the latter's integrity, or his confidential intercourse would confer the chance of a more signal and direct betrayal. Before Clanton could prepare to follow the directions and perform the villanies against Stewart that were now expected of him, the latter had returned from his southern jaunt, and was on his way to Madison. He had therefore no immediate duties, except to return home and strengthen his hands against the youth's return. In this view, he determined to make an instrument of Vess. This was not difficult. Vess was a grossly ignorant and weak-minded man, and Clanton was a very artful one. A word dropped by the latter into the former's ear, that Stewart had been too familiar with his wife; served the purpose of making him a willing agent, and from a state of nerveless indolence and indifference to Stewart, Vess became his desperate and determined enemy.

Stewart's stay in Madison was, as has been seen, protracted to an unusual length. Putting this fact in connection with the expeditions that had started to cut him off, and the additional fact that not a line had been received from him for several weeks, Clanton became convinced that Stewart had fallen a victim to assassination. Under this impression he instituted inquiries among some of his associates, and had the satisfaction to learn that a letter had been received by one of the party, that Stewart had really fallen by the hands of a stryker named Rodgers, who was reported to have overhauled him between

La Grange[1] and the line. This report was greedily devoured by Clanton, for it relieved him of the perilous treachery allotted to him, and it afforded him an opportunity at the same time, of possessing himself, without dispute, of much of Stewart's property which remained in his custody. Believing implicitly in a rumor that was so congenial to his hopes, he spread it throughout the neighborhood, and having done this, divide the property of the supposed deceased, between himself and his instrument Vess, taking care, however, to reserve to himself the lion's share.

In the mean time Stewart, whom we left at the conclusion of the last chapter, starting from Madison for home, was proceeding cautiously on his way to the purchase. Meeting with no accident or detention on the route, he arrived in due time at his destination, but on entering the village was taken all aback by the general astonishment which greeted his appearance. This reception, though his mind was prepared for any change, sadly puzzled him at first, but when the cause was explained, and he detected the advantage which had been taken of his rumored death by his two pretended friends, he was at no loss to discover the source of the report.—The strangeness of the circumstance, the indecent avaricious haste of the self-instituted administrators upon his effects, and numerous evidences which he had recently received of the baseness of mankind, smote his mind with a suspicion of Clanton's connection with his enemies; and the coldness of the latter when questioned as to the motives of his conduct, justified him in its firm adoption. He did not betray this revolution in his sentiments, however, but

1. LaGrange, Tennessee was located in southeast Fayette County.

pretending to be satisfied with Clanton's explanations, he made no change in his demeanor, nor adopted any striking alterations in his arrangements. On the contrary, he simulated perfect satisfaction, and even went to board again with Vess. He, however, took the wise precaution to sleep in his own house, now finished, which stood near by, that he might not be exposed to treachery at night. To make himself the more secure in this way, he procured bolts and fastenings of the firmest character, and fitted them to his doors with his own hands, and kept fresh loaded weapons always prepared for use.

There was need for these precautions. Immediately on his return, the neighborhood became subject to the visits of numerous suspicious characters, and rude looking-men, who never before had been seen in the vicinity, were observed to squat around and locate themselves among the mean cabins in the neighborhood.

This state of things excited surprise in the uninterested, but it struck alarm into the breast of Stewart, and every unfamiliar face was a warning for him to stand upon his guard. These fears were justified by several more definite indications of danger, and one circumstance, in particular, determined him to take prompt and decisive measures for his safety.

When leaving the house of Vess one evening shortly after supper, he discovered in the dusk two figures slinking along the hedges in his rear. He sharpened his pace and soon was safely inside his door. After keeping a light burning for a reasonable time he put it out, and then cautiously drew himself up to the window. The gloom outside was so deep in contrast to the previous light of his apartment, that for a few minutes he could

THE ASSASSINS WATCHING STEWART'S HOUSE

discover no object, but melting to his strengthening vision, the darkness at length revealed two figures standing in front of the house and occasionally walking up and down before it. They would now and then step round to the rear and then again would look up and clown the front, as if in search of some vulnerable point. Half an hour elapsed in these manœuvres, when a third party joined them, who after holding a close consultation for a few moments, went away, taking one of the pair with him. In a few minutes the absent man returned with a small ladder. After a proper pause, and a careful survey of the road to see that no person was near, the ends of the ladder were muffled with handkerchiefs, and were softly placed against the house under the window where Stewart stood sentry. Kicking off his shoes, and feeling in his bosom as if to see if his weapon was free, one of the men began to ascend. The movements of the ruffian were so stealthy and artistical, that hat! not the intended victim been upon the watch, his lightest slumbers would not have received a whisper of alarm. The climber at length reached the window, but he was doomed to proceed no further, for as he laid his hand upon the frame to raise it up, a sharp streak of flame shot through the glass, and the adventurer reeled backwards to the ground. He was neither killed nor mortally wounded, however, for he rose to his feet after a moment's pause, and holding his shoulder as if that had been the point of the wound, ran off after his companion. They had not been gone an instant when the third man, plunging forward with a curse, seized and bore off the ladder, which his companions had left behind them in their flight. Stewart regretted this movement seriously, for he was about to secure possession of the ladder in the belief that it would afford him a clue to whom he was indebted for the attempt.

This atrocious effort to assassinate him, convinced Stewart of the necessity of taking active measures to turn the tables upon the wretches who were thirsting for his life. He therefore started out early on the following morning, and having related the transaction to the better class of his neighbors, organized a company of Regulators for the expulsion from the neighborhood of all suspicious characters, including loungers and idle persons whose means of living were unknown. The first who experienced the effects of the stringent adjudication of the Regulators, was a man named Tucker, from Arkansas, who was overheard in drink to threaten Stewart's life, and who, when questioned as to his business in the neighborhood, could give no satisfactory reply. Having no friend to speak in his behalf, and being a vagabond by his own showing, he was dealt with most summarily, and publicly expelled the country— being forbidden to return on pain of a pair of cropped ears. Another man, named Barker, who proved to be a counterfeiter, and a third, who proved also to be one of Murrell's men, were dealt with in the same way. A fourth, however, named Glenn, and a most depraved and dangerous character, gave more trouble, and Stewart found that he was to experience thenceforth greater difficulties in his investigations than he expected. He discovered that there were several among his company who gave evidences of friendship to the marauding clans, and he wisely concluded that a company accessible to such materials had better be dissolved at once. He, accordingly, withdrew from its command on Glenn's acquittal, expressing himself satisfied with what had been done, and declaring his belief that the organization was no longer necessary, as the neighborhood had evidently been completely purged of its obnoxious visitants.

The danger that had threatened Stewart, though apparently abridged, was only changed for a peril of a far more subtle and insidious character. It was the danger of poison—a danger that threatened him every time he sat at Vess's board, and which forced him to confine himself to the simplest food, and to the tea and coffee which was shared by his host and hostess in common with himself. There were many reasons for these suspicions, and a strange vomiting which he had been seized with after drinking coffee prepared for him alone at a late supper, justified him in his doubts.

It will be said by many, that a man so hemmed in and beset with peril, should have abandoned the neighborhood which had no ties but those of pecuniary interest, and which had now become so hostile as to discourage even those of business. Indeed, so said Stewart's judgment to itself, and he decided that after he had arranged his outstanding affairs, invested his money in the most available public lands then in the market, and bore testimony at the Court in Madison, he would put a sufficient sum in his pocket to take him to the East, and there remain until the excitement which surrounded him had passed away, and the desperadoes who were thirsting for his life had been dispersed. With these views he devoted the time which intervened before the trial in disposing of all his remaining goods, in examining the character of all the unappropriated lands in the purchase, and in preparing a journal of Murrell's conversations, accomplices and plans, for the vindication of his own course, and as a warning to all villains in future.

Returning home late one afternoon from one of his land-hunting excursions, a man rode up from his rear, and drew up in company with him. The stranger was a man of large size, and brawny muscular frame. He was about thirty years old, but his rugged, weather beaten face, heavy whiskers, and a sweeping scar which measured his entire cheek, gave him at first sight an appearene of greater age. Perceiving that this formidable looking character was armed with a heavy bowie-knife, and a holster on each side of his superb horse, Stewart put himself upon his guard, and feeling that his weapons were ready for' use, made his calculations for danger.

The stranger on riding up, commences with the usual common-place of travellers, and after the exchange of a few ordinary remarks, asked Stewart if he had any acquaintance in the neighborhood. The latter replied in the affirmative, and mentioned several.

"Are you acquainted with a man in this part of the country by the name of Virgil A Stewart?"

"Yes, sir, I am; and just about as well as I wish to be with all such fellows."

"You don't like him, then!" said the stranger, brightening."

"I have seen others I have liked as well!"

"If you've no particular objections, I should like to know why you're down on him—for I dislike him very much myself."

"Well, for one thing," said Stewart, flinging his head contemptuously, "he's altogether too smart. He's one at your fellows that knows more than anybody else, and he, interferes with things that don't concern him. He's been taking advantage of a man lately that's a better man than himself, and who never gave him any provocation!"

"Who do you mean," said the stranger, "do you allude to Murrell?"

"It don't matter much who I mean," replied Stewart; and then, as if an idea had struck him, he turned round to his companion, and looking him full in the face for a moment, he flung up his hand with the private sign which he had learned in the morass.

The interrogation was answered in an instant by the stranger, and both the men instantly leaned towards each other, and grasping hands in the warmth of brotherhood passed another signal in the clasp.

"Why, damn it, I *thought* you was one of us from the start!" exclaimed the robber with a grin of confidence and gratification. "What is your name?"

"Well, I make Tom Goodin suit me just now."

"Mine is George Aker," said the robber. "I'm on a mission from the Grand Council to stop this Stewart's wind, and I guess you can help me in the business."

"Well, I don't know but I might, but I didn't know there had been a meeting in the matter!"

"Oh, yes, a dozen. We think we've got him pretty straight now, *for he's living with his enemies and our friends*. If I succeed, however, all our trouble is ended, and he is out of the way. But if I don't, our plan is to get Murrell out of prison, and let him off till the session of court comes round. In the meantime there will be men here to prefer a charge against Stewart for counterfeiting, that will defame him before the world.—When the trial comes on, Murrell will appear of his own accord, and while this speaks in favor of his innocence, the infamy of the charge against Stewart, will kill his testimony. There is a party on their way to Madison now to release him, and on my return, if I don't succeed in killing Stewart, they will set out for this place to make the charge against him for counterfeiting."

"The plan is a magnificent one, and must succeed. I suppose it comes from the boss."

"Certain. And I guess Jackson jail is racked by this time. God help Stewart then. I would like to carry my part through, for I should take a pleasure in laying him out. There's been a man here before me on this same business, but he couldn't do anything. When he came away, he engaged an old man and his wife, with whom Stewart was living, to put him through by poison.—He gave them a hundred dollars for the service, but for some reason or other they ha'nt done it. The council got tired of waiting, so they made up two hundred for me, and here I am ready to take the first chance to do up the work."

"Is there anyone about here whose help you calculate upon?" inquired Stewart.

"Well, I don't know as there is," replied Aker. "There's a family of Glen's, near Troy,[2] that I have made some calculations on, and there's a '*big fish*' whom Stewart thinks one of his best friends, that ought to help me; but he's of little account just now, for he'll take no step until Stewart is dead. When that takes place, he has agreed to defame him for the purpose of restoring our folks to credit. But that kind of assistance is of no good to me now. I want a willing hand and a good nerve, and 1 think you're the man.—I'm not greedy, and will divide

---

2. Troy, Mississippi

the price, and if you think you can do the business, you shall have a hundred down."

They had now arrived within the precincts of his neighborhood, and Stewart, for the purpose of keeping up the delusion of the robber, agreed to his proposals, and received the hundred dollars, at the suggestion of Aker that he had better take it, as he might be obliged to fly precipitately after the commission of the deed. He then promised to undertake the business that very night, and advising Aker not to proceed any further in his company, as he was under some disrepute in the neighborhood, made an appointment to meet him on the following morning at ten o'clock, at an indicated point on the road between Troy and Commerce.[3]

"Good night, then," said Aker, as they separated. "I will take your advice and not go to Glenn's to-night, but in the morning I shall expect to hear that the work is done.—If you can do no better, shoot him as he sits by the fire, but don't fail! Good night!"

"Good night!" said Stewart, riding off with the blood-money and prize of his own life in his pocket.

---

3. Commerce, Mississippi

CHAPTER XXII.

Plans for Arrest of Aker—Dangerous Hospitality—The Poisoned Beverage—The Appointment—The Secret Departure—Change of Scene—Murrell in his Cell—Gathering of the Marauders in Jackson—Preparations for Escape—Progress of the Plan—The Open Air.

The conversation with Aker the assassin, had conferred upon Stewart the most important revelations. He saw every point of his position. What before had been mere surmise, took the shape of fact, and he was satisfactorily convinced that be was not only living with his enemies, but that an attempt had really been made to poison him. He shuddered with terror as he reviewed the perils through which he had passed, and contemplated those which he had still to weather, but still, in the midst of his discouragement and gloom, he could not forbear admiring the paramount genius, which from the empire of a prison cell could command the service of a king, and direct designs which would have defied the ability of most other men, with all the advantages of personal liberty and action to assist them. He felt a slight twinge at times, in the shape of a reproach, that he had measured himself against such a terrible opponent. It was not a touch of conscience, but a rebuke of judgment; and there were moments when he would peevishly condemn himself as a fool, for having involved his life and prospects for the cause of others. It was too late, however, for these reflections to be either wise or salutary. The steps which had been taken were irrevocable; the combat was in progress, and he must fight it out like a man.

The first matter which claimed his attention was the disposal of Aker, and the next the adoption of measures to turn the information of Aker to the best account.

As to the disposal of Aker, it seemed to be plain what course to follow. A communication to some trusty neighbor of what had happened, and the preparation of an ambush party for the following morning, which should overhear the atrocious mission of the emissary, and then arrest him, appeared to be the only proper plan to adopt. But there was one strong objection to this course. It was difficult to find that trusty neighbor, and the best exercise of his discrimination in the selection of a confidant, would leave him but an equal chance of entrusting his secret to a friend or an enemy. Friends he had, and many of them, but he had been most grievously betrayed, and he was excusable in doubting all mankind. It was impossible for him to carry the affair through alone, however, and he therefore determined to trust once more to human nature, and to take the risk that was connected with the most effectual mode. If the plan failed, he would then have nothing to reproach himself with. With this intention he drew up at the house of a Mr. Saunders, on his road home, but notwithstanding he remained there for an hour, he wisely, as subsequent revelations proved, abstained from carrying out the purpose of his visit. The coldness of the manner of his host, and his affected disbelief of the truth of Aker's communications, was the occasion of this change of his intentions, and Stewart felt a relief when he left the door, that he had not betrayed his designs into *that* neighbor's hands.

It was now past the supper hour of the Vess family, and having no appetite for food, Stewart concluded to go directly to his own house and retire for the night; but a thought struck him which induced him to alter his mind. In the energy which always accompanies an exasperated state of feeling, he resolved to push his investigations against his boarding house keepers at once. The time was apt for a satisfactory solution of the poisoning problem. The lateness of the hour would induce Mrs. Vess to prepare a special supper for him; and then, if ever, the poison would be put into his drink.

As he expected, Mrs. Vess invited him to sup and notwithstanding he affected to have supped already, she insisted on his taking at least *a cup of coffee*. Some bread and the remains of a joint were put before him.—The first of these he merely tasted, but when the coffee was poured out he gently pushed it back, complaining that he felt unwell, and filling a glass with milk, drank it off instead. At this a glance was exchanged between the woman and her husband, and the atrocious beverage was taken from the table with the rest of the provisions. Stewart had not been able to detect any suspicious movement in the preparation of his drink, but he was not the less convinced that it contained an enemy to life, and as there remained a chance to satisfy himself upon that point, he withdrew on the pretence of going home, and concealed himself in some bushes opposite, where he could observe all that took place in the apartment. On his retiring, his hostess stopped short in her occupation, and commenced what appeared to be an earnest and angry conversation with her husband. She then resumed the disposal of the supper ware, and having cleared the board, took the coffee pot and carried it to the light. After looking into it and smelling it somewhat anxiously, she called up Vess, and made him go through the same examination. She then turned to him as if asking his opinion, whereupon he shook his head, as if deciding that there was nothing in the appearance or smell of the beverage that could have given their guest alarm. This point having been settled, the female took the vessel to the door and threw the contents upon the ground. As she did so, a favorite cur put his nose down to the steaming liquid, whereupon she drove him suddenly away with the remark of, "Look out, you rascal, that was intended for a spy!" She then called the animal in and closed the door.

"Well," said Stewart, as he turned off home, "I find my friend of the road has told me the truth about these people, and I shall therefore take his word for all the rest."

After arriving at his house he sat down and addressed a letter to the Hennings, and one also to the Sheriff of Madison, detailing all the particulars of the intended rescue of Murrell which he had learned from Aker, urging them to take precautions against the danger. In the morning, after due preparation, he set out on horseback to the pile of logs on the Commerce road, designated as the place of meeting with the assassin. It was not his purpose to arrest him then, but to make some further inquiries in relation to Murrell's plans, to ascertain the part of country the chief intended to strike for when he should escape, and he also wished to ascertain with certainty, whether the enemy spoken of by Aker as a "big fish" was Clanton.

The eagerness of his purpose brought him to the rendezvous long before the time, but he waited with patience for the hour of ten. Ten o'clock came, however, without bringing the robber with it; eleven o'clock passed, and still he did not make his appearance; and at length, when morning had nearly verged into meridian, Stewart concluded that the villain had been apprised of his mistake, and had determined not to keep the dangerous appointment. The momentary appearance of a figure at some distance off, which he recognised as Glenn's, strengthened this impression, and he concluded that any longer stay upon his post would only afford derision to concealed observers. He therefore released his horse from an adjacent tree where he had been fastened, and mounting him rode on to the post office, and sealed and deposited the letters which he had prepared the night before.

He returned home disappointed and gloomy, and reviewing the whole condition of his affairs, resolved to leave the Purchase at once, not to return until after the trial, when he would take leave of it forever. Having formed this determination, he securely stowed his goods, and putting all his papers in his saddle bags, set out on the second day afterward for Madison. He gave no notice of his intentions to a soul, nor did he venture to depart until darkness protected him from discovery.

Fear changes the color of every thing it touches. It robs manhood of its boldness, and it makes honor take the hue of crime.

Aker had given Stewart a true statement of the machinations of the clans. A determination had been taken in accordance with Murrell's directions to have him released at all hazards, and a number of the most daring and experienced of the confederacy had proceeded north for the purpose of carrying it into effect. Before the period of Stewart's departure from the Purchase, numbers of them had already skulked into Jackson, and placed themselves in communication with the prisoner through the agency of his wife, who had taken up her residence in the town from the time of the imprisonment of her husband. Occasionally some of his clansmen would obtain access to the prison, and be allowed an interview with the lion of the place, but this favor was always obtained on their pretences of a natural curiosity to see, and to speak to a man who had rendered himself so terribly notorious. These visits afforded vast satisfaction to Murrell. They gave him a substantial and face to face assurance of the fidelity of his adherents, and enabled him to communicate directly, and without the intervention of a feminine and inexperienced mind, with those on whom he would have to trust for the execution of his commands.

The atmosphere of the prison became more elastic, and the sunshine which found its way into his cell seemed to increase at every visit, with a superadding brightness that promised soon to melt away the very bars.

The men who visited him did not attempt to convey him any implements of escape. The wife was made sole agent of this duty. It was she who took him in a small and finely tempered file, a watch spring to saw the bars, a small cold-chisel and a slim but strong cord to lower him to the ground when he should have removed all obstructions to his egress. These things were hidden with the utmost adroitness from the scrutiny of the keepers, during the period of their visits. A hole was bored in each of the lower legs of his bunk. These, after his implements had been placed into them, were stopped up with two admirably fitted plugs, and for the better disguise of this last specimen of mechanism, a lot of hard brown soap was rubbed over the ends of each and then ground into the dirt of the floor to give a superficial coating of "old times," that would satisfy even the most pertinacious and experienced scrutinizer. He had only received his instruments one at a time, for it was necessary that each in turn should be carefully disposed of before the next one came. The watch spring when it arrived was confined to the same depository with the file, but the cord which came last of all, was wound round his body, next his skin, during a visit of his wife.

We find him at length possessed of all the necessary implements to secure an egress, provided he could have tolerable luck in concealing the progress of his operations. But there were other matters to be considered beyond a mere escape beyond the walls. A retreat was to be secured and the dangers of a re-capture provided against. Murrell had not slighted any portion of his plan. He was a good general, and having contemplated a deliberate campaign, was determined to make sure and solid the advantages he should gain by a first surprise. He therefore ordered relays of horses to be prepared for him in the direction of the Mississippi line, at ten mile intervals for the first night. This would enable him to reach the cabin of a friend who lived thirty miles distant, by daylight.—There, he was to receive the refreshment of a hasty meal, and then be driven on towards the line in a covered waggon drawn by two swift animals. This waggon was also to be relieved with a relay of a similar character, to be followed by another and another while the day lasted. The teams were to be kept up at their speed except when in sight of travellers on the road, or when passing through a village, or by a house. On these occasions they were to assume a business jog-trot, and the fugitive was to remain concealed under some light sacks of bran which were to cover the waggon bottoms for that purpose. At night the saddle relays were to be resumed. These would carry him beyond the line and place him out of the danger of arrest on any process except a requisition from the Governor of Tennessee. So much for the flight.

The pursuit was also to be the object of some management, and that portion of his friends who were not to be used in assisting the escape, were to be employed in misleading the chase.—These were to be at hand when the first alarm occasioned by the prisoner's disappearance was given, and were to endeavor to induce the belief that the fugitive had turned either north, east, or west—in

MURRELL ESCAPING FROM THE BAGNIO

short, to any direction but the right one. Appearances were to be contrived to encourage this impression, by the discovery of the fugitive's handkerchief in one direction, his tobacco-box or pocket-comb in another, and if such contrivances as these would not suffice, then a few men were to be stationed on the direct route, to report a man of Murrell's description as having turned off either to the right or left—for the Cumberland Mountains or the Mississippi. A number of the clan were also to ride in company, to aid these chance descriptions by creating diversions in their favor.

After this plan had been arranged, promulgated, and its several branches duly assigned to the various bands required for its consummation, Murrell had only to wait until the decay of the moon should bring round a night of early darkness to favor the first period of flight. This, however, occasioned so delay, for the pause was occupied with the outside preparations of which we have previously spoken.

The night arrived. The weakened bars received their final wound, and the open air which had been so long cancelled to his hopes, at length flowed in upon his face without a check. He strove through the narrow aperture, he slid swiftly down the cord, and dropped in the arms of two stout men below. Seizing him by each shoulder, these friends ran him across fields for half a mile, with scarcely any intermission in their speed, but coming to a wood at the end of that distance, they found a ready saddled horse in waiting to take up their task.

Receiving an assurance that every thing upon the road was "right," the marauder vaulted in his saddle, and striking his spurs into his horse, waved a brief "good bye," and commenced the chase that was to cost justice many a weary stride to overtake.

CHAPTER XXIII.

The flight—Disaster in the First Heat—The Second—The Third—The Pursuit—Progress of Stewart to the North—The Inn at Springhill—The New Acquaintance—The Owner of the Black Horse—Unconscious Separation of the Robbers and Their Foe—Progress of Murrell East and of Stewart North—Fresh Pursuit.

Desperately did the fugitive marauder ride. The night was pitch dark, but he tore over the ground as recklessly as though the meridian sun were blazing in his path. The wind was sharp and cutting, but it was tempered with the breath of liberty, and its severity was therefore blandness to his cheek. It screamed at times through the tall leafless trees that bordered the roadside, and now and then made him turn to listen if it were not the halloo of pursuit.

In the eighth mile he was startled by an imitative sound of this description. It came rushing through the trees like the confused voice of a distant multitude, and the flying horseman, with an involuntary impulse, again challenged the powers of his flagging steed. The faithful animal responded promptly to the deep plunge of the bloody spur into his already sorely wounded side; but in descending a slope under a shaking rein and a desperate pace, he suddenly stumbled and pitched headlong in the road, throwing his rider several feet beyond him, and tumbling himself over and over two or three times with the tremendous impetus.

The marauder had landed fortunately, and after rising stiffly from the ground, found that he had escaped with two or three slight bruises about the shoulders. But the horse was irretrievably gone; both his knees were broke and his neck was wrenched. The fugitive took him by the bride and tried to coax him to his feet, so that he might lead him from the road to prevent his carcase being an evidence of his route, but the effort was without success. The poor beast raised its head and mane one fruitless motion with its broken limbs, and then sunk helpless back. The robber now decided promptly on his course. He drew out his knife and cut the throat of the animal, that he might not have to show the accident was very recent, and he then took off the saddle and the harness and carried it with him, that its ownership might not be identified. He had got a little over two miles to run to his next relay; so tying the saddle on his back with the bellyband, and taking the reins and head gear in his hand, he set out on a run to complete the rest of the distance. The feat was accomplished with considerable difficulty. His long confinement had softened his frame, and he found himself frequently obliged to rest to humor his recent hurts. When he arrived at his ten mile rendezvous he was very much exhausted, but he refused any delay, and was satisfied with the refreshment of a single draught of spirits that was tendered from the flask of one of his henchmen. He then mounted and started on again.

By dint of faithfully performing his three ten mile heats, Murrell arrived in the gray of the morning at the cabin of a trusty friend at about two miles distance from the main road. He now found himself very stiff and sore, and during the preparation of a meal employed himself in examining his bruises and in bathing them with spirits. His stay did not exceed an hour and a half, and the latter division of his time was spent in a sound sleep before the fire, during the preparation of the vehicle that was to convey him further on. At seven o'clock he was roused up and took his place in the covered waggon. A soft mattress had been spread upon the bottom, a bag of bran was his pillow, and bags of meal were piled over and around him. A cross stick protected his head from the pressure from above, and a hole in the bottom of the waggon afforded him a supply of air. Thus lodged, the weary traveller disposed himself to rest, and soon resumed the sleep which be had commenced within the house.

About an hour after the commencement of this portion of Murrell's journey, the discovery was made in the prison that the land pirate was gone. The greatest consternation instantly prevailed, and in the first confusion of the calamity the keepers were at loss what course to take. Recovering from their surprise, however, they ran

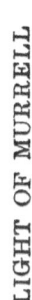

FLIGHT OF MURRELL

out, gave the alarm and set the towns-people to work searching every barn and out-house. Horses were then got out, and several pursuing parties were formed. The whole town was in commotion. The citizens flocked into the streets, and debated the affair in little knots, in every direction. All sorts of opinions were advanced as to the marauder's course of flight. Some conjectured that he was still burrowing in the neighborhood; some thought he had struck North and was already many miles away, and others insisted that he had gone towards the river. There were those who advised immediate pursuit, and there were also those who derided the idea of attempting to run down such a stag hound as the pirate chief, with a start in his favor of several hours.

In these debates and conflicting agitations, the adherents of the fugitive exercised their influence, but the main of their efforts were directed to the parties which were organized for pursuit. They thrust distracting councils upon these circles, and by mounting with them and joining the parties, exercised an equally distracting influence upon the chase.

It is unnecessary that we should attempt to describe the results of the efforts of the pursuers. The masterly arrangements that had been previously taken to baffle and mislead them, proved effectual, and the day was spent in idle coursing and idler speculations. All the scouting parties returned back at the close of the afternoon, beaten out with exertion and dispirited with failure.

While this was going on, Murrell still lay in the bottom of the vehicle in which he had taken his lodgings that morning, comfortable in the assurance of a space between him and immediate danger, of some sixty miles.

At nightfall he was across the line, but pushing onward for ten miles more, he reached a spacious cabin, where he found comfort and safe refuge. Considerable preparation had been made at this place to receive the chief. A sumptuous table was spread, a profusion of liquors covered the board, and eight or ten trusty clansmen invited him to sit down and help them celebrate his escape by a night-long revel. But Murrell had little appetite for frolic. He knew too well the value of time, to be enticed into the loss of a necessary minute, and having slept well through the day, he felt capable of "expressing" himself still further on that night. He therefore acceded to their request to join them, for a time only, on the condition that he might remain temperate in his drink, and be allowed to set out at twelve o'clock that night. These terms were at last agreed upon, and after a few hours of enjoyment the chief arose and withdrew.

Mounting his horse he took a course eastward through Tippah county, with intention of making his way to Florence, Alabama. He had got but half a mile on his way, however, when he was warned to stand upon his guard by the sound of hoofs approaching from behind, and he turned to find one of his roystering companions following him for the purpose of insisting upon sharing his journey. Murrell made no strenuous opposition to the offer, and the two marauders jogged along together.

From the nature of the country their journey was necessarily slow, and when morning dawned they had accomplished but a few miles from the starting place of the night before. The day likewise was one of tedious progress, from the necessity of taking a circuitous route to avoid the main road and when they arrived, at evening, in the vicinity of Springhill, they decided that it was necessary that their beasts should have the refreshment of a full night's rest. To secure this, they concluded upon entering the town and seeking entertainment at the inn.

The day after Stewart left the Choctaw country, his absence was noticed by Clanton, and communicated at once to the Glenns. It was at once suspected by these latter parties, that he had set out for Madison, and that his purpose was to finish the mischief he had brought upon the band, by giving evidence against the chief at the trial. 1t beho[o]ved a faithful clansman, therefore, to follow him at once, and endeavor to intercept this final danger. Glenn accordingly set out in hot pursuit of the young man, but with a miscalculating judgment he took the directest road, on the presumption that Stewart would depend for safety on the policy of haste. The pursuer therefore selected the route through Lafayette and Marshall counties, while Stewart with a cautious judgment, had chosen Pontotoc and Tippah.

But Stewart was approaching a peril far greater than a meeting with Glenn, or the one he had with Aker, the special assassin of the band; for he was about crossing the track of the arch enemy himself.

He entered Springhill on the same evening as Murrell, though at a later hour, and, singular enough, selected the very tavern or inn at which the robbers had put up an hour before.

Alighting at the door, he inquired of the landlord if he could afford him accommodation for the night?

Receiving a reply in the affirmative, he handed his bridle to the black ostler, and followed him to the stable, to personally observe, according to his habit, that his horse was properly attended and cared for. This task occupied him several minutes, when having satisfied himself with the boy's arrangements, he turned to leave the stable.

"Fine beast that, you got there," said a man of singular appearance, who, with his hands in his pockets, blocked up the passage way.

"Yes a good animal;" replied Stewart, attempting to pass on.

"You've seen mine, I suppose," said the man, and taking Stewart by the arm without any further ceremony, he led him to the furtherest stall, and bidding the boy hold up the lanthorn, challenged his admiration for a really fine chesnut horse.

"It is indeed a fine horse, sir," said Stewart, now observing that this new acquaintance was slightly touched with drink. "Rather a better animal than mine, I should say."

"Well, I don't know about that," replied the stranger, "but here's the cretur that bents the field." Saying this, he took the lanthorn from the boy and held it to the adjoining stall.

The animal thus classically alluded to was a superb black gelding, of remarkable elegance of form and coat, and displayed an extraordinary combination of the points which are most prized for speed, for strength, and for endurance. The encomiums of Stewart were sincere, and were so earnestly expressed that his new acquaintance was flattered in such a high degree, that handing the lanthorn back, he proposed that they should return to the tavern and take a drink. On entering the bar-room, Stewart observed three persons sitting near the stove whose dress and appearance betokened them to be the usual local loungers of a village tavern. This trio, with the landlord's wife who leaned upon the counter, and the landlord himself who stood before it, formed the entire of the inmates of the apartment.

"Dead heads!" said the stranger, in an under tone, motioning bis hand towards the trio at the stove, and winking significantly to Stewart at the same time. "Dead heads, they are! Come, let's have a drink."

"Your invite suits me right well," said Stewart, adapting his language to the style of his companion. "I'm dry as a preacher."

At this moment a colored boy entered the room and made a communication to the landlord. The landlord, after receiving it, turned and informed the stranger "that his friend had gone to bed, and requested to see him for a moment up stairs!"

"In one moment!" said the man, and bolting his liquor hastily, he left the room wiping his mouth with his sleeve.

"What is the name of that gentleman?" said Stewart to the landlord, as the stranger disappeared.

"Well, now, I really can't tell," said the landlord, with a bland what'll-you-have sort of a smile; "I really can't tell; but I believe—" and here, the landlord, overcome by the magnitude of the consideration, looked towards his wife for aid.

The lady, to whom this sort of appeal appeared familiar, took up the reply, and remarked without circumlocution, but in a respectful manner, that the stranger was a traveller, and had arrived with the owner of the black horse a little after dark. The tall pale gentleman* had gone to bed almost immediately on his arrival, but this one seemed to be fond of his glass and his joke."

At this moment the stranger returned.—His countenance was graver than before, and he evidently bestowed on Stewart a thorough professional scrutiny as he approached him. A smile followed this examination, however, and it was apparent that his mind felt satisfied that any further inquiry was unnecessary. Some idle conversation followed, and Stewart, after the exchange of another drink, retired to bed.

When he rose in the morning, he proceeded down stairs with the intention of ascertaining something more about the owners of the black and chesnut horses, but his purpose was defeated by the information that the travellers had mounted and set out at earliest dawn.

Puzzling himself therefore no more about them, he partook of his breakfast and continued on his journey. In due time he reached Madison without a hostile encounter, and it was then that he obtained a confirmation of the rumor which he had heard during the previous two days, that Murrell had escaped. He had refused to believe this report at the first, but now that the fact was plain, he became instantly impressed that the owner of the black horse at the Springhill inn, was the fugitive murderer and land pirate of the west.

He communicated this opinion to his friends, and on the strength of it two trusty men secretly set out for Springhill, in the hope that the trail could be taken up at that point and followed to success.

---

* Murrell must have been bleached at this time by his imprisonment.

CHAPTER XXIV.

The Southern Trail—The Pursuers at Fault—The Robber's Destination—"Buzzard's Roost"—Tuscaloosa—Plans of Business—Alarm—Reward for the Land Pirate—Precipitate Movements—The Clue—The Chase—The Moonlight Night—The Spy—The Capture.

Stewart spent several days with his old acquaintances in Madison, but after a stay prolonged somewhat by a slight indisposition, he prepared to set out for Lexington, Kentucky. He had selected that place for the publication of his book concerning Murrell and his clan, and believing, now, that a long time would elapse before the marauder would be retaken, if indeed he were taken at all, he felt it incumbent upon him to be as expeditious as possible in laying before an unconscious population, those wide-spread and terrible designs, which yet threatened the country with conflagration, murder, and rapine. The postponement of these disclosures while the marauder was encaged, was a mere question of policy; but now that the arch enemy was abroad, and acting doubtless with that almost superhuman energy which vigorous minds are capable of displaying in making amends for lost time, the question changed into a command of imperative duty.

He had selected Lexington as the place of making his publication, as well from the fact of his having two sincere and attached friends in that town, as from the facilities which would be afforded to the business portion of the work. He could, moreover, consider himself personally safe there, and being thus relieved from one great source of anxiety, would not only be likely soon to regain his robust health, but to achieve also an equanimity of mind, which the troubled scenes of the previous three months had almost made him hopeless of again. He set out, therefore, full of his purpose, and immediately on his arrival, commenced his task.

The two persons who started out in pursuit of Murrell on the hint of Stewart, were, as we said before, shrewd and capable men. They made direct for Springhill, and there, by dint of well directed but apparently careless inquiries, got a full description of the travellers, even to the smallest article of their dress that had appeared in sight. Being confirmed by this that Stewart was correct, and learning from the ostler that the travellers had gone East, they followed on the trail. They traced them to several inns, and in the last were fortunate enough to get the clue from a housemaid, who by listening to the conversation of the robbers had overheard them speak of Florence, Alabama. This was encouraging to the pursuers, and paying less heed to the minutiæ of the chase, now that they had got a clue to its point of direction, they made directly forward with very slight delays. In this policy they erred. Their information was correct, but its continuous value was dependent upon the fluctuations of a human mind, and they might better have, closely perused the road to see whether that intention had not altered or diverged, than to have relied so implicitly on what was so extremely liable to change. The result of their spirited descent upon Florence was—nothing.— They slid through the town to no purpose, and smelt in every corner without avail. They scoured the neighborhood and made inquiries at every cabin on the roads, but the mysterious travellers were as impalpable to their inquiries as to their sight. It was plain that they had lost the trail, and that to take it up again they must fain ride back to the tavern where they had got misled. But even this proved idle. The elusive fugitives appeared to have descended into the earth some where about this spot, and to trace them any further on its surface appeared to be a hopeless task. Indeed, it was proved so on the following morning by the arrival of a public proclamation of the escape of the notorious John A. Murrell, and the offer of a large reward for his apprehension.—The pursuers therefore gave up their adventure, and returned home discomfited.

It now becomes of interest to know what really did become of Murrell and his fellow traveller. The last place they had been traced to by the men from Madison was Waterloo, a little town situated on a bend of the Tennessee river, just east of the Mississippi line. We must, therefore, take them up at this place, and follow them, for our own satisfaction, to their destination. The two marauders had left the inn at Waterloo,[1] at day-break, after their night's stay, with the intention of proceeding directly on to Florence. Murrell, however, by one of those sudden and apparently capricious changes of determination which men in praiseworthy causes are apt to call "providential," resolved to cross the river and strike another course from the one previously decided on.

He communicated the alteration of his determination to his companion, and pointing out a raft or flat boat that lay fastened to the bank of the river by a stake in front of a cabin door, stated that he should cross the river at that point, and desired that his companion would pursue his journey on to Florence by the direct road and await him there.

This change of arrangements did not suit the volunteer traveller, for he had promised himself the fortune of remaining the companion of the chief, but his remonstrances fell upon an unalterable purpose, and he was fain to yield to a resolution that appeared as fixed as it was fresh.

"You can say to any who expect me," said Murrell, "that in less than a month I will be in Florence to see them all, and to thank them for their preparations to assist me; and be sure tell them that nothing but a sudden necessity now draws me off."

Saying this the marauder bade his companion goodbye, and turned down to the cabin at the river side. Here he soon made a bargain for himself and horse to be ferried across; and in an hour afterwards had landed on the southern bank of the river.

---

1. Waterloo was in Lauderdale County, Alabama. The location of the original town is now at the bottom of Pickwick Lake.

The marauder directed his course to a place called "Buzzard's Roost," a little to the south of which, in a sheltered and retired cove of a small tributary of the Tennessee, he lifted a friendly latch and claimed the hospitality of an old campaigner, on whose experience and prudence he could place a reliance as perfect as he could upon his own.

Here he took a day's good rest, and having recruited himself fully, and obtaining a thorough new disguise, he left his coal black stallion in temporary exchange for a staunch and wiry chesnut colt. Thus remounted and caparisoned, he struck south another stage. He passed in succession through Marion, Fayette, and Tuscaloosa counties, until he came to the capital of the last. Here he found, in accidental congregation, a nest of his congenial friends, and feeling, from the distance which he had placed between himself and those who would pursue him, a tolerable confidence in his safety, he yielded to the temptations which were held out to him on all sides, to enter into the enjoyments of peace. The pains of caution and the restraints of prudence were all swept away in the impulsive fever of violent enjoyment which again revisited him, and in the three days following his arrival, he made full amends for the austerity of his confinement in Jackson jail. But at the end of that time the whirlwind was at an end, and the most patient student or most eager follower of silence could not have exceeded him in close elaborate devotion to his professional combinations.

The course of Stewart in reference to the insurrection, and also of the numerous murders of which Murrell stood confessed the bloody and brutal perpetrator, puzzled the robber not a little. He wondered why an enemy, so dire and uncompromising had withheld charges of such superior heinousness, to the selection of the comparatively trivial complaint of negro stealing. It was true that of the others he had no direct proof; but why had he not even breathed them in private gossip, if for nothing else than private satisfaction, or to challenge the horror of some listening friend? It was evident that he had not done so, but had preserved the momentous burden sacred within the limits of his own private breast, as though he hugged the danger from bursting on a friend! There was something so strange in this that almost impressed his mind with awe, but the marauder at length construed the apparent contradiction into a secret design on the part of Stewart, to withhold every portion of the detail until he had secured evidence to sustain the whole development at once. This was a startling thought, and as soon as Murrell became duly impressed with it, he dispatched directions to every quarter to counteract any efforts that might be made to get testimony as to his criminal acts, and even purposed to go in person down to Mobile, where he had murdered the unfortunate gambler, and where himself, and Crenshaw had robbed the brig, to take precautions in that quarter.

This latter portion of his decision, however, he was not able to put in operation, for on the day previous to the one he had selected for his departure, the city teemed with the reports of the escape of the great land pirate of the West, and handbills were distributed describing his person, and offering a heavy reward for his apprehension. In addition to the alarm naturally occasioned by this proclamation, he imagined he had already attracted the suspicious observance of more than one person in the place. He therefore promptly decided to leave without even waiting for the night, and selecting an opportunity, withdrew to the outskirts of the town, and sought a place to assume a new disguise which he had procured the day before. Having effected a transformation to his satisfaction, he took his seat in a stage to New Lexington, with the intention of proceeding boldly back upon his trail to Florence. His calculations for this course were, that where the cry first starts it first subsides, and that it would be the height of absurdity to take the excitement in its head and run before it, at the best with but a few hours in advance, all the way down the river.

Acting upon these bold and judicious calculations, the robber pursued his way rapidly and directly along the regular stage route, taking the capital town of Fayetteville in his way, and finally bringing up at Florence, on a fine evening in the month of May, without mischance of any kind. But his sudden disappearance from Tuscaloosa immediately on the publication of the handbill, had excited a suspicion in several minds which, when strengthened with the description of the handbill, induced inquiries as to the manner in which he left. To ascertain this much pains were taken, and at length the effort was rewarded by the information from the driver of one of the stages which ran to New Lexington, that a gentleman had taken passage about four miles out of town on the northern road, on the date in question: and that he was pretty much of the description given in the handbill, though he was dressed very differently from the person there described. This information led to a trail, and the trail brought the pursuers straight to Florence in five days after Murrell had arrived there.

On arriving in town the party from Tuscaloosa waited upon the Sheriff, and making him acquainted with their suspicions, obtained his assistance to hunt up the fugitive. Some days elapsed, however, before they well successful in establishing the hope even of the marauder's presence in the city, and discouraged by the doubts of the sheriff's officers, they were even then several times on the point of giving up their enterprise in despair. One of the Tuscaloosa officers, while matters were at this stage, was concerned with uneasy meditations on the discomfiture which appeared in store for them and that after having retired to his bed for several hours without the power to sleep, he left his uneasy couch, and betaking himself to the window, sought to calm himself by taking a view of the rich moonlight which flooded the roofs and streets.

It was past midnight, and every thing was still as death. Presently he heard a firm and heavy footfall advancing up the street, and by that species of clairvoyance which so often makes "the wish the father to the thought," he imagined he could distinguish in the swagger of the man, as he approached, the identical gait and movement of his mysterious friend of Tuscaloosa. A few seconds more proved he was not mistaken, and drawing on his trowsers, slipping on his coat, and diving into his hat with the dexterity of a comedian who has long practised sudden transformations, he ran out in his stocking feet in time to catch the clear footfall before it had entirely died away. By slinking in the shade, and holding a respectful distance to the object he pursued, he was successful in tracking the night-walker to his home, when returning to his lodging, he woke up his friend, and set out with him to the house of the sheriff. A party of officers were soon collected, and marching under the direction of the spy, the posse soon pounced upon a secret den of the marauders, and secured possession of the grand object of the expedition.

The fugitive robber was again in custody, and spent the remainder of the bright May moonlight night in the sheriff's prison.

The game had turned finally against him, and the robber chief appeared to be conscious that the fortune of his hand was out. He therefore calmly submitted to his fate, and bore it with a philosophical equanimity that almost amounted to cheerfulness.*

Information of the recapture of the marauder was sent to Tennessee immediately on his arrest, and promulgated throughout the country. In due time officers from Madison arrived at Florence, with a requisition from the Governor of Tennessee upon the Governor of Alabama for the body of the prisoner; Murrell was therefore duly embarked upon a steamboat at Florence, and conveyed by the river as far as Carrollville,[2] opposite to which place he was debarked, under a strong escort and conveyance, rapidly to Jackson.

---

2. Carrollville, Tennessee, located in Wayne County. According to The Tennessee Gazetteer, it was a villiage situated "directly on the road between Waynesboro and Lexington, on the east bank of the Tennessee [River]." The *Gazetteer* spells it Carrollsville. *Tennessee Gazetteer*, 126.

* It was at this time that the plan of Murrell for the decimation and destruction of Stewart, as drawn out by his own hand, and published in a previous chapter, was discovered. It was found on his person by the sheriff of Florence, while searching him, and was afterwards forwarded to Madison, to be used in evidence on the trial.

On his arrival there, he was placed in the custody of Mr. Deberry, the sheriff, who, in consequence of the dilapidated state of the jail, was forced to hold him prisoner in his own office, and keep him under constant guard. The marauder was however securely chained, and the deputies who guarded him were armed.

On the day after the arrival of the prisoner at Madison, Mr. Henning despatched his son to Lexington, Ky., to acquaint Mr. Stewart with the fact of his arrest, and to request him to return at once to Madison, as the trial would be hurried on for the purpose of bringing matters to a final close as soon as possible.

Things now appeared to be approaching to a climax.

CHAPTER XXV.

The trial—Arraignment of Murrell—Testimony of Stewart—Sensation of the Audience—Second Day—Unexpected Heading off of the Defence—Summing Up—The Verdict.

For fourteen days Murrell remained in the personal custody of Mr. Deberry, the Sheriff, at his office, but at the end of that time he was removed to the county jail; which in the meanwhile had been put in a state of complete repair.

"During the time that the prisoner was in my custody," says Mr. Deberry, in a letter under date of September, 1835, "he excited great curiosity, and many persons visited him, as well strangers, as the citizens of our county. On these occasions, the subject of his route with Stewart was one of the most common topics of conversation, and though he was frequently morose and taciturn, he would now and then talk freely on the subject. When thus disposed, he would admit, in accordance with his statement on arrest, that Stewart was a perfect stranger to him until he met him at the bridge at Estanaula, and that he then only knew him by the name of Hues. This refuted the idea that Stewart could have been an associate marauder, who had betrayed his confederate or chief through motives of envy or revenge, as has been charged against him."

After Murrell had been transferred to the jail, he appeared to have lost a great portion of that elasticity of mind which had previously sustained him: a circumstance that may have been attributable in part to an extra strictness of confinement, and also to a denial of all communication even with his wife, except through his counsel.

At the opening of the July term of the Circuit Court of Madison County, the Grand Jury, under the direction of Alexander S. Bradford, Esq.,[1] Prosecuting Attorney of the District, and on the evidence of Virgil A. Stewart, brought in a bill of Indictment against John A. Murrell, for the crime of "negro stealing" and in a few days afterward the case was called on for trial.

The Court house on the day of trial was crowded to overflowing with deeply anxious spectators. All thronged to hear the mysterious crimes that were to be unravelled, and all were eager to see that daring marauder, and no

1. Alexander Bradford (1799–1873) was one of the earliest lawyers in Jackson, Tennessee, and the first district attorney of Madison County. His father-in-law, Pleasant M. Miller, was himself a respected attorney, former U.S. Congressman, and first chancellor of the Chancery Court of West Tennessee.

less daring witness, who had occupied so large an attention in the public mind. Among the audience could be detected here and there several strange-looking faces, which appeared to be marked with a concern that was not entirely made up of curiosity. When Murrell was brought into Court, all eyes were fixed upon him. He was dressed with scrupulous neatness, his step was firm and confident, and he wore upon his face a complacent smile, which a stranger to his character might have easily mistaken for a mark of conscious innocence.

Having made his way across the Court Room in the midst of the officers, the prisoner sat down in front of the bench beside his counsel. Of these, he had four; but the most distinguished, and the one on whose eloquence the marauder most relied, was Milton Brown, Esq.,[2] the representative in Congress from Tennessee, who rendered his name so famous in 1844 by the presentation of the memorable resolution which annexed Texas to the United States. This gentleman was to be the advocate of the case, and to him was consigned the responsible duty of making the concluding argument in behalf of the prisoner.

Stewart sat close by the prosecuting officers. His appearance was a marked contrast with that of Murrell. His countenance was pale and anxious, and it seemed as if, to him, the approaching ordeal threatened consequences much more serious than it did to the accused. The contrast marked the difference between Innocence and Guilt. To the robber, the danger was but the common

---

2. Milton Brown (1804–1883) became judge of the Chancery Court for West Tennessee a year after the Murrell trial, served as a Whig in the U.S. House of Representatives from 1841 to 1847, and later became president of the Mississippi & Tennessee Central and Mobile & Ohio railroads.

alternative which every rogue embraces when he sells himself to crime. He could therefore resign himself to chance and its results, with a professional philosophy. To Stewart, the crisis was charged with a thousand unknown consequences. His good name was at stake. He was surrounded by desperate and subtle enemies, and he was responsible for the completion of a task, the results of which were to affect his whole future life. Good reason had he then to seem concerned.

The hour having arrived for the commencement of proceedings, Murrell was arraigned, and the Clerk proceeded, in the usual form, to propound the question of "guilty," or "not guilty."

"Not guilty," said the prisoner, looking firmly at the clerk, and then composedly sitting down.

The prosecuting Attorney, after opening the case to the jury at considerable length, called Parson Henning to testify as to the loss of his negroes, on the night of the 16th of January, which evidence being given in, he next called Mr. Stewart to the stand.

Mr. Stewart commenced his evidence by a relation of his adventure from the time of his meeting with the accused at the bridge of Estanaula, Ala.;[3] regularly and methodically developing all the circumstances and occurrences which grew out of that meeting and giving the conversations along the road and frequently the very language of the prisoner, as we have detailed it in the previous chapters of this history. Proceeding step by step through all the incidents of the excursion, he included all those feats of villany, so vividly narrated by the prisoner as the exploits of the elder brother, and then described

3. Estanaula was located in Tennessee, not Alabama.

to the jury, in exact terms, the manner in which the prisoner had finally made himself known to him, as being that elder brother himself.

The relation of this testimony excited the strongest sensation in the Court-room, and at times the horror was so audible, that the knuckles of the clerk were obliged to be put in requisition, to restore order. The occasional interruptions of the counsel, and the pauses required by them to take the testimony accurately down, occasioned considerable delay, and though Stewart had ascended the stand at the commencement of the afternoon, he continued until dark without half finishing his story. The Court then adjourned till the following morning, to abide which time the robber was conveyed back to his cell by the officers, while Stewart retired home in the midst of a circle of friends. The audience dispersed—each fortunate member to retail to wondering ears, the dark developments which he had heard that day.

On the following morning Stewart resumed his place upon the witness-stand, and continued his evidence. He took up his narrative where he left it off the day before, conducted the jury into the haunts of the Arkansas, and related the particulars of the return. It was during this latter portion of the testimony that he undesignedly sprung a mine upon the defence which disconcerted all their plans, and so unhinged their arrangements that their case became hopeless from that moment.

It will be recollected, that while in company with Murrell, Stewart had carefully made memorandums of every piece of information of note, and had been particularly careful to jot down the names and localities of those whom the marauder had signalized as his associates.

By carefully transferring these to a list, as opportunity offered, he had obtained the names and residences of the most influential of the clan. Now, it so happened that Murrell, unconscious of this fact, had, in arranging his scheme of defence, selected several of these very men to bear important testimony in his favor, and, also to contradict the most essential points advanced by Stewart. An exposure of their characters in advance therefore, as a mere portion of the narrative, and made evidently without any consciousness of their intended introduction in the case, told with tremendous effect upon the prisoner and his counsel, and as Stewart read their names in connection with the story, the latter looked at their client as if reproaching him with having misled them by disingenuousness in relation to the real position of his witnesses. Murrell, however, had no answer to make, for he was more astounded than his counsel.

The circumstance made no marked impression upon anyone else, and even Stewart (who was ignorant of the plan which he had broken) did not attribute the simultaneous withdrawal of several persons from the audience, as the effect of the disclosure.

The direct testimony of Stewart, embracing most of the disclosures related in the preceding narrative, occupied nearly the whole day, and it was not till late in the afternoon that the prosecuting attorney delivered him over into the hands of the opposing counsel for examination.

Relying entirely upon the integrity of his story, and being perfectly self-possessed, the skilful efforts of the counsel to confuse the young man, and to entangle him in contradictions, were of no avail, and his statement stood unharmed in any part. He finally descended from the stand, after having given perfect satisfaction to all in the Court-room, except the prisoner and his friends.

On the following morning an attempt was made to impeach the evidence of Mr. Stewart. but owing to the non-appearance of nearly all the witnesses whom counsel called for that purpose, it resulted in a signal failure; the character of Stewart being triumphantly sustained by the first people of the county. The last chance left, was the destruction of his evidence by proving him interested in the conviction of the prisoner. But in this, as in other points, the defence had lost its staunchest reliance, in the strange disappearance of the witnesses of the accused. A man named Reuben McVey was obtained, however, who was induced to come into Court and swear that Stewart had confided to him the fact that Parson Henning had hired him to detect Murrell, and was to pay him handsomely if that person was convicted; but the fellow's statement was so full of contradictions and absurdities, that it fell upon the jury with no force, and, as several of them stated afterward, it was discredited altogether.

The testimony having been all put in, Mr. Brown rose, and, turning to the jury, commenced summing up for the defence. He had a hard task; but he was pre-eminently capable of hard tasks, as he has very conclusively shown by the Texas resolution. He commenced his address by stating, that the whole evidence against the accused consisted in the testimony of a single witness, and that witness, a person of more than doubtful reputation, and, as had been shown, of interested motives. He then proceeded to take up Stewart's testimony point by point, and insisted, that from the whole character of the brief relationship which stood admitted as existing between him, and the prisoner, there doubtless had been a previous intimate connection between them, and that, therefore, be Murrell as bad as he might, Stewart must of necessity be worse for adding to his original crimes the despicable guilt of treachery. But even if, this were not the case, continued the lawyer, he still had acted towards Murrell with a falseness and deception, inconsistent with the character of an honest man. He had, of his own motion, represented himself as a horse hunter, and as a graceless villain; and it was but reasonable to believe, that a man who could so cheerfully concoct a falsehood, and so naturally practice a deception, would, in the next step, not hesitate to swear to the integrity of both. That the great cause of Justice rejected and disdained the aid of subterfuge and treachery, and that the man who could contemplate making falsehood a recognised agent of truth, deserved the execration, rather than the respect and consideration, of his fellow men.

The learned counsel having continued in this strain for about two hours, sat down and resigned the case into the hands of the District Attorney and the Judge.

The charge of the Court was brief. The complaint was stated, the testimony briefly rehearsed, and the jury were told that if they concluded to credit Mr. Stewart's testimony, they must find against the prisoner. Retiring under this charge, the jury soon came to a conclusion, and on signifying to the Court that they had agreed, declared their verdict to be *against* the prisoner, whom they found *Guilty of Negro Stealing*.

The Court then called upon the prisoner to receive his sentence; and after a few appropriate remarks upon his heinous course of life, gave him the extreme penalty of the law, by consigning him to the State Penitentiary *at hard labor for the period of ten years.*

"Thus," says a report of the case published at the time, "ended the trial and conviction of the great 'Western Land Pirate,' a human demon who had reduced murder and robbery to a system, and who had steeled his heart against the whole human family."

When the verdict was rendered, the audience evinced their satisfaction at the result by an applause which could not be repressed, and an indignant crowd thronged around the convicted felon as he was conveyed to his prison, and assailed him with insults and reproaches.

Stewart, on the other hand, received the warm congratulations of the principal persons in attendance at the court, and returned to his temporary dwelling-place, surrounded with a mob of friends.

The struggle had ended in his favor; but though the winner of a moral triumph, he had, as we shall see, by no means gained a victory over personal danger.

CHAPTER XXVI.

State of Public Feeling after the Trial—The Treacherous Letter—Success of the Snare—The Eastern Trip—Suspicious Acquaintance—The Gloomy Path—The Ambuscade—The death struggle—The Result—The Bivouac.

The excitement which succeeded the conviction of Murrell, was wider and wilder than during the progress of the trial. Those who before had been too stolid for the romance of conjecture, were now profoundly moved by the actual developments of the testimony; and those who had relied upon a tolerable share of horrors, were even distanced by the facts, and challenged for an increased surprise. Nothing was talked of for days but the bloody deeds of the marauder, while the romantic courage and singular devotion of Stewart furnished an equally absorbing contrast. The fever ran high against the convict, and had there been some leading spirit to give the general indignation an aim, the robber would have been torn piecemeal by the mob ere he had been removed from the town to the State Prison at Nashville. The verdict and the sentence, therefore, though the first was just and the last was to the extent of the law, gave general dissatisfaction, and the regret was universal that the criminal had not been tried upon his more sanguinary crimes, and mulcted of his life. But the rage was idle, and the law bore off its victim without further harm. Having accomplished the conviction of his enemy, Stewart had but one more duty to perform, and that was to give an extended publicity to the proceedings of the trial throughout the western region and the whole country. This was necessary, for the reason that no report, had been published, and the probability was that none would be unless through his agency. He had, besides his most important revelation to make in the details of the intended insurrection, which yet had not been publicly referred to.

Accordingly he commenced arranging his papers for his final task, and was engrossed for several weeks in the laborious work of writing out the notes he had taken from time to time into a consistent history.

While thus engaged the alarm and infuriated emissaries of the gang were actively employed devising means to deter him from his undertaking. They knew that he possessed full minutes of the embryo rising, and that he would be able also to call to mind, in a deliberate narration, many names, which he might have overlooked in the confusion of the trial. Every leading man was therefore in a state of the utmost sensitiveness and the whole band watched him, with an unmixed anxiety, for the stroke that was to frustrate the elaborate design of years. Private agents of the clan were sent to him in the guise of friends, to represent the dangerous position he would inevitably place himself in by publishing the meditated disclosures to the world; while others, still more insidious, hinted the possibility that the clan might be willing to advance a large sum of money to ensure him to secrecy. Stewart, however, as might have been expected, scouted at all these semi-threats and propositions with contempt, and remained steadfast in his determinations.

Finding him entirely intractable to either fear or gain, the conspirators were obliged at last to fall back upon the old policy of force; and having ascertained that the volume could not well be prepared in less than three or four months, they devised a means of getting rid of him before that time. They knew that he intended leaving the country shortly after the publication of his book, and they also knew that he was extremely desirous of selling all the property he owned in Mississippi. Adapting these facts to their purposes, they had a letter written, and mailed in Perry county, Tennessee, purporting to come from a gentleman who wished to purchase a tract of property which Stewart owned in Mississippi. The writer stated he had learned that the land could be bought on reasonable terms, and as he was desirous of emigrating to that part of the country, he would be glad to hear from Mr. Stewart on the subject, or to receive a call from him if he could make it convenient to come in that direction.

Deceived by the plausible character of this epistle, Stewart readily fell into the snare, and being about to depart for Lexington, Ky., with his papers, now all prepared for the press, he resolved to take an eastern direction, and go through Perry county.

Accordingly he packed up his papers, and stowing them snugly among his clothing, on the 28th of September, somewhat more than two months after the trial, took his departure from Madison county forever. Towards evening he reached the house of Mr. Deberry and accepted his hospitality for the night, but early on the morning of the 29th, he again resumed his journey. On the evening of the 29th, just as the dusk was inviting in the stars, he espied a neat-looking and retired little inn, at which he calculated he would not only find comfortable quarters, but be able co escape scrutinizing observation. The inside of the tavern kept the promise to his hope, but he had not been long enjoying its quiet comforts before his anticipations of repose were suddenly disturbed by the arrival of four ill-looking and coarse behaved men, whose demeanor was of that swaggering style, which is so commonly assumed by ignorant and ill-bred persons, in the idea that it shows their independence. What struck Stewart as somewhat peculiar, was the fact that for some moments, and during their conversation with the landlord, they affected not to scrutinize him at all, and, indeed, seemed scarcely aware of his presence. Things did not remain in this condition long, however, for after they had satisfied themselves as to their accommodations for the night, and ordered a glass all round, the man who was doing the honors, took his glass in his hand, and wheeling his back against the counter, fixed his eyes upon our friend, and with a rough courtesy invited him to drink along. The invitation was one that could not well be refused without offence between travellers, and Stewart, with an assumed cheerfulness, complied.

What the men had overlooked in scrutiny before, was made up now, and Stewart almost felt assured by an intuitive admonition, that the eight eyes which were travelling so sharply over every portion of his person, were studying him as the betrayer of Murrell.—He carefully prevented his uneasiness from becoming manifest, however, and when the leader of the party commenced to press him with interrogatories, he evaded them by vague replies, and by occupying their time with amusing stories. They managed nevertheless to probe him with several direct questions as to what part of the country he intended journeying; whether he purposed crossing the Tennessee river; if so, by what ferry, and what direction he would then take. But their interrogatories were answered by the replies that he had business in the immediate neighborhood that would occupy him several days, and that he could not say what he should thereafter do.

The careful management which thus successfully baffled all the efforts of inquirers, was, however, destined to be overthrown by one of those chance oversights, which the shrewdest and most cautious men will oftentimes be subject to, for after a long pause in the conversation, in which Stewart had fallen into a profound reverie, he suddenly turned his head, and forgetful of all that had passed, inquired of the host the nearest road to Patton's ferry. He was conscious of the slip as soon as it was committed, but he did not apprehend, notwithstanding his doubt of the character of his pot companions, that he was destined to pay so dearly for it as the sequel proved.

At daybreak the next morning, the four strangers paid their bill, and left the house together, as they came; but Stewart remained to breakfast, and did not depart till ten o'clock, for the purpose of giving his friends of the previous evening, as wide a separation as possible. He then set out, and improving his time, arrived in the afternoon at the house of a friend, named Gilbert, whose hospitalities he enjoyed until the 2d of October, when he again proceeded on his journey.

Mr. Stewart had determined to cross the Tennessee river at Patton's ferry, and pursue his journey eastward to Columbia, in Maury county, and from thence to take a line to Lexington, Ky., by the way of Nashville. He had chosen this indirect and rather circuitous route, to avoid observation as much as possible, and to elude the pursuit of any who might perchance have suspected his original destination.

The wild and desolate region of country extending along the road for several miles westward of Patton's Ferry, was calculated to engender the most gloomy thoughts in the mind of any solitary traveller. To Stewart, therefore, whose mind was almost morbid with dark forebodings, it may be supposed to have been depressing in the extreme. He grew heavier and heavier in spirit as he proceeded, and at length, as if obeying a direction which a perceptible danger had rendered imperative, he drew his single pistol from his saddle-bags, and after carefully examining it, placed it in his side pocket. He had until now placed more reliance on the hope of eluding danger, than in successfully resisting it, but having taken all the precautions within his power against the last resort, he continued his journey through the cheerless solitude, without meeting with an object to disturb the monotonous gloom which weighed like an incubus upon him. In this state of mind he journeyed along until it had reached the hour of four in the afternoon, by which time he had arrived within some eight or ten miles of the ferry.

It was at this portion of the road that he was surprised by the sudden appearance of three men who had been concealed among the trees which bordered that portion of the road-side.

He was for a moment startled and confused by the suddenness of the apparition, but in a moment more be recovered his self-possession, and was by far a better man than he had been in any previous portion of the day. The visions vanished from his mind, a tangible danger had taken their place, and his manhood, no longer stupified and perplexed by shadows, seemed to rejoice in the exchange of misty dread for actual danger.—His qualities were roused within him. His eye sparkled with rage, and a formidable frame dilated as he recognised in the assassins, three of the men whom he had met at the inn on the evening of the 29th.

The miscreants had disposed themselves in a firm triangle. One stood on either side, at a distance of some two rods from the spot where he had brought his horse to a halt, and the third had taken his position in the centre of the road a few yards further off. The two first were armed with rifles, and the latter held in his hand a very heavy pistol.

The assassin who was stationed on the right, and who appeared to be the leader, ordered Stewart to dismount.

The young man made no answer, and did not alter his position or give token of resistance, whereupon the robber kept slowly advancing towards him, continuing in an angry tone to order him down from his saddle. When he had got within six paces of Stewart, he appeared to falter slightly at the firmness of the young man's gaze, and making a pause, demanded to know whether he intended to come down or not?

Stewart still kept his lips firmly set, when perceiving him intractable, the wretch made a movement to level his piece. Before, however, he could bring it to his eye, the young man dexterously drew his pistol and discharged it in his face. The ball entered his forehead, and the ruffian dropped lifeless to the earth. As he fell, his piece went off, but the charge passed harmlessly under the belly of the horse, and lodged in the ground a few yards distant. The miscreant on the left levelled his rifle, but owing to a sudden plunge of Stewart's horse at the first report, the bullet wounded nothing but the intrenchant air. There was now but one armed assailant left, and striking spurs to his horse, the young man intended to ride him down. Unfortunately the animal recoiled from the charge, and the villain was allowed a deliberate aim, but happily his pistol snapped, when, taking advantage of the mishap, Stewart pressed upon him, and raising aloft his own empty pistol, he hurled it in the man's face with such sharp and sudden force as to strike him to the earth with the blow. He had no chance, however, to follow up the advantage, for as he rose from the bending position he occasioned by the action, he received a tremendous blow across his neck and shoulders from the butt of the heavy rifle in the hands of the robber on the left, and as he turned to answer the assault, the villain whom he had stricken to the ground regained his feet, and seizing a heavy piece of rock dashed it in his breast with a force that made him reel backward in his saddle. The severity of these blows, and particularly the latter, occasioned a sickening sensation which threatened a swoon, and for a moment Stewart had but power enough to challenge once more the good will of his horse by striking his spurs into his sides.

This time, however, the frightened animal obeyed, and giving a willing bound cleared the circle of immediate danger, and then striking an honest gallop fled like the wind along the road. The third assassin burst into a savage curse at the escape, and picking up the pistol which had refused fire, levelled it again at the flying figure. The weapon proved truer than before, and, taking fire, sped a ball through the fleshy part of the arm of the rider, who, almost swooning with his hurts, sagged nerveless and helpless into the saddle. The horse flew on like mad, and it was not till after the lapse of several minutes, that his master, revived by the cool air streaming in his face, raised his head and grasped the flapping rein.

He turned to look behind, and saw the two men, though at a considerable distance, running after him, as if they expected to behold him fall from the saddle at every bound of the horse. Seeing this, he directed his course to a thick wood that offered itself at about a quarter of a mile ahead, on the left hand, and plunged into its shadow to avoid further observation. After he had entered it to the distance of a few hundred yards, a vale opened to his right, which he followed for about three miles. The immediate appearance of danger now no longer sustaining him, he began to grow quite sick, and found that he would not be able to continue his flight much further. He accordingly directed his course to a small bayou, along which he proceeded till he fell upon a spot that appeared entirely secluded and hidden by the thick surrounding foliage. Here he dismounted, and tying his horse amid the thick underbush, took out his portmanteau and spread his blanket for a cheerless bivouac.

The sun had not yet gone down, so he was obliged to keep unwilling watch until the evening had set in. But at length the charitable darkness came, and draining his spirit flask of the whole of its contents, the unfortunate young man resigned himself to such repose as the agony of his mind and body would permit.

CHAPTER XXVII.

The Night in the Woods—Change of Purpose—Resumption of Journey—Physical Surrender—The Amiable Hostess—The Warning—Blood Hounds on the Track—Renewed Flight—Disasters—Rescue and Final Accomplishment of the Grand Object.

The prominent part borne by Stewart in the latter and more stirring portions of this history, and the interest which has naturally been created in the mind for a character so distinguished by generous and heroic qualities, renders it proper for us to follow him to a satisfactory condition of affairs, before leaving him forever to resume our more especial task of tracing the career of the miscreant hero to its close.

We left the young man sorely wounded, stretched in a jungle with no roof above him but the stars, seeking the repose and shelter which were so necessary to his condition. The manner in which he passed the night is thrillingly described in the following extract from a letter, which he shortly afterward wrote to a friend in Georgia:—

"Never did I pass so terrible a night. While the light lasted my only care was the physical agony of my wounds, but when the heavy darkness fell around me, every fear, and every gloomy thought of my intensely agitated mind became aggravated into actual forms, which appeared to be hovering around me, and threatening my life. Whether I fell asleep, or whether I only became unconscious through delirium, I cannot say, but at different times through the night, I found myself crawling in terror through the brush and thicket to avoid some hideous demon, who seemed to be pursuing me. Starting awake, I would then lie down and soon lose all thought again. I am inclined to think that I must have passed several hours in this terrible state of nightmare or delirium, for when I finally awoke it was nearly noon, but, notwithstanding the length of my sleep, I felt none of the effects of a repose. I awoke in almost indescribable pain. My neck was much swollen, my wounded arm was very stiff and sore, and pains racked my frame from head to foot. Added to this, I found I had considerable fever, which operating with my other ailments, made my condition forlorn in the extreme. I laid for a long lime a prey to the gloomiest reflections, and my desire to rise was checked by mental depression and debility, and by a mistrust of my power to continue my journey.

"I at length did rise, but not without the greatest difficulty, and by an extraordinary effort I managed to saddle and mount my horse. I was then, as you may imagine, in no little doubt what next to do. I was no more than five miles from the scene of the previous day's affray, and I could not hope that such bloodhounds as then assailed me would relinquish the chase because they had received a check, or content themselves to let me off, after I had slain one of their confederates. At whatever point I might attempt to issue from the wood, I ran the risk of again fulling in their hands, and the attempt to obtain shelter at a house, might deliver me a helpless sacrifice into the hands of some of the resident confederates, who had already been put on the look out for the wounded traveller. Danger and death seemed to stare me in the face on every side; and in this gloomy state the conviction again smote my mind with double force, that even if I should now be fortunate enough to extricate myself, I would never dare remain in the South or West after the disclosure of the horrible transactions, and of the names of the actors, which yet remained a secret in my bosom. I came, therefore, to the conclusion, in that moment as I sat so sick upon my saddle, that it was my duty to leave America entirely for a few years, and for the purpose of being enabled to carry out this intention most speedily and safely, I determined to strike south to Mobile, and from thence to take ship to Europe. This resolution being formed, I shook the reins of my horse, and commended myself to the care of Providence for protection from the perils which surrounded me."

It was late in the afternoon before Mr. Stewart, as we are informed by him in a subsequent and more extended narrative, left the place which had served as a couch and a hiding-place throughout the night, Having eaten nothing, nor even cleansed himself for want of water, he felt an additional motive to proceed as hastily as possible. After an hour's travel he found a small pond where he refreshed his horse, and broke his own fast with a few fragments of food which he drew from a small store in the saddle-bags. His appetite, however, made but slight demands upon his larder, and he was soon at liberty to cleanse his garments and his face from the blood which covered them. He then changed his dress, and after removing every vestige of the previous day's affray, resumed his journey. He passed near a farm-house just at dark, but gave it a wide berth to avoid coming in contact with any of its inmates. During the night he met with several roads, but none of them running in the direction he wished, he crossed them arbitrarily, and continued on his solitary journey through woods and unfrequented paths till midnight.—Then, overcome with fatigue and faintness, he pulled up at the border of the creek, and dismounted with the intention of seeking what repose he could, as on the night before. His half-famished beast was turned loose (tied head and leg) to tear a repast from the niggard and reluctant surface of the earth, while he, the master, found his inhospitable couch upon it.

In the morning, though he had suffered less than on the previous night, he awoke with a heightened fever, and with his limbs cramped and aching from the dampness of the ground. It therefore became necessary for him to seek the comforts and relief of some house at once, without regard to the considerations which had previously made him avoid the dwelling of his fellow man, as he would have shunned the ambush of the panther. In accordance with this resolution he struck out in the open country, and soon fell upon a road, which after an hour's travel brought him to a house. He there briefly explained his condition, and asked for refreshment for his horse and accommodations for himself. His requests were granted after some hesitation, but as soon as he received an assent to his wishes, he hurried to bed without pausing to speculate upon the reluctant manner in which it had been granted by the host. He was kindly treated in his new lodgings, nevertheless. The wife of the cabin was a woman whom nature had blessed with a kind heart and a large share of the domestic virtues, and the distressed condition of the pale and trembling stranger claimed at once all her sympathy, and secured the most notable attentions.—She had a dish of gruel made for him at once, and having ascertained the state of his fever, produced from her medicinal stores an anodyne to tranquillize his nerves, that he might enjoy a quiet and refreshing sleep.

This treatment was attended with a genial effect, but with the assuaging of his pains came a feebleness which threatened to keep the invalid a prisoner to his bed for several days. The thought of this delay caused a momentary irritation which almost threatened to recall the fever, and his uneasiness was not a little aggravated by the perseverance of his good-natured nurse, in seeking to learn the name and history of her patient. There was but one way to get along with her without seeming to maintain an ungrateful taciturnity, and that was by telling her a fictitious history instead of a true one, and gaining confidence by a false ingenuousness, instead of distrust by a cold and reserved demeanor. Stewart, therefore, called himself Cowan, and represented himself as a planter from Brandon, Mississippi, accounting for his bruises by stating that he had been thrown from his horse on the night before. This was perfectly satisfactory to the hostess, who, having traced the causes of the fever to suit her mind, set about completing the cure of her patient without further inquiry.

Under these circumstances it might be expected that Stewart would resign himself to tolerable ease of mind, and patiently await the return of sufficient strength to enable him to resume his journey, but there was a strange sort of dread that kept thumping at his bosom and protesting against the stay. He tried to define this feeling and to account for it upon rational grounds, but failing to recognize anything that had transpired during his visit as suspicious in the least degree, or deserving of the slightest uneasiness, he discarded the warning as a bugbear of his depression.

On the afternoon of the second day, however, a circumstance took place which gave a different aspect to affairs. He had fallen into a sleep shortly after his hostess had left his chamber. During his slumber he dreamt that the door slowly opened, and that he saw a person peep in the room cautiously, and after taking a thorough survey of the apartment, softly step inside. In a moment this person seemed to be followed by another, and the two, drawing up beside each other, paused, to listen for the third time, whether the sleeper was sound. It was at this period of his dream that Stewart aroused to a half consciousness, which convinced him that his vision was but the dull impression of an actual state of things, at that time in existence in his chamber. His change of condition from sleep to consciousness was so gradual that it made no perceptible effect upon his countenance, and by a strange self control he was enabled to maintain a simulated sleep, as natural in its appearance as that which had stood god-father to his dream. Though he dared not open his eyes he felt convinced that there were two persons in his room, and he also felt satisfied, that, from their stealthy manner, they were there for no honest purpose. Presently the visitors advanced until they reached the bedside, but there they paused, and a long minute elapsed in perfect silence. During this interval the agony of Stewart's mind was intense. He momentarily expected to feel the plunge of a poniard in his bosom, but he dared not express the slightest agitation, and the necessities of the case would not permit him to take a single precaution against the danger. The crisis passed, however, and the unseen pair turned and slowly moved towards the door. It was then that the sick man ventured a momentary glance, but it was a glance that only furnished him with half an answer, for though he recognized in one of the parties the form of his landlord; the other figure seemed a total stranger. The cold drops of perspiration burst from the invalid's skin as they vanished from the chamber, and he leaned forward to listen if he could hear the conclusions of their visit. His sharpened organs were not without their satisfaction, for through the crack of the door, which had not been entirely closed, he caught the following whispered sentences:—

"Well," said a voice, which the listener took for the landlord's, "is it him?"

"Yes."

"I suppose you are not likely to be mistaken?" continued the first voice.

"No, he was down to the Arkansas among us for two days. I was first introduced to him there, and noticed a small scar he has got on his left temple. I can't be mistaken."

"Is he worth anything?"

"He's not a rich planter exactly, but he's got some stuff—perhaps a couple o' thousand."

"What—with him?"

"It may be, for he's on the move; but I suspect he's got some papers of still more value than that, in the portmanteau which he keeps under his head."

Here the speakers moved, and after a word or two more, which was rendered indistinct by the increased distance they went down stairs.

It was now plain to Stewart that he had been traced out by Murrell's bloodhounds, and that his death was certain unless he could effect an escape. How to accomplish this he scarcely knew. It was doubtful if he could find means to obtain egress from the house, and if he did, it was then more doubtful, if he could sit on his horse to ride away. His wounds were better and his fever was allayed, it was true, but his debility had been humored by his invalid indulgences into an artificial feebleness which rejected every invitation to effort. The crisis was desperate, however, and after some deliberation he decided to summon strength, and make the attempt to fly.

Three hours elapsed before his hostess entered the room again to inquire after his condition. Stewart drew her into conversation, and asked incidentally who the visitor was whom they had received during the day. The good lady informed him with a smile, which seemed to infer he had been misled by his weakened mind, that be was mistaken, that they had received no visiter at all; that she herself had been out visiting all the afternoon, at the request of her husband, who sent her with a message to a neighbour who lived about two miles off.

This reply convinced Stewart of the integrity of his nurse, and also convinced him that a person who had thus to be sent out of the way of evil deeds, would be a friend to him who was marked out as a victim by the evil doers. He resolved to make a demand upon her assistance, and to explain as far as he could, without impugning the motives or conduct of her husband, the nature of his peril. He accordingly informed her of what had occurred during her absence, and told her that he had recognized in the person of the stranger whom her husband had introduced to his chamber, a bitter personal enemy, who had long sought his life, for having crossed his prospects with a young lady of Columbus,[1] to whom he (Stewart) was betrothed. He believed, he said, that her husband had introduced this person under proper motives to the chamber, but that he was convinced the whole object of the stranger was to ascertain his identity, that he might hover in the neighbourhood until his departure, either to assassinate him in some lonely place along the road, or to challenge him to mortal combat.

The heart of the kind landlady entered deeply into this story, and she was at once eagerly desirous of making her husband acquainted with all the touching particulars of the romance, and of securing his protection to the journey of their guest whenever he should wish to set out. But this would not do for Stewart, and he was obliged to labor earnestly to convince her of the impropriety of making a confidant of a man whose notions might have been prejudiced by a previous story, and who might, perhaps, also, stand bound by a solemn promise to acquaint the stranger with all his movements. This argument had

1. Columbus, Mississippi

the desired effect, and after a world of protests and of warnings against his leaving a sick bed to go a travelling in the night air, the hostess agreed to let him out of the house after she and her husband had retired to bed, and also to see that his horse was all ready to his hand.

At eight o'clock in the evening Stewart rose, and dressing himself and muffling himself up warmly, lowered his saddle bags and portmanteau out of the window with a string, so that they might not make a noise by falling on the ground. He then descended softly to the back door, which, as the kind creature who had nursed him had promised, he found ajar. He proceeded to the stable and found his horse giving evidence of being full, by standing with idle jaws before a well filled rack. The saddle and bridle were at hand, and soon the traveller was prepared to start. Sprinkling the stable floor thick with hay, even beyond the door sill, that the hoofs of his beast might make no noise, he led the animal slowly to the bars, and from thence several hundred feet beyond the house. Then mounting, he turned and gave a blessing to his benefactress, and rode off, encouraged to his journey by the genial atmosphere, and enlivened by the mellow moonlight which flooded the whole drowsy landscape with a sheen of gold. Sustained by a false exhilaration, the young man made good progress throughout the night, but towards the morning, the gathering damps had saturated his lungs, and provoked a relapse of the worst features of his illness. At length his ailments triumphed, and just at the break of the morning, he reeled from the saddle under the influence of a swoon, and tumbled into the road in a state of perfect insensibility. In this deplorable situation he remained some time, and doubtless would have perished there, had not a waggoner passed by, and humanely transferred him to his van. By the humane exertions of this man, Stewart was soon restored to consciousness, when finding that the vehicle was bound for the Chickasaw settlement, Mississippi, he bargained for a passage, and directed his horse to be tied behind. In this way he secured a safe deliverance from Tennessee, and an arrival on the second day at a fine and comfortable inn at Ripley.[2] While recruiting himself at this place he met with an old school-fellow, named Walton,[3] who was on his route to Memphis, Tennessee, and who, after some persuasion, induced him to relinquish his notion of leaving America, and to remain firm to his original intention of going to Kentucky, to publish his exposure of the marauders. Stewart agreed to follow his advice, on condition that his friend would take his papers into his custody, and have them published in case he should not survive to direct their publication himself. This being agreed to, the two friends separated, to meet again at Natchez at a given time. By degrees Mr. Stewart pursued his journey south, until he arrived at the house of Mr. James Moore, to whom he bore a letter from Walton. At the house of Mr. Moore, the invalid remained for several days, during which the hospitable care and kind attentions he received promoted a rapid progress of returning health. He was soon enabled to keep his appointment at Natchez, where, on meeting his friend, he

2. Ripley, Mississippi

3. Augustus Q. Walton, Esq. It was to him to Stewart supposedly entrusted his account of Murrell that was published in 1835 as *History of the Detection, Conviction, Life and Designs of John A. Murrel, the Great Western Land Pirate*. It is believed that Walton was either Stewart's ghostwriter or (more likely) a fictional persona adopted by him.

held out inducements for the latter to accompany him to the North.

In the early part of November, Mr. Stewart took passage at Natchez for Louisville, in company with his friend Walton, but on arriving at Cincinnati, his health had suffered so serious a relapse that he was obliged to debark and lay by until the ensuing spring. In the meantime, however, his friend prepared his book for the press, and published it in the latter part of February following (1835).[4]

By the 1st of May Stewart had recovered his health sufficient to travel, and after devoting himself to several jaunts up and down the Mississippi, mainly to see that the pamphlet had a thorough dissemination, he settled up his affairs, and transferred himself and fortunes to the Atlantic border.

Since the date of the foregoing events he has been resident, for the most part, in Pennsylvania, and by the exercise of a strict and persevering attention to business, has made himself master, as we understand, of ample means.

---

4. This work was published as a small pamphlet under the weighty title of *History of the Detection, Conviction, Life and Designs of John A. Murek, the Great Western Land Pirate, Together With His System of Villainy, and Plan of Exciting a Negro Rebellion, and a Catalogue of the Names of Four Hundred and Forty-Five of His Mystic Clan, Fellows and Followers, and Their Efforts for the Destruction of Mr. Virgil A. Stewart, the Young Man Who Detected Him, to Which is Added a Biographical Sketch of Mr. Virgil A. Stewart.*

CHAPTER XXVIII.

Great Revival among the Marauders—The Gathering of the Council—The Conspirators of Mississippi—Progress of the Plot—Approach of the Crisis—The Scope of the Tornado—Alarm of the Country—The "Committee of Safety"—The Glimmering of Vengeance.

The publication of Stewart's pamphlet and its dissemination throughout the region which its exposures saved from a threatened devastation, produced a sensation, in comparison with which the excitement, attendant upon the arrest of Murrell and the revealments of his trial, were but small. The dark and sanguinary scheme of massacre was then laid bare in all its hideous details, and a thrill of horror, such as is only elicited from men who gaze back upon some appalling danger from which they have miraculously escaped, ran through the shuddering communities of the West and South. But following the electric shiver came a warming of the blood which grew into a rage for vengeance, and in the first madness of the fever many a dissolute and suspicious character, fell victims to the sudden and fatal indignation of excited citizens. Some were smitten down in casual encounters which, if noticed at all, were merely chronicled as chance affrays, and others perished under the more deliberate but equally savage adjudication of the Regulators.

These results were not immediate upon the publication of the pamphlet, but were provoked by a subsequent series of events which have became a portion of the history of the West, and which, from their connection with the imprisoned marauder and his class, it is our duty to narrate.

The incarceration of Murrell and the exposition of the grand scheme of the insurrection, seemed at first to threaten the utter disorganization of the band, and, dismayed and discomfited, the miscreants of the morass cowered in their dens, while the leading members who were established reputably in society, abstained from any system of correspondence with each other. The paralysis, however, did not last long; a fragment of the more daring spirits, grasping at hope even in the very depth of gloom, conceived the daring policy of carrying out the plans of the chief, by precipitating the insurrection which had been previously set for the 25th December. They conceived that the country, relying upon the statements of Stewart, would not enter into a general system of precaution against the rising, until shortly previous to the indicated time, and that therefore if they could hurry the crisis as early as July, they might still command success by taking the country unawares. This plan was proposed by one of the most distinguished of Murrell's personal friends, named Andrew Boyd, of Hinds County, Mississippi, and was sustained by Rural Blake, Joshua Cotton and two brothers Earl, who were situated in the adjoining counties of Madison and Warren in the same State.

These men were the leading spirits of Mississippi, and boldly answered for the readiness of the one hundred and fifty adherents of the clan in that State, and they also unhesitatingly asserted that the negroes could be as easily made ready for the rising in July, as they could for the first appointed time or a year thence. Indeed, Boyd declared the earlier date ought originally to have been chosen, and it surprised him, he said, that the advantages of the fourth day of July had not struck the acute mind of their chief, nor suggested itself to the thoughts of any of the confederacy. By selecting the afternoon or evening of that day, they would avail themselves of all the advantages arising our of the general assembling of the negroes of the various plantations for the celebration of the national holiday, and they would also derive no small assistance from the exhilarated state of mind which would be produced by this temporary taste of freedom, as well as by the suggestive character of the occasion. Opportunities would be afforded, too, for the distribution of spirits, of fire-arms, for intercourse between the white emissary and the slave, and the alarm when given would not spread so rapidly as on any other occasion, as the events of the day would have familiarized the drowsy overseer and planter with the reports of musketry and pistols.

This brilliant proposition of Boyd's, as it was afterwards called by Murrell, found the same favor with every councillor to whom it was broken as it had gained from Blake, Cotton, and the Earls; and the result was, that after it had been agitated among the leaders in the various States, a general council was summoned to meet at Columbus, in the State of Mississippi, to take it into deliberate consideration.

The council met, as appears from certain revelations subsequently made in the trial of Cotton, in the month of March, 1835, and from this fact it is plain that Boyd must have hit upon his idea immediately upon the appearance of Stewart's pamphlet and the apparent frustration of the whole design of the insurrection. At the meeting of the council, Boyd explained his plan in *extenso*, showed the feasibility of accomplishing all they had to do in the three months which they had before them, and predicted that if the other States would but display the same alacrity as Mississippi, the rising would be crowned with success, and they might calculate upon a liberation of the chief and restoration of the band, not only to its former state, but to a condition of power and influence which had not been comprehended in the scope of their previous hopes.

These views met with an enthusiastic reception, and after being adopted, the council broke up, each delegation departing to its own State, charged with the most momentous duties. We now find the plan of the insurrection thoroughly revived, and starting on its new progress with a threatening energy. Some of these appearances, however, were deceptive. The delegations of most of the districts being deprived of the management of the arch demon who had inspired and sustained their efforts for years, became mistrustful of the issue, and feared to trust themselves so wide at sea under any lesser guidance. The consequence was, that in all but Mississippi, the plan began to droop after the first impression of Boyd's energetic views had worn off, but in the latter State, the activity of the local leader and his adherents kept the enterprise moving forward, with a vigor that did not pause even long enough to observe the dangerous apathy which had fallen upon every other quarter. The eventual result of this state of things was, that the explosion and its consequences were confined to Boyd's district, and its rage and retribution to the members of his following; we must therefore abandon any attempt to trace the gradual progress and frustration of those portions of the plot, which were stifled without violence, or went out of themselves in the other States, and confine ourselves to the recorded developments of the horrors which darken the archives of the State of Mississippi in the summer of 1835.

The events which we are about to chronicle are principally confined to Madison, Hinds, and Warren counties, of Mississippi, and our attention is therefore called particularly to the condition, arrangements and operations of the conspirators in that quarter of the State. Of the character of Andrew Boyd, the leader and director of these operations, the reader has already had on opportunity to form some idea. Next to him in importance and ability was Ruel Blake, of whom we have previously spoken. This man was a native of Connecticut, and according to his own statement had followed the sea for the greater part of his life. He had resided in Madison some three years, but notwithstanding this length of residence he could claim few, if any friends. He was of a cold, unsocial temperament, which joined to a forbidding countenance and notoriously cruel habits, rendered him detested by those who had opportunities of frequently observing him.—From his revengeful and savage disposition, there were many who credited the vague report, that the dosing passages of his career upon the sea had been scenes of piracy and bloodshed.—On his arrival in Madison he had adopted the trade of ginwright, and worked at it during his residence with much success up to the time of the conspiracy.

A.L. Donovan[1] was the name of another active conspirator. He resided at Beattie's Bluff, on Big Black River, and had, in company with a man named Moss and his two sons, receivers of stolen goods, made numerous adherents among the negroes of that place. In Warren county, the Earls, two daring brothers, and three other men named Rawson, Lofton and Donley, spread the fever of sedition, while in Hinds, Boyd himself held in control a set of spirits, who, if they did not equal him in talent, at least were not inferior to him in wickedness or daring.

Men thus associated and impelled, could not fail to make rapid progress in any undertaking in which they might engage, and by the first of June the conspirators had infused their dangerous plans into the simple minds of half the negroes of the three counties. Hinds county

---

1. Angus Donovan, a vagabond known for his gambling habits and acquaintance with slaves at Beattie's Bluff, Mississippi. Lal Penick, *Great Western Land Pirate*, 113.

was to be the rendezvous and head quarters, and a place known as the Old Agency,[2] situated near the border of Madison, had been fixed upon as a depot for arms and ammunition. Madison it was supposed would yield without a struggle, as it was principally divided in large plantations, on most of which no white man, but an overseer, was to be found during the summer months. The absence of the wealthiest planters and their families to the north in the month of July, would, therefore, not only relieve the ignorant negroes from one great restraint, but would give them a preponderance of fifty to one over the whites who remained. A row of rings at specified plantations from one end of the country to the other, were to give the simultaneous signal for the general onslaught, and the knife and pistol, the hoe or axe, was to end all opposition by unrelenting massacre. While the work of slaughter was in progress, the white leaders of the servile bands were to gather the plunder of the place, and having thus finished the first chapter of destruction, march on to Hinds. There they were to be joined by Boyd and his forces, also flushed with slaughter, and to receive a new distribution of cutlasses and fire-arms. The leaders were to mount at this place, and from thence proceed at the head of their forces in the direction of Vicksburg, plundering the various plantations on the road, and swelling their numbers at every stopping place. By the accessions from Warren county, the marauders expected to be able to march into Vicksburg and Natchez, and to take possession of both places, intending, subsequently, to establish themselves at the former, and from that

---

2. Old Agency refers to the Choctaw Indian Agency that was located there. The Old Agency Road was part of the Natchez Trace.

point despatch their bands both north and south, and overrun or command the upper and lower country. The negroes who contributed to this movement were promised revenge for past wrongs, possession of the delicate-skinned daughters and wives of their former masters, and a final transportation to free States with enough money in their pockets to start them handsomely in the world as their own masters. With such temptations as these, it is not to be wondered at that the subtle white men had bewildered the credulous minds of their simple dupes, and moulded them to their atrocious purposes. Day by day the dark sedition widened, and Boyd, Blake, and their sanguinary satellites, while gazing with satisfaction upon this promising state of things, chafed for the tardy hour that was to consummate the bloody hope of years. Destiny, however, was working across their purposes, and while they thought themselves secure of their aims, a fatal web of death was slowly dropping its meshes upon them and their torrid plans.

The nature of the plot and the necessities of the case had obliged the marauders to confide largely in the blacks and although the utmost discrimination and experience of negro character was invariably exercised before the details of the design were committed to any slave, yet injudicious selections had been made. Some of the black leaders had confided their hopes and brilliant prospects vaguely to their wives and sweethearts, and passing from them, the momentous secret had become the subject of mysterious gossip among the workers of farms. Some of these conversations among the blacks, were now and then overheard by unfriendly ears, and by degrees a rumor got abroad that an insurrection of the slaves was meditated. The rumor was an alarming one; but as it came unsustained by any authentic information, and as it could not be ascertained how or where it had originated, most of the citizens were disposed to regard the report as utterly unfounded. Towards the latter part of June, however, the citizens of Livingston ascertained that the rumor had emanated from Madame Latham, a wealthy lady residing at Beattie's Bluff, whereupon it was at once proposed that a committee of gentlemen should proceed to her plantation, for the purpose of ascertaining upon what ground she had given publicity to such a fearful statement. The lady, in compliance with the request of the committee, informed them that her convictions were the result of several circumstances, but mainly rested on parts of alarming conversations overheard by her among her house girls. She remarked that her suspicions were first awakened by a strange insolence of bearing in her servants, and by the threatening language that they would use whenever punished or rebuked for it. These expressions induced her to scrutinize their conduct very closely, and it was not very long before she overheard a conversation, during which one of them was heard to say to another, that she "wished to God it was all over with—that she was tired of waiting on the white folks, and that she wanted to be her own mistress the balance of her days, and clear up her own house." Soon afterwards she heard the same girl in conversation with a negro man, belonging to a neighbor named Mr. Landfair. From the low and guarded tones of the speakers, she could not for a time distinguish what they said, but she observed the girl hold out her (Mrs. Latham's) babe toward the black man, and heard her ask him "if it were not a pity to kill such a pretty and innocent little creature as that." The man shook his head, and answered that "it was a pity, but that it must be done." These facts Mrs. Latham communicated to her son, who summoned the girl before him in the evening, and informed her that her conversation had been overheard. Conceiving, in her terror, that the whole of the dialogue had been detected, she fell upon her knees and begged for mercy, but being promised forgiveness on the condition that she should make a full confession, she stated that Mr. Landfair's man, her sweetheart, had informed her that there was to be a rising of the black people in a few days, and that they intended to kill all the whites, and take possession of the country, and become ladies and gentlemen themselves. "These were my reasons," said Mrs. Latham, in conclusion, "for giving publicity to the report of a threatened rising."

The committee were deeply impressed with the strength of these facts, but for the purpose of obtaining further confirmation of the statement, they summoned before them the other female servants of the household, and separately examining them, found their statements to correspond in every particular with the relation of the lady. The committee then charged Mrs Latham to see that the girls were prevented from having communication with any person whatever, until she heard again from them, and then proceeded to Mr. Landfair's and had two of his men taken into custody. By examining these men, though the culprits did not fully confess, the committee gained fresh evidence of the existence of the plot, and also were enabled by some collateral facts that were elicited, to fix their suspicions upon some of the white men, who were its secret instigators.

With these facts in their possession, the committee returned to Livingston, and reported their solemn convictions that a frightful insurrection was in progress, and advised the immediate organization of a Committee of Safety, with power to try, condemn, and execute, and the instant establishment of patrols and regulating squads.

This report was made on the 26th of June, eight days before the contemplated rising; but the unfortunate miscreants to whom it threatened retribution were blindly unaware of the danger that was gathering around them. They were dreaming of a successful rapine, the restoration of their clan, and the liberation of their chief; but in the midst of their delusion, death was sweeping towards them with a speed which defied escape, and mocked their blind and savage hopes.

CHAPTER XXIX.

Proceedings at Livingston—Alarming returns—Arrest of negro conspirators at the Bluff—Confessions under the lash—Horrible revealments—Disclosure of the names of the white leaders—The judgment and its execution.

The report which was made by the Investigating Committee on their return from Beattie's Bluff, on the afternoon of the 26th June, aroused the leading citizens of Livingston from their lethargy, and a secret circular was prepared that evening and despatched at once to the principal planters of that vicinity, calling upon them to assemble together on the following morning to devise measures to meet the alarming condition of affairs which hall been so providentially disclosed. The notice thus distributed, received the prompt attention of every person to whom it was directed, and on the following morning a large number of the most influential citizens of the county of Madison, were observed to arrive in Livingston, and to proceed to the house of Colonel D.H. Runnels, of that place. There, after a long sitting, during which the facts elicited by the Committee of Investigation were duly discussed, various measures of precaution were adopted, and committees appointed to investigate the state of affairs in the different districts of the county.

Having made arrangements for the due organization of patrols, and charged the committees with their several duties, the Council adjourned until the 30th June, when the committees were expected to report the results of their proceedings.

Though these measures and movements were intended to be kept secret until the proper rime should arrive for action, they necessarily leaked out in part, and filled the community with dark surmises, and vague alarms. It fortunately happened, however, that these proceedings escaped the reach of Boyd, who had summoned a final council of all the conspirators at the Old Agency, in Hinds county, on the very day when these ominous proceedings were in progress in the town of Livingston. It was owing, therefore, entirely to this providential coincidence, that none of the band detected the threatening movements that were sweeping out and around their intended circle of operations.

The main of the conspirators who were present at this miscreant gathering, were Ruel Blake, Doctor Cotton, the brothers Earl, Donovan, Rawson, Lofton, and Donley, whom we have before mentioned, and a Doctor

Saunders,[1] Lee Smith, and Albe Dean, whose subsequent fate entitle them to a special mention now.

Doctor Joshua Cotton, was, like Blake, an eastern man, and had some years before emigrated from Connecticut to Tennessee. At Memphis, in the latter State, he had committed some crimes shortly after his arrival, for which the was sentenced to Nashville penitentiary. While there he formed all acquaintance with Murrell, who was serving out a term on his first conviction, and he subsequently became an active and important member of his band. He married in Tipton county, of that State, and remained there until the trial and conviction of his chief, when, fearing arrest and a similar punishment, he abruptly set out with his wife and child in a southern direction. In a few weeks after his departure, he appeared at the Old Agency in Hinds county, Mississippi, alone, and from the time that he left Tennessee, his wife and child were never heard of. Shortly after his arrival at the Agency, he set up as a steam doctor, and married a worthy young girl, the daughter of an overseer; but he had not been possessed of her more than six weeks before he made a proposition to an accomplice to carry her off to Red River, in Arkansas. and abandon her to her fate. The diabolical project, however, never was carried out, as the revival of the insurrection suggested a better opportunity and a more effectual mode of divorce.

Saunders was a native of Sumner county, Tennessee, and had also been one of Murrell's adherents in that State. A few weeks after the arrest of the chief, he also started precipitately South, and directed his course through the

---

1. William Saunders

middle counties of Mississippi. At Livingston he ascertained that a planter in the neighbourhood required an overseer, and presenting himself promptly for the place, succeeded in obtaining it. He was soon discharged, however, his loose deportment being considered incompatible with that system of severe respect required from the negroes to their masters. It was about this time that Cotton set up as a steam doctor in Hinds, and getting wind of the fact, Saunders struck towards him, and was promptly taken into partnership as soon as he made his presence known.

Lee Smith was also a native of Tennessee, but had for some time previous to Cotton's arrival been a resident at the Agency. He was a man of good character and habits, and though poor was generally respected. Cotton perceived that he might be of service to the insurrection, and for the purpose of seducing him into the plan, offered him a partnership with himself and Saunders. This effected the conversion of Smith to their designs, and being a man of weak and inferior intellect, he soon became a most active coadjutor in all the schemes of his partners. Dean, the last mentioned of the above list, was a native of Connecticut, and the son of a highly respectable family. He had left home in 1831 or 1832, in consequence of some criminal act, and had found his way in 1833 to Madison county, Miss. On his arrival, being destitute, he took up the trade of making washing machines, and continued it until after the arrival of Cotton and Saunders. Then he made propositions to enter their co-partnership, which being favourably entertained, he found himself the fourth member of the firm of "Cotton, Saunders, & Co., Steam Doctors."

The operations of this firm, through their familiar intercourse with the sick negroes and their families, were eminently serviceable to Boyd and to the plot. Its principal members were, therefore, treated with the most extreme deference by the temporary leader of the insurrection.

The council at which these men were present was composed of some forty or fifty persons. It was held at night, and its deliberations continued for several hours. Finally, having examined and re-examined the whole nature and condition of their arrangement, it was decided that every thing would he ready on the fourth of July, and that no postponement need take place. The various departments of the bloody work were duly assigned to the several leaders, and the method of the movements marked down. The operations were to be commenced first at Beattie's Bluff, under the directions of Donovan, the Earls, Rawson and others; Blake and Cotton were to light the torch in Livingston, and to Saunders, Dean, and Smith, were assigned the destruction of those districts where their influence among the negroes was paramount. Having settled these and other important matters, the council formally separated to meet again in the blood and smoke of rapine and insurrection.

On the 30th of June the committee at Livingston met pursuant to adjournment, and with closed doors received the report of their committees. Their secret session was a short one. The returns laid before them by the committee, which had confined its investigations to Beattie's Bluff, were of a nature so alarming, that an additional member was added to that body, and they were despatched post haste whence they came, commissioned with full powers to try, condemn, and adopt whatever penal measures the contingency might seem to them to require in that locality. The committee then issued orders for the arrest of suspected white men, and having satisfied themselves that their commands were in the way of prompt execution, threw open their doors to the citizens, and commenced the public examination of some criminals whom they already held in arrest. Who these criminals were, and how they were disposed of, we will not for the present inquire, but follow the committee which was despatched to Beattie's Bluff; and overlook their operations.

The committee of which we now speak was composed of Capt. Beattie,[2] James M. Smith and Mr. Mabry,[3] all residents of the Bluff, and citizens in whom the community had the most implicit confidence. Their first proceeding was to arrest the two girls belonging to Mrs. Latham and publicly re-examine them, so that the citizens, being convinced themselves by direct evidence of the existence of the plot, would be prepared to sustain the committee in the stringent measures which they contemplated. The testimony of the first girl produced the most extraordinary excitement, and when she repeated that portion of the scene with the babe between herself and Mr. Landfair's man, the rage was uncontrollable, and a large portion of the crowd burst away in the direction of Mr. Landfair's place to drag forth the monster who had had the heart to say that the innocent must die.

---

2. Andrew Beattie

3. Jesse Mabry (1791/92–), a local merchant and one-time cotton planter. Joshua D. Rothman, *Flush Times & Fever Dreams: A Story of Capitalism and Slavery in the Age of Jackson*. Athens: University of Georgia Press, 2012, 100–101.

While this movement was going on, a Mr. Lee came forward and stated, that he had heard a seditious conversation between two of Captain Stanberry's slaves, one of whom was a blacksmith named Joe, and the other of whom was a black preacher named Weaver. The arrest of these men was immediately ordered, and also the arrest of a mulatto man named Sam, the property of Mr. Mabry, whom Mr. M. felt convinced must be implicated in the plot, if the blacksmith Joe was a participant therein. He formed this opinion from the close familiarity which had always existed between the two men, and also in consequence of the shrewd and vicious disposition of his slave culprits.

The first of the three culprits who was produced was the blacksmith. The negro at first appeared slightly daunted by the array of excited faces which enclosed on all sides, but soon regained his composure. Mr. Mabry who conducted the examination, commenced by asking the prisoner when he had last seen Sam, and what had been the purport of their last conversation together. For a time the African stoutly denied that any thing of an improper nature had passed between him and his friend, but having his hands bound with cords preparatory to a threatened whipping, he consented to make a full confession on the condition that he should not be punished. This being promised, he commenced by telling Mr. Mabry, that he knew he wanted to find out all about the "rising," and he would now tell him what he knew, protesting, however, that he had nothing to do with the business. He said that all the information he was possessed of on the subject, he had obtained through Sam, who, in the way of gossip only had told him that the negroes, under the directior of certain white men, intended to "rise" on the evening of the 4th of July, and burn and destroy and slaughter all the whites. Sam had further told him the names of some of these men, and had pointed out at various times several others whose names he did not know. The names of the white men which he recollected, were those of Ruel Blake, Drs. Cotton and Saunders, and the only negroes whom he knew to be implicated in the plot were Sam, Weaver, and another negro preacher named Russell. These he had been told were to be captains.

While Joe was going on with his confession, Weaver was brought in. He was immediately called upon to answer for himself in like manner with Joe, but to the surprise of all, contented himself with a general denial of Joe's statement, and firmly refused to make any replies to the questions that were put to him. The consequences of his obduracy were explained to him, but still he was inexorable. No offers of lenity could shake his courage, and he remained steadfast under the torture of the lash, when even his executioner was nigh to fainting with his task. At length the whipping ceased, and the preacher was stood aside for further deliberation.

Russell, the other preacher, came next, but being made of baser stuff, a few strokes soon disposed him to make a full revealment of all he knew. His statement implicated Weaver and Sam, and agreed in all its parts with the testimony of Joe, with the exception that he went further into the particulars of the plot.—His theory of the rising was, that the first movement was to be made at the Bluff; it was to proceed to Livingston, where they expected heavy reinforcements from Hinds, it was then to advance to Vernon, and from Vernon to go South to

Clinton. On arriving at the latter place it was calculated the insurgents would be strong enough to march into Natchez, and to sack the place. Having killed the inhabitants of that city, and plundered the banks and warehouses, they were to retire to a strong position called "*The Devil's Punch Bowl*,"[4] and establish themselves in force.* This testimony was carefully taken down by the committee, after which Russell was bound and stood beside Weaver.

Mr. Mabry's man Sam was then brought forward, but he stoutly denied everything that Joe had alleged against him, and like Weaver maintained his position under all the torture of the lash. The day being now far spent, it was decided not to dispose of the three criminals until the morrow, and as it had been ascertained that Mr. Landfair's negro had made his escape, the fatigued committee postponed the continuation of the investigation until the following morning, putting the prisoners meanwhile under the charge of a strong guard for the night.

On the morning of the 2nd a number of slaves were brought before the committee, but most of them having been produced on mere surmise, were soon disposed of. One, however, named Jim, who is described by Mr.

---

4. "The Devil's Punch Bowl" was an unusual five-hundred foot wide depression of thick woods and underbrush along the bluffs of the Mississippi River north of Natchez, Mississippi. An ideal place for hiding, it was reputed to be an enclave for river pirates and escaped slaves.

* This line of march differs slightly, as will be seen, from the one before laid down. A similiar variance appeared afterwards in the confession of another of the conspirators. The probability is, however, that each line had been proposed in council, and remained subject to the contingencies of the actual march for its adoption.

Mabry in his official report of the proceedings, as a very sensible and fine looking young fellow, proved to be an important conspirator. For a long time he refused to make any confession, but being cruelly lacerated with the whip, he at length gave in, and promised to tell all if the flagellator would hold his hand. His statement was similar to Russell's, but he implicated more white men than either he or Joe. Among these was young Donovan, whom the writhing slave pointed out among the spectators, and also Moss the receiver, and his two sons, who were likewise present. These men having been secured, Jim described in full their method of corrupting the slaves. Of Moss and his sons he related several acts of villany, and described them as the worst men who could exist in any community. He could not say that they were connected with the insurrection, but he knew that they kept a receiving shop for all the goods which the negroes could steal from their masters, and thus encourage them to pilfer by finding a market for the plunder; he also knew that they were in the habit of harboring Donovan and the bad white men in the neighborhood, who inflamed the slaves with vicious thoughts, and set their brains on fire with whiskey. Jim further stated that it was the object of the insurrection to slay all the whites, except some of the most beautiful women, whom the white men told the negro captains they might keep for wives. That intoxicated with this prospect, he had picked out a very beautiful lady for himself, and that he and his wife had already had a serious quarrel in consequence of his having informed her of his intention and of his choice.

The excitement of the crowd at this portion of Jim's story was intense, and it was feared at times that the infuriated audience would yield to the impulses of its rage, and burst in upon the miserable culprits and tear them to pieces. The high character of the committee, however, kept the turbulent in awe, and the tribunal was allowed to proceed without any serious interference.

The last man arraigned was a negro named Bacchus, belonging to a planter near the Bluff. He confessed without punishment, and corroborated the evidence that had been put in before.

The work of investigation appeared now to be at an end. Conclusive evidence had been produced against the five negroes in custody, and it but remained to decide upon the punishment and command its execution.

There could be but little hesitation as to the course to be pursued. There was no jail in the county that would hold more than six or eight persons, and those but insecurely, and if the prisoners were dispatched to any other county, the large guard required would weaken the defenders of the place, and leave many families entirely unprotected.—An imminent and pressing danger existed, to which the civil or regularly constituted authorities of the State were inadequate, and which nothing but the most prompt and signal measures—measures that would strike an equal terror to the heart of the ringleader and the misguided instrument—could repress or check.

There was still another consideration which contributed to the ultimate decision of the committee. The enraged populace expected the summary execution of the victims, and if their fury were denied a prompt requital, they might take the recompense of their wrongs into their own bands. If this should happen the committee would have more to answer for, perhaps, than the lives of five guilty men, for no rage is so merciless as the rage which springs from fear, and no havoc so undiscriminating as the fury of a mob.

Moved by these considerations, as well as by the legitimate necessities of the case, the committee therefore condemned the preachers, Weaver and Russel, and the men, Jim, Sam and Bacchus, to be hung by the neck within the hour.

As soon as this award was given, the mob set up a shout which rent the air, and before the Court could assign sheriffs to execute their orders, they burst in upon the the prisoners and bore them off with repeated huzzas of ferocious exultation. They paused at a large tree within two or three hundred yards of the scene of the previous examination. In the next instant a man was seen crawling on hands and knees along a horizontal limb, and then, holding down his hand for a rope to be slung up to him to be made fast. Brief time elapsed before the fatal cord was fixed, when, heralded by a yell which might have come from a chorus of fiends, a black object was seen dangling above the heads of the crowd and writhing in unsightly spasms in the air. When the body had spent its mortal agony and was worthless of any further pain, another victim was strung up with another shout, and another and another and another followed, till the sturdy old limb creaked and groaned with the frightful weight, and the whole five Africans hung side by side.

The spirit of the audience was for the time tolerably appeased, for they had made the most of the slaughter by enjoying it in instalments, but there was something yet in store to give a handsome finish to their sanguinary jubilee. Just as they were on the point of dispersion, a shout was heard from the direction of the river, and in a few moments afterwards a crowd of excited men came rushing forward with a negro in their midst, whom they had just taken in the swamp, and who proved to be Mr. Landfair's man who had escaped the day before. The whole spirit of the inhuman revel appeared to revive at once, and amid shouts of the most boisterous delight the dusky culprit went aloft beside his grim companions, and his grotesque agonies wound up the performances of the horrid holiday.

LYNCHING OF THE NEGROES AT BEATTIE'S BLUFF

CHAPTER XXX.

Investigations at Livingston—The water carrier—The affray—Flight of Blake—Arrest of Saunders—Arrest of Boyd and Cotton—Appearance of the conspirators before the tribunal—Decision of the committee—Boyd's evening expedition—Proceedings of the 2d of July—The desperate chase.

While the committee and citizens of Beattie's Bluff were engaged in the examination and executions described in the last chapter, the citizens of Livingston and the adjacent country were no less active in ferreting out the sources of the rebellion. On the adjournment of the Central Committee of Safety, on the 27th of June, each member of the meeting retired to his plantation, or his district, and commenced investigations. in the hope of eliciting some facts worthy of presentation at the re-gathering on the 30th. With this view,

Mr. William P. Johnson, a wealthy planter, instructed a favorite slave, whom he had made a driver, and in whom he could place implicit reliance, to singly examine all the negroes of the place, and see if they knew anything of the conspiracy. The driver, in compliance with this direction, set about his task, and on the following day fell in with an old water carrier, who cautiously admitted that he had heard there was to be a rising throughout the State, though he could not say when it was to take place. To make up, however, for his deficient knowledge upon this point, he, in confidence, referred the driver to a negro man, named Peter, belonging to Ruel Blake, who, he said, was thoroughly acquainted with all the details of the plot. The driver, persisting further, and affecting to be favorable to the plan, asked the old man if he could tell him where he should get powder and shot, and to whom he should apply to join the malcontents; but the water carrier's knowledge appeared to be limited upon the subject, and he again referred to Blake's man, adding that he supposed Peter could soon furnish powder and shot without going further, as he had heard him say that he had found out there was a large lot of powder in kegs in Wm. M. Rice's store, in Livingston, which place he should break open as soon as it was wanted.

The driver communicated this information to his master, who, however, prudently abstained from taking any immediate action in the premises, preferring to submit the further direction of the development to the judgment of the committee, than to take the risk of putting the negroes on their guard by a premature arrest.

On the 30th of June, the committee met at Livingston, agreeably to adjournment, and were soon convinced, from the nature of the reports which were laid before them, that their alarms had not been unfounded. Among other communications, the names of Cotton, Boyd, and Saunders were handed in as suspicious persons, and though nothing definite had been elicited against any of them, it was recommended that each should be arrested on the strength of his known habits of intimacy with the negroes of the plantations. Orders were, therefore, made to that effect, which, having been issued, the committee proceeded with their investigations.

Mr. Johnson then presented the evidence of his driver, in relation to the water carrier and Ruel Blake's man, Peter. Blake, who was present at the meeting, and who had been a deeply anxious observer of the proceeding, expressed the most unfeigned astonishment at this revelation, and with a well assumed earnestness volunteered to produce the culprit for instant examination. On this pretence he left the room, but contrary to his wishes he was followed by two or three officious assistants, who appeared to be actuated by an equally ardent desire with himself, to aid in the prosecution of justice. Though thus trammelled and observed, Blake, nevertheless, found a chance, while bearing the slave back to the court-house, to whisper an exhortation in his ear, begging him to remain firm in his denial, as that would be his only chance of safety. When Blake re-entered the court-house with his negro, he found the water-carrier already there, and about to undergo examination on the points which inculpated his slave. The old negro was asked to confess what he had told Mr. Johnson's driver, on the morning of the 29th, but though confronted with the accusing African, he stoutly denied having held any such conversation as was alleged against him. Persuasion and threats were used without avail, and the obdurate old fellow was at length consigned to the actual terrors of the lash.

A biting thong wielded by a strong and practised hand, is the most irresistible of human arguments with those whose minds have not been refined to that pitch of intelligence which is capable of martyrdom; consequently, after suffering a most severe chastisement, the wincing victim yielded to the physical infliction, and made a full confession. He admitted the truth of the driver's story in every particular, repeated that he did not know when the rising was to take place, but stated that Blake's man, then present, had told him it would be in a few days. Peter was then put under examination but mindful of his master's caution, professed to be entirely ignorant of a contemplated rebellion, and denied the whole statement of the water-carrier from first to last. Finding him determined against mild inducements, the committee condemned him to be whipped, and in courtesy to his master, requested that he would personally inflict the chastisement.

Upon this, the gin-wright took the whip, and deliberately repeating all the charges of which the culprit stood accused, advised the slave if he was guilty, to spare him the necessity of punishing him, by making a confession. The negro, however, stoutly denied his guilt, whereupon Blake commenced to apply the cat to his back, pausing at intervals, and inquiring if he was yet prepared to confess. The manner in which the whipping was laid on, however, did not give general satisfaction to the spectators, and it was not long before it was perceived by every one present, that Blake, so far from wishing to hurt the negro, only struck him a hard blow now and then to keep up appearances. It was plain to the committee that nothing would be got out of him at this rate, and believing, in addition, that his presence acted as a restraint upon the culprit, they requested Blake to withdraw, and allow somebody else to try a hand at managing the slave. Blake could scarcely conceal his deep chagrin at this command, but relinquishing the whip he sullenly withdrew to a short distance. His agitation was extreme, and he kept walking to and fro upon the outskirts of the crowd, but drawing closer and closer every time, he heard the sharp sing of the thong descend upon the moaning sufferer's back. At length the slave spoke, whereupon, unable to stand it any longer, and determined to stake every thing upon a single chance, Blake rushed into the centre of the crowd, and swore that his negro should not be touched another lick, and that those who wished to carry the torture any further, would have to whip him first. At this expression, the man who was whipping the prisoner, taking the remark as a reflection upon himself, drew back the cat as if to strike the gin-wright, but quick as thought the enraged conspirator caught the handle of the thong with one hand, and knocked his assailant down at the same moment with the other. Two or three sprang forward to interfere, whom Blake assailed in the same manner, and a most bloody affray would have been the consequence, had not some of the coolest of the bystanders dragged the conspirator out of the crowd, and begged him to run for his life. Blake took the hint, and making the most of a light pair of heels, succeeded in getting safe away.

Being a slave-holder, no one at that time had the most remote idea that Blake was at all connected with the conspiracy, but attributed his interference entirely to sympathy for his negro, and a disposition to believe too easily in his protestations of innocence.

When Blake was gone, the lash was again resumed, and the interrogation of the negro again commenced, but the wavering crisis between the soul and body of the slave had passed, and the devotion of his master to save him made the will of the simple but grateful negro superior to all the powers of pain. He was more steadfast than at first, and his examination ended as it had begun. But though Blake thus fortunately escaped the detection of his connection with the conspiracy, the affair had involved him in a peril, from which it was necessary for him to fly. Taking the advice therefore of a gentleman for whom he was working at the time, he set out that evening in the direction of Vicksburg, with the intention of staying away from the country, until the excitement should blow over.

Leaving Blake to pursue his Course of flight according to the contingencies of the time, we must return to the committee.

Immediately after the affray we have described, Saunders was brought in and put under examination. He justified himself against the charges that were made against him, of intimacy with the negroes, by pleading the necessity of his business as a doctor, which obliged him to be familiar with the humblest residents of the plantations. This was considered plausible, and the point was not pressed. He was interrogated as to the character of Cotton, when, either for the purpose of revenging himself for some secret wrong, or, through the natural impulse of a base mind to relieve itself by impugning others with higher faults, he accused Cotton of the most odious traits of character, and made no hesitation in declaring that he kept up a trade with the negroes by exchanging spirits, for whatever they might steal and bring to him. He could not say whether he had anything to do with the conspiracy, but would leave it to the committee to decide whether such a man would be likely to have part in it or no.

Upon this evidence Saunders was released, and a guard thrown forward on the road towards Hinds county, from whence Cotton was expected to return on the following morning. He had not yet come back from the council at the Old Agency, having delayed a day at the request of Boyd, who was desirous of accompanying him to Livingston, where he wished to superintend certain important preparations, with his own eye.

Having secured his own release as a witness, and placed matters in shape for the arrest of Cotton, Saunders (though he did not dream that his conduct was compromising Boyd), selected the second hour of the evening for precipitate flight to the banks of the Mississippi. He had seen enough to know that the rebellion was nipped and destroyed, and that the best chance of safety for himself, as well as for all who had been concerned, was to put wisdom in their heels and fly.

On the following morning, while Boyd and Cotton were jogging leisurely along, about ten miles from Livingston, they espied a band of armed men approaching them. The circumstance was so unusual, that it was Boyd's first impulse to turn and fly, but a moment's thought restrained him, and the two horsemen suffered the regulators to approach.

The purpose of the scouts was soon explained, and the travellers made to understand that they were prisoners. Struck with surprise, but affecting a perfect unconcern, they cheerfully agreed to submit to the directions of the party, and Boyd pleasantly congratulated all hands that their journey should lie so exactly to the same point.

On being ushered before the committee, Cotton contented himself with a simple protest against his arrest, defying the committee to produce a jot of evidence that would warrant, even by implication, the slightest shadow upon his character. The committee were somewhat shaken by the confident bearing of the steam doctor, but recalling the points of Saunders' testimony from their minutes, they informed him that his partner in business, William Saunders, had made charges against him of the most heinous character, which he was ready to substantiate under oath. Upon this Cotton burst into a violent fit of rage, denounced Saunders as a worthless and lying scoundrel, and told to the court, that he thought he could with little difficulty explain to them the reason and motive of the rascal's charges. He then went on with admirable quickness and ingenuity, to state the pretended fact that Saunders had two days before opened a small private desk belonging to him, and stolen two hundred and seventy-five dollars; that finding out he was suspected, and meditating flight, the villain had laid this information in the hope that he, (Cotton,) would be prevented from pursuing and overtaking him.

The committee listened patiently to this admirable fabrication, and then ordered the witness, Saunders, to be brought forward to substantiate his charges. Saunders, however, did not appear, and it being soon ascertained that he had really fled the night before, Cotton's story was credited, and he was discharged for want of any evidence against him.

While Cotton's examination was going on, Boyd had had a good opportunity to look through the crowd for the purpose of sifting out a friend. His efforts were successful for he was fortunate enough to observe the two Earls among the audience, and to manage to give them a signal that he should require their assistance. When he was arraigned and interrogated, he frankly admitted that he had heard of the conspiracy, and further admitted that he was inclined to believe in its existence. He qualified these admissions, however, by explaining that all he knew about it was from the common rumor among his neighbors, which was probably similar to the one that had originally drawn the committee together. He further stated, that having a large family of children who might fall victims to the ferocity of the negroes if a rebellion were to break out, the the reports had impressed his mind with the most profound alarm. Indeed, the prospect of the terrible slaughter of his wife and little ones had haunted him like the nightmare for the last three or four days, until unable to endure it any longer, he had accompanied his friend Cotton to Livingston, with the special intention of satisfying himself of the truth or falsity of the reports, and of offering his services to the committee, if need for them should exist.

This story was told with strong effect upon the credulity of the listeners. As soon as it was concluded, the two Earls stepped forward, and in succession informed the committee that they knew Mr. Boyd to be one of the most respectable of the citizens of Hinds county, and assured them it was entirely out of the probabilities of the case to suppose, that a man bound as he was to society by such substantial interests and ties, could meditate or countenance, much less aid or abet, such a terrible conspiracy as was under consideration.—This prompt and earnest evidence, being clinched with a concluding remark of Cotton's, that nothing had ever been said against Mr. Boyd, except what had proceeded from the secret slanders of the villain Saunders, conquered the judgment of the committee, and induced them to release the miscreant leader, on the same ground as they had discharged his associate, the steam doctor.

The day being now well spent, the committee adjourned, and Blake and Cotton retired to an inn in the outskirts of the town. There, after nightfall, they were joined by the two Earls, and a consultation was held as to the best mode of proceeding. It was the general opinion that the rebellion was defeated for the time, though in the ignorance of the developments which had taken place that day at Beattie's Bluff, the daring mind of Boyd would not yet relinquish all hope of its successful prosecution. This, however, did not provoke much debate; measures for personal safety being considered as entitled to paramount consideration. A thousand little circumstances might tend to a development that would compromise them all, and they were surrounded by an excited populace, whose fears qualified them to become the most unscrupulous of executioners. The true policy of the conspirators, therefore, was to fly—if they could get away.

Some management was to be observed in this, however. It would not do for the whole four to leave at once, or to take the same routes. In this view Boyd proposed that the Earls should leave that night, striking north and south, and that he and Cotton should remain till next day, and after quelling all suspicions by appearing at the meeting of the citizens in the morning, take their chance to slip away into the woods, and gain the advantage of part of a day, as well as of a whole night, on the start. As soon as this was agreed upon, the party broke up, and the Earls set out according to previous agreement. In an hour afterwards, Boyd stealthily left the house, and winding himself in the shadows of the road, for a distance of some half mile, he sprang over a fence, and cautiously approached a small negro-cabin which stood in the enclosure. Tapping as stealthily as a cat, at the rough window-shutter, on the dark side of the shanty, he, after the pause of a few minutes, was answered by the appearance of a large woolly head thrust out of the aperture.

"Gor a mighty, Massa Boyd, dis you! What bring you here?"

"Hush, Sam," said Boyd, laying his finger on his lips impressively. "Lean your head down, I have a word to say, and then I must leave you. Is your wife asleep, and all still?"

"Yes, all sound as a roach. No one list'ain," answered the negro, in a low tone.

Having satisfied himself that all was safe, Boyd then communicated to the negro that he wanted him on the following morning to call at Warren's tavern and get his horse, and lead him to a designated and somewhat distant point in the woods, and there to tie him. That having done this, he was to station himself at some convenient point on the edge of the wood, to await his approach, and conduct him by the nearest route to where the animal was tethered.—To all this the negro faithfully agreed, without questioning the object of the order, and after exchanging a few more words in recapitulation of the details, the singular conference was broken off, the woolly head shrunk back into the scarcely darker gloom of the cabin, and the conspirator wound back to his inn without having been missed.

On the following day the committee again resumed their investigations, and examined several negroes without eliciting any thing additional, or implicating any white man as being connected with the plot, and it began to be thought by most of the citizens, that the intended rebellion was confined entirely to the blacks, among whom the negro preachers were, doubtless, as in all previous in stances, the main instruments and instigators. Boyd and Cotton were present, and participated, as may be supposed, quite largely to the satisfaction occasioned by the growth of this conviction. Indeed, they began to hope that the entire danger would pass without explosion, and it became a matter of some question in their minds, whether it were necessary to abandon Livingston so surreptitiously, under the then favorable aspect of affairs. They were not long left to hesitation on this point. however, for while they were tranquilly contemplating the improved condition of their prospects, a shout was heard coming up the road, which on being explained, announced that Saunders had been retaken, and was then being brought towards the court-house on the shoulders of the approaching crowd.

The instant this intelligence was made known to the conspirators, their faces took the hue of fear, and exchanging a look of dismay, they separated without a word, and withdrew in different directions from the throng.

Their alarm was not without cause. Saunders had been met on his road to Vicksburgh, by one of the firm of Ewing, Maddux & Co. of Livingston, to whom, while in drink, he had imparted the fact, that it was the intention of certain men whom he could name, to rob one of that firm who was then supposed to be on his return from New Orleans with a large amount of money.

The gentleman, by plying the rogue with liquor, and flattering him adroitly, next learned, that a conspiracy of the negroes was in progress in Madison County, in which certain white men were supposed to be leaders, and that though he, (Saunders,) would not name names, he would say, it would be well for the people of the country to keep a sharp watch on Doctor Cotton, Ruel Blake, and a few of their associates. These hints were sufficient for the gentleman to whom they were given, and convinced that Saunders must be a participant in schemes of which he knew so much, he made no hesitation in having him arrested and carried back.

As soon as this gentleman arrived in Livingston with his prisoner, the committee ordered the re-arrest of Cotton and of Boyd and also directed the arrest of Blake. Those who had stood next to the two former in the crowd, turned to lay hands upon them, but lo, they were gone! The assemblage was sifted in all directions, but it was plain the rascals had vanished from the ground. The circle widened, and peering citizens ran to the turnings of the streets, but without obtaining any definite satisfaction.

One of the searchers, however, being called to by a female who was leaning out of a window, had his attention directed to a distant figure, which appeared to be running across fields at top speed for the woods. The hint was taken, and waving his arm and leading off down the road, the man called upon his companions to follow him. The summons was instantly obeyed, and dashing forward, some twenty or thirty men, accompanied by two track dogs, or bloodhounds, that had been held in leash to hunt the negroes out of the swamps, gave chase.

The fugitive turned his head, and perceiving that the wild halloo was up, increased his speed to the highest mark of fear. He was near the wood, and already heard the cheering welcome of his sooty friend.

"Hi! yi! dis way, Massa Boyd, dis way, de track-dog is eaten up de ground like fire! Dis way, Massa Boyd," saying which, the faithful negro sprang from a branch on which he had been perched, and seizing his white brother by the hand, ran at full speed with him through the tangled chapparal. Closer and closer came the bounds of the fierce dogs upon the trail, but ere they could reach their prey, the panting robber had sprung into his saddle, and gathered the bridle in his hand. As he struck the spurs into the horse's sides, the curtain of foliage that stretched around him, was broken by a plunge, and the next instant the negro was pulled to the earth by one of the savage hounds.

The other dog followed in the next instant, but as he sprang upon the white man in his saddle, he received full in his skull the entire contents of a huge horse pistol, which the robber had just time to draw. Then spurring his horse, the marauder tore from the jungle, and rode for dear life in a direction which had previously been given him by the negro.

In a few minutes the pursuers came up, and found the slave still in the custody of one faithful hound, while the other lay dead and brained a few feet further off. The clog was taken off the African, and the captive was bound and taken back to town by one more portion of the party, while the other, with the remaining hound, pursued the fruitless chase a short distance further on. They finally gave up the hunt, satisfied that their prey had made a good escape, but ignorant whether it was Cotton, Boyd, or Blake.

THE BLOODHOUNDS SCENTING BOYD'S TRACK.

CHAPTER XXXI.

The ecstacy of Slaughter—Pursuit and Arrest of Cotton—Enforcement of the Code of Necessity—Expiations of Crime—Sequestrations of the Conspiracy.

Though Boyd's courser had flung distance from his heels so fast as to mock the most desperate efforts of his pursuers, he could not disappoint them of a bloody compensation. The negro Sam, from the circumstances under which he was found, had evidently been an abettor of the unknown horseman's flight, and this fact, to minds exasperated with but one idea, condemned both him and the fugitive as accomplices in the rebellion. Surmise is fact to an excited mind, and rage makes but slight pause between proof and punishment.

The helpless African was seized by the infuriated regulators, and while they ran him at full speed to the town, they swore that no forms of law or tedious process of inquiry, should baffle them of his execution that afternoon.

As they approached the Court-House, with this determination, they were unexpectedly met and borne back by an immense crowd, which appeared to be agitated by the most intense excitement, and which, with shouts and yells, and violent gestures, was sweeping its way towards an open space a few hundred yards distance off. Awed for a moment by agitation which so far eclipsed their own, the returning party fell a few paces back, but stimulated in the next, by a scene so congenial with their feelings, they dashed at the edge of the rushing mass to learn the cause of the unusual movement. A glance revealed two negroes in firm custody, with halters around their necks, their dusky faces ashey grey, and their eyeballs nearly starting out with fear. This prologue to a bloody pastime could not be mistaken by the captors of Sam, and plunging into the centre of the throng, they contributed their victim to the coming spectacle.

The cause of this extraordinary tumult, was the arrival of the intelligence of what had transpired on the previous three days at Beattie's Bluff. This news, not only comprised an account of the execution of the five negroes, but embraced the revelations of their dying confessions, and the confirmation of the worst suspicions in relation to the extent and seriousness of the plot. The wondering and horror-stricken spectators were apprised for the first time of the exact period fixed for the insurrection, and they shuddered when it fell upon their ears, that but one day intervened between them and their danger. Most terrible of all, it was now made plain that they were not to contend alone with a few discontented and desperate negroes, but that the servile malcontents were to be led and stimulated in the work of carnage by the most abandoned white men of the country. White men, consisting of highway robbers, murderers, horse thieves, counterfeiters, slave-stealers, and other desperadoes, who had for years infested the thin districts of the South and West and who were generally dreaded throughout these portions of the country, as the "Murrell Gangs."

As these terrifying details fell one upon another, the feelings of the audience rose almost to the pitch of frenzy, and finally, when it was stated that all the whites were to be slain, except the most beautiful females, who were to be reserved as mistresses of the negro captains, the listeners lost all self command, and with cries of "put them to death!" "put them to death!" seized upon Blake's slave and the old water-carrier, and bore them from the custody of the committee. It was in vain that the leading members of the temporary tribunal represented the dangerous effects of the example—in vain that they sought to intercept the informal slaughter, by the promise of a summary condemnation on the following day.—The blood of the multitude was up. They were jealous of their prey, and regarding the committee as envious of their assumption of independent jurisdiction, were deaf to all propositions of delay. Hurrying along as if apprehensive even that the softer portions of their own natures might relent, or that reflection would be unfaithful to that rapture of destruction, that ecstacy of slaughter, which is the fiercest of all human joys, they dashed blindly on with unlistening ears, entertaining no dream but that of vengeance.—When the captors of Sam met them in their mad career, they made no inquiry as to the nature of the man's offence, nor asked a question as the character of the proof against him. A hearty joy manifested itself at the providential capture of another monster, and amid shouts of exultation, the crowd arrived with the three captives at the spot which they had selected as the place of execution.

Spreading themselves all around a huge tree, lookers on of the multitude sought the most convenient positions to observe the coming spectacles, and then subsiding into silence, the mass waited the completion of the preparations which occupied a busy few in its centre. At length the bustle at the foot of the tree ceased; an opening and expanding of the inner circle took place; a simultaneous whisper between proximate by-standers, of *"now they are going up!"* buzzed through the throng, and then, after a slight rustling from hange of place and rising on tip-toes, there came a short pause, during which reigned a silence so profound, that the twinkling of the broad leaves above might have been heard as they turned lazily over to the soft embraces of the evening breeze. But that pause was short, for in another moment the three dusky sacrifices were snapped aloft above that white sea of human rage, and as they squirmed and twisted in the air, there broke forth a shout so fierce and quick, that the branches of the old tree, waved up and down as if agitated by a tempest.

That shout was heard by Cotton, as he lay crouched at three miles distance in the morass. He did not know its meaning, but it smote upon his guilty soul like a knell of death, and as the fearful reverberation again and again rung upon his ear, he grovelled still closer to the damp and slimy earth.

For four hours had he remained in this seclusion. He had withdrawn from the court-house at the same time as Boyd, but not having been so provident in preparing means for flight, he was obliged to take a circuitous path to the swamp, and being baffled several times in his course, struck it in a place which was separated from the route he designed to take, by a space of open field in view of the town which he dared not cross in the daylight. Cowering in the grass, he gazed alternately at the heavens to mark the approach of darkness, and then listened with the most lively and feverish fear, to every sound that disturbed the surrounding stillness. No wonder then that the shout which hailed the execution of his deluded dupes, pierced his cruel and remorseless heart with a prophetic terror, or that an instinct of approaching fate should have whispered to his soul that the tempest he had helped to raise was about whirling back upon himself.

Several minutes elapsed, but still those terrible hurras came booming in his ears. He found no relief by lying prone upon the surface of the ground, for the very earth seemed to have taken part against him, and conveyed still more acutely to his ears those warnings of impending retribution. Believing at length that he was the victim of all overheated imagination, he raised himself upon his knees and listened eagerly towards the town. Sure enough he had been deceived. The reverberation was only in his tympanum, and the air was vacant of any dreaded sound. He had been a fool, a child, the victim of a bugbear, but what was that? Suddenly the steam doctor

COTTON LISTENING TO THE SHOUTS AT THE LYNCHING OF HIS ACCOMPLICES.

paused. A faint halloo come singing down the breeze, of a different tone from the huge roar which had at first so terrified him. It was very faint—so faint that there was room to doubt whether it might not be a mere illusion. He listened again. Alas, it was no fancied sound, but became clear, distinct, and sharp, as if it had won upon the distance.—He drew a long breath, and inclined his ear for the third time. Then, after a moment's breathless pause, he turned and fled. Diving this way and that, he plunged deeper and deeper and deeper into the morass, yet the pursuing cry mixed with the deep bay of the relentless track-dog, came nearer and more near upon his trail. Despairing of the chances of flight, exhausted with fatigue, and enfeebled with the throes of fear, the wretched fugitive cast himself beneath the undergrowth, and seizing the rank and tangled grass, drew himself deep into the slime that nourished a dense thicket. There the hounds seized him, and from thence the hunters of men drew him forth. For a moment the captors could scarcely distinguish, from the solid and begrimed figure before them, who they had taken prisoner, but on perceiving it was the steam doctor, and one of the main instigators of the rebellion, they grasped him eagerly and turned back to the town. Being dusk when they arrived, they were met by the regularly appointed evening patrols, which had been appointed by the Committee, who took the prisoner into safe custody to protect him from the vengeance of the mob.

On the same evening the Committee met, but great dissatisfaction having been occasioned among the members by the lawless proceedings of the afternoon, they declined any further investigations at that time, and postponed the examination till the following morning.

At ten o'clock on that day, Cotton was arraigned for trial.

The first witness called against the wretched man was his treacherous accomplice, Dr. Saunders, who, under oath, confirmed all his previous statements of the 30th June, and detailed, in addition, the prisoner's mode of making converts among the negroes. Other evidence was produced confirmatory of Saunders' statements, by persons who had seen Cotton lurking suspiciously about the plantations at Livingston, Vernon, and Beattie's Bluff, on pretence of hunting horses, which Saunders affirmed he had purposely turned loose to gain access to the different estates where they might have strayed.

A negro of Beattie's Bluff who had been tampered with by Cotton during one of these excursions, was sent for by the committee, to see if he could recognize the white emissary in the person of the prisoner on trial before them.

The African being introduced into a room where Cotton was, after taking a glance at all present, readily selected and pointed out the steam doctor as the horse hunter who had accosted him in the prairies, who had given him spirits to drink, and who had then sought to make him swear a horrible oath to join the insurrectionary bands in process of formation.

This positive identification deprived Cotton of all courage. He turned ashy pale when the boy recognized him, and came near to fainting as he related the incidents of their conversation. The trial lasted throughout the day, and was resumed on the following morning by the introduction on the record of the confession of the negroes hung at Beattie's Bluff, in which the prisoner had been indicated by name as one of the ringleaders of the insurrection. After some other corroborating testimony, the committee retired to deliberate upon the case, and to arrive at a decision. Immediately upon their leaving the room, the Doctor uttered an exclamation of despair, and expressed his opinion that he must be convicted. Taking this as a virtual admission of his guilt, some of the bystanders advised him to confess whereupon he seized eagerly upon the request, and offered to reveal the whole conspiracy, on condition that the committee would not have him hung immediately. This offer was communicated to the committee, who, however, rejected the proposition peremptorily, sending word that they were satisfied of his guilt, whether he should confess or not, and that the future welfare of his own soul made it more important for him to make a clean breast, than it was for them to receive his communications. Baffled thus of his last hope, the conspirator made the following voluntary statements, which were taken hastily down as they fell from his lips.

COTTON'S CONFESSION

"I acknowledge my guilt. I was one of the principal ones with Boyd and Ruel Blake, in getting up this conspiracy. I am a member of the Murrell clan, and belong to what we call the Grand Council. I have counselled with them on an island in the Mississippi, and once near Columbus, this spring. Our object in undertaking this clan, was not to liberate the negroes, but get plunder. It has been in contemplation several years, but fell through on Murrell's conviction and imprisonment, We sought to revive it on the plan laid down in

Stewart's pamphlet. From the exposure of our plans in that publication, we feared the citizens would be on their guard on the night of the 25th December, so we thought we would take by surprise on the night of the 4th July, and it would have been to-night (and may be yet), but for the detection of our plans. There are about one hundred and fifty of our clan in this State. Boyd is the leader, and the Earls, who swore for us on the 1st, were his main men. Saunders was in the plot. Blake's boy, Peter, was justly punished, for he was active in corrupting his fellow negroes. There are arms and ammunition deposited in Hinds County, near Raymond.

(Signed) JOSHUA COTTON."

July 4th, 1835.

This paper having been signed by the condemned, he was sentenced to he hung within the hour, in order that the news of his execution might be circulated extensively for the purpose of intimidating his accomplices and dupes.

When brought to the place of execution the wretched man again confessed his guilt, and his last words were "Take care of your selves for to-night and to-morrow night."

The trial of Saunders was taken up, and much of the evidence against Cotton bearing also upon his case, he was convicted, after a brief examination, and hung upon the same day.

This was the manner in which the good people of Livingston celebrated the national anniversary, and truth to say it was scarcely less a holiday than if the proceedings had been peaceful. At night every man and boy capable of carrying a musket, was under arms, and the women, feeling an equal interest in the impending peril, took measures for aiding, if need should be, in the defence of their domestic dwellings. Fortunately, however, the night passed away without alarm, and the weary citizens on the following day felt as if the crisis of the danger had gone by.

Still no precaution was abandoned, the patrols were kept up as strictly as before, and the committee maintained its daily sessions. Several suspected persons were arrested and discharged on insufficient proof, but on the 7th of July, Albe Dean, the third partner in the firm of Cotton, Saunders, & Co., and Donovan, of Beattie's Bluff; were taken and condemned. They were both executed on the 8th of July, on which day, by a singular coincidence, the notorious Ruel Blake was brought in as a prisoner from Vicksburg. He had been arrested on the 5th instant, and arrived in time to behold Dean and Donovan expatiate their offences on the scaffold.

Blake was put on trial on the 9th, condemned and executed on the 10th. He went to death protesting his innocence, and angrily repulsed all invitations to confess.

The next man put on trial was Lee Smith, the remaining partner of the firm of Cotton, Saunders, & Co. There was little that was definite against him, and though the committee were inclined to believe in his guilt, they acquitted him, on condition that he should leave the State at once. This he eagerly agreed to, but while he was fulfilling the obligation with all the fidelity of fear, he was intercepted by the citizens of Hinds county, and cut to pieces. He probably owed this vengeful visitation to the fact of having been connected with the three executed members of the firm.

Two men, William Benson and Lunsford Barnes, were next tried and acquitted, and ordered to leave the country. The former was a native of New York, and came from the neighborhood of Albany. He was a simple fellow, and was suspected chiefly from the fact of having been in the employ of Blake. Both made good their retreat, and were never afterwards heard of in that part of the country.

The last duties of the committee were performed, in the examination of the two brothers Earle, who had been arrested in Livingston on the 17th of July, under a strong escort. The committee were not in session when they arrived, and before they met, William, the younger, made a voluntary confession developing all the proceedings of himself and brother from first to last. They were committed to custody, separately until the following day.

During the night, William committed suicide by hanging himself with his handkerchief to the round of a ladder that stood in his room. John was then tried and found guilty, but owing to the arrival of a despatch from the Committee of Safety of Vicksburg, (that Committee which had so summarily fined the gamblers, on the 6th,) requesting that the prisoner be delivered to their custody, he escaped execution. What became of him does not appear from the papers in our possession, but as we do not find his name among the summary executions of that excited period, the probability is that he was consigned to a long term of imprisonment.

Thus ended that bold and terrible conception which had sprung from the daring mind of the great robber chieftain, and which had occupied the councils of his band for years. In a spirit of infernal malice it had been conceived; silently, and with consummate skill and perseverance, it had been extended over the whole Southwest; and when accidental adverse combinations seemed to render its consummation hopeless, it was desperately precipitated by inferior hands, and the torch already kindled that was to light the train. Fortunately it exploded on its engineers, and conferred, by its retributive inflictions, safety and protection to the region which it had threatened with slaughter and conflagration.

CHAPTER XXXII.

Entrance of Murrell in the State Prison—The Felon Gang—The Blacksmith Shop—The Philosophy of Signs—Destruction of the Plot—Despair—Moral Resolution—The Convict's Wife—The Demon of the Cells—Release—Death.

We left the Evil Genius of our narrative, the robber chieftain, a convicted captive loaded with chains, and holding his reluctant way to those gloomy portals which open to the earthly sepulchre of crime.

Ten years struck from a man's life, to be filled with an appalling shadow which bars the future and half drowns the past, is no trifle for the most stoical imagination to contemplate; yet the strong mind of the robber submitted to the dismal prospect without an absolute surrender to despair. Indeed, to judge from his bearing he scarcely seemed conscious of the swift approach of the impenetrable cloud that was about enveloping him, perhaps for ever, in its misty folds, but approached his destiny like a man, who, condemned from the joyous beauties of the earth to the hideous darkness of a cave, walks backward to his doom and drinks in sunlight to the last.

So with the robber. Though disheartening shadows piled themselves in front, the past unrolled before him the flashing wake which he had claved through the tempestuous billows of the world's despite, and in this lurid train of bloody fortune sought the hope that was to light him through the threatening blackness, that overhung his future path.

His effort was not entirely without success. There were many things which spoke comfort to his soul. He was no poor, bungling, friendless felon, who had committed his first crime through the frenzy of distress, and who was therefore devoid of profession accomplices outside to labor for his release.—No; though a captive, he was chieftain still of the powerful confederation, composed of hundreds of desperate men who would dream only of his deliverance, and whose social influence, in many cases great, would, if force or stratagem should fail, in due time effect his manumission from his bonds, by pardon. Flattered by these vain and misleading visions, the convict conquered all despondent thoughts, and made himself master of a false content. Poor fool—far braver would he have been had he trembled like an aspen before the bloody picture of the past, and sought by penance and condition to expiate the crimes which now pledged Heaven to everlasting vengeance!

The convict entered the portal of the prison. He entered it to learn how vain is the conceit of guilt. His insolent composure faltered as he touched the threshold; there was a trepidation in the step, before so confident and bold; and as the closing gate creaked a malicious mockery on his ear, his heart sank, his lips turned white and faint, and his relaxing sinews for a moment threatened to become traitors to his will. But a glance ahead, which revealed a troop of prisoners about to file past him to their cells, recalled his pride, and a powerful effort made him as cold and placid as before.

There were looks of wonder cast from some of those who tramped in that felon gang, as their eyes fell aslant upon the man whom they had once served with the obedience of clansmen; but no glance of recognition passed between them and the fallen chief, whom they now for the first time met on equal terms. The file passed on; the tramp died away; the dull crash of an hundred ponderous bolts penned up the members of that miscreant household in their seperate dungeons, and surrounded by many with whom he had shared all the savage luxury of evil doing, and with whom he was now destined to atone, the doomed marauder cast himself upon his narrow bunk to enjoy without restraint that strange extacy which is found even in absolute despair.

Murrell was for a time doomed to solitary confinement, but the initiatory period of punishment having passed, he was brought out to be assigned a department in which he should labor for the State. He had been reared to no business; but while in Murfreesborough prison some years before, he had worked in the blacksmith shop, and he now made blacksmithing his trade. To the blacksmith shop he was therefore consigned, and in its employments and variations he experienced reliefs, which were denied to the narrow scope and dull monotony of a solitary cell.

He was now within reach of direct information of the great world outside, and by means of his digital alphabet, before noticed as common among convicts, he could converse freely, not only with the workmen, but with members of his band, who would now and then gain access to the prison in the character of visiters. These men, while passing through the establishment, as if guided only by an idle curiosity, would be sure not to omit the blacksmith shop, and while there would seek an opportunity, when unobserved, to relate with rapid fingers the information which they had brought, and then take back from the sooty digits of the smith his orders in return. In this way the marauder had learnt all the operations of Stewart, and directed the attempt, in which we have heretofore recorded, to bride him from his purpose of a full exposure of the more atrocious passages of his career. The suppression or defeat of those of the details, which would prove him to be a demon and a monster, rather than a man, the imprisoned miscreant knew was essential to his hope of pardon, and we, therefore find him, in addition to the advice to buy the manuscript, directing the close pursuit of his strange enemy and the defeat of his intentions by the violent suppression of his life. We have seen with what alacrity this advice was followed out, and the providential manner in which its devilish aim was foiled.

After the publication of the pamphlet,[1] there was a wide break in the stream of outside communication. The

---

1. The "pamphlet" was *History of the Detection, Conviction, Life and Designs of John A. Murrell, the Great Western Land Pirate...* by Augustus Q. Walton, Esq.

bands were paralyzed by fear, and though they did not disperse and scatter, they kept themselves concealed, and abstained from any active intercourse or correspondence. Murrell, therefore, experienced a season of neglect, and received not the slightest intimation of the movements of his clans, until the bold revival of the exploded insurrection by Boyd and Cotton had been agreed upon in the councils of the Mississippi. This brilliant resuscitation of his daring scheme, struck the mind of the convict with unqualified admiration, and his practised judgment perceived in the very daring of the movement one of those assurances of success which he had always found attendant upon the most desperate exploits of his own career. There was one point in the movement, however, which his acute and subtle mind regarded with some uneasiness. The plot had been revived, debated, and adopted without consultation of his wishes, or so much as seeking his opinion. This augured a disfranchisement from his influence, and the gradual advance among the confederacy of some other leading mind, which was to occupy the place left vacant by his own incarceration. The result was natural, but still it was mortifying, and a burning and feverish discontent set in, which worked incessant torture upon his proud and aspiring mind.

A faithful emissary, however, soon set his mind at ease by placing him in possession of the true details, and when he learned that one of the main objects of the rising, was the bursting of his bonds, he reproached himself deeply for his distrust.

Having possessed himself of the scope of the new plot, Murrell dwelt with the most intense interest upon every detail of which he had been apprised, and his restless scheming brain, worked its parts into the wildest speculations. As the fourth of July advanced, communications were had with him under great difficulties, and only at long intervals, and for the six weeks immediately previous to the intended outbreak, he received not an item from outside. The most feverish anxiety took possession of his mind on the designated night, and listening at the bars of his cage, he expected every moment to see the lurid glare of the conflagration flicker on the walls, or to hear the roar of the insurgent bands as they thundered at the portal. But the night passed away undisturbed, except by the voice of some noisy reveller or an occasional pistol shot from some holiday patriot.

During the next night, and the next, and the next, the miscreant listened with painful eagerness for the shout of blood; but night after night went by without a breath of turbulence, and worn out with watching, and sick with his fierce thirst for slaughter, he would in the morning hours angrily cast himself upon his miserable settle, and curse himself into a short and feverish sleep. Thus passed away a fortnight, and still the fever grew more tense. No word came how matters had progressed outside. Not the slightest intimation could be drawn from the demeanor of the officers of the prison, that anything unusual had taken place. All was tranquil, regular, and commonplace, except the raging tempest of the robber's mind.

On the morning of the 19th July, however, he had the satisfaction of hearing himself accosted with a curse, as he was turned out to his work. This was a relief. He looked around and perceived that the keepers wore a look of care, and as the day passed on, the officers of the prison were seen gathering frequently into knots, and gravely discoursing some matter of absorbing interest. It was plain that something unusual had happened, and the frequent sidelong glances which were cast on him, confirmed his mind that the plot had broken out, and that its operations were of magnitude. Night came, but still the tantalizing riddle remained unread, and he who felt most deeply interested in its solution, went back to his cell in a state of excitement bordering on frenzy. But the livelong night gave to his faithful ear no token of hope, no sound of promise. No axes smote the sullen gates, and no tumultuous shouts of maddened hordes spake terror to the honest and cheer to the depraved. The morning broke; the hour of release arrived; and every bolt shot back but that which guarded the cell of the marauder. His breakfast was served, but he was left in torturing solitude until an advanced hour of the forenoon, when two of the chief officers of the prison entered, and sought to elicit information from him on the subject of the plot.

The robber regarded his inquisitors with a disdain which he made no effort to disguise, and after listening to all their inquiries, bluffly informed them that if they came to him to assign him tasks within the range of prison discipline, he was ready to perform them, but if they meant to solicit a favor, they must bear in mind that the application raised him to a level with themselves, and they must therefore treat him like an equal.

"We do not exactly understand what you mean," said one of the visitors.

"I mean," said Murrell, in the same tone which he had used before, "that if you expect any information or advice from me, you must first give me your confidence. In plain terms, you must let me know why you pay me this visit, and the whole state of the case which agitates you, without reserve."

Seeing there was no choice but to gratify the prisoner's whim, the visitors gave a full history of the proceedings at Livingston and Beattie's Bluff. As the course of the narrative brought forward the different directors of the plot, the narrator would question Murrell if he knew the man alluded to, but the robber evaded the interrogatory by a demand to hear the whole story before he spoke. Thus he gathered a full history of the death of his last hope. When the relation was done, he denied all knowledge of any of the parties concerned, pronounced Cotton a perjured man, and declared that it was now his firm belief that Stewart was himself the secret instigator of the plot which he had pretended to expose and charge on other hands. He further declared that the villains who had perished were Stewart's emissaries, who, with persevering malice, forgot not to seek to injure him, by connecting his name with their villaines, even in the hour when vengeance had so justly overtaken themselves.

This was all that the utmost ingenuity of the visitors could draw from the stubborn prisoner, and they left him as unenlightened as they came, except in an additional knowledge of his strange character.

This tragic denouement of the grand drama of his life, dropped the curtain on all the false hopes and vain illusions of the past. The gloom behind was now as dense as the shadows that rose up before, and the despairing wretch, for the first time, felt that he was completely enveloped by his fate. Several days passed, and Murrell remained in a state of mental torpor, which was followed by a fever, that transferred him to the hospital, and left him prisoner to his bed for several weeks. During this period he calmly weighed his situation, and rejecting entirely the idle hopes which had previously misled him, he resolved upon a stoical content which should comprehend nothing but the present. The past was woe, the future was despair, and there was, nothing left him but the passing hour. With that facility of adaptation, which we have before observed, the cold-hearted calculator became the most amiable of the inmates of the prison, and at once rose to favor by his cheerful alacrity in the performance of his tasks. He soon became a sort of pet of the keeper who had charge of his department, and was raised to the position of foreman of his shop, on the expiration of the term of the convict who had previously held that place. He was again a leader, even though in an humble scope.

Five years passed away without any circumstance transpiring to alter his condition. About the middle of his term, it was made known to him that his wife had become dissolute among the lowest characters.[2] This was the severest blow which he had received during all his degradation. Sooth to say, it was a stinging thought for one who had commanded respect from a thousand satellites, and spread terror throughout nearly half a zone, that he might be dishonored by the meanest of his troop.

In a year or two after this occurrence, a visible change took place in Murrell's appearance. His robust form grew thin; the strong substantial flesh upon his cheeks

---

2. Elizabeth (Mangrum) Murrell had indeed become destitute in her husband's absence, and she was convicted of petit larceny. Her twelve-month sentence to the state penitentiary was suspended, however, owing to her circumstances. Lal Penick, *Great Western Land Pirate*, 28–29.

grew soft and pale; his eyes, before so cold and penetrating, became drowsy and evasive; and instead of the firm, resolute step which had marked the confidence of great physical powers, his gait became loose, shuffling, and uncertain. The prison demon had seized upon him. The evil spirit which haunts the solitude of the depraved adult, had gained the mastery over his stern thoughts, and the strong man wilted under its assaults as parchment shrivels before a consuming fire. Weakening continually under the vital drain, his mind became accessible to influences which it had before disdained, and by degrees the convict gave an increased attention to the gentle counsels of religious visitors, who, with a generous devotion, sought the redemption of his begrimed and blood-stained soul. At length the pertinacious kindness of the christian visiters won its reward; the dull patience of the convict changed to an inquiring interest, which at length quickened to conversion, and the cruel-hearted and remorseless land-pirate of the west became a meek and sighing methodist. This was so signal a triumph for religion, that straightway the convert became an object of absorbing interest to those who had effected his salvation; and not content with recommending him to favor in his confinement, these new friends agitated the abridgement of his term, and strange to say, accomplished his release in 1845, some few months previous to the legal expiration of his sentence.

On coming out of prison the repentant robber did not seek his wife, or cast one thought upon his former friends. Ambition had died within him, and resigning himself into the hands of his religious benefactors, he retired to a little piece of land prepared for him in Pikeville,³ set up a forge, and sought to gain a livelihood by tinkering, mending ploughs, and chance blacksmithing, for the neighbours round.⁴

But his course was run. The seeds of dissolution implanted by the demon of the cells, had germed within him, and a swift decay—more swift for its great triumph—soon stretched the sometime robber a cold fragment of mortality before a crowd of chattering doctors, who, with rolled up sleeves and glittering scalpels, surrounded a dissecting table.⁵

Thus closed the mortal career of John A. Murrell, the Great Land Pirate of the West.⁶

THE END

---

3. Pikeville was the county seat of Bledsoe County, Tennessee, located on the Sequatchee River 109 miles southeast of Nashville.

4. Murrell was released early from the pentitentiary in April 1844, having contracted tuberculosis during his incarceration. Lal Penick, *Great Western Land Pirate*, 28.

5. Murrell died on November 1, 1844, just seventh months after his release from prison. Supposedly before his death, he admitted "he had been guilty of almost every crime charged against him except murder." *Ibid*, 28.

6. Murrell is buried at Smyrna Cemetery northeast of Pikeville, Tennessee. His grave is marked by a plain marble tombstone with the inscription: JOHN A. MURRELL. His grave was supposedly desecrated after his burial and his head was removed from his body, which was left behind to be mauled by hogs. The head was put on display at carnivals. *Ibid*, 31.

INDEX.

Africa, 108
Aker, George, 236, 248–253, 254, 256, 268
Alabama, 43, 44, 64, 129, 129, 198, 280
Alabama River, 56
Albany, New York, 365
Arkansas, 30, 64, 110, 120, 121, 127, 128, 144, 168, 170, 171, 177, 179, 182, 201, 212, 218, 226, 229, 232, 245, 286, 307, 326
Arkansas River, 97, 116, 163
Augusta, Georgia, 93

Bacchus (slave), 334, 335
Barataria, Louisiana, 33

Barker, 245
Barnes, Lunsford, 365
Barney, Jehu, 194, 197–199, 229, 230
Bayliss, Col. William H., 170, 171, 206, 232
Beattie, Capt. Andrew, 329
Beattie's Bluff, Mississippi, 318, 321, 328, 329, 331, 334, 338, 347, 355, 361, 362, 374
Bellefont, Alabama, 46, 46fn
Benson, William, 365
Benton, 114
Big Black River (Mississippi), 318
Billy the Kid, vii

Blake, Rural, 315–317, 320, 325, 326, 328, 331, 339–343, 350, 352, 356, 362, 348, 364
  see also: Peter (slave of Ruel Blake)
Boyd, Andrew, 129, 315, 316–320, 325, 328, 340, 344–345, 346–352, 354, 358, 362, 363, 371
Bradford, Alexander (prosecutor of Murrell), 283, 283fn
Brandon, Mississippi, 305
Brazil, 108
Brown, Milton (defender of Murrell), 284, 284fn, 288–289
"Buzzard's Roost" (Alabama), 276

Comanches, 163
Campeachy, Yucatan, 107
Capote, Truman, 56fn
Captain Slick's Company, 124–127, 143
Carrollville, Tennessee, 280, 280fn
Carter, 66-68
Centerville, Tennessee, 24, 24fn
Central Committee of Safety, 321, 338, 339,, 360–361
Champion, John, 178, 181–183, 197, 204, 230, 232
Charleston, South Carolina, 93
Chickasaw Bend, 186
Chickasaw Bluff, 177
Chickasaw settlement (Mississippi), 311
Choctaw Nation/Purchase (Mississippi), 66, 71, 72, 114, 147, 154, 156, 204, 226, 233, 236, 238, 239, 255, 256, 268
Choctaw Pass, 205
Cincinnati, Ohio, 30, 31, 34, 35, 93, 312
Clanton, Matthew, 147, 147fn, 226, 233, 237–242, 255, 268
Clinton, Mississippi, 331
Columbia, Tennessee, 62, 66, 296
Columbus, Mississippi, 64, 309, 316, 362
Commerce, Mississippi, 250, 255
Committee of Investigation (Livingston, Mississippi), 324, 328, 329
Committee of Safety (Vicksburg, Mississippi), 365
Connecticut, 317, 326, 327
Cotton, Dr. Joshua, 315, 316, 325, 327, 328, 331, 340, 343, 344–350, 352, 357–360, 371, 374
  confession to insurrection, 362–363
  executed, 363
  and Murrell, 326
Cotton, Saunders & Company, 364
Crenshaw, Harry [David], 13–22, 108, 277
  meets Murrell, 13–18, 18fn
  murder and robbery of Woods, 36–40
  reunites with Murrell, 31–47, 51–66
  robbery of the mail carrier, 66
Crow Creek, 45
Cumberland Mountains, 36, 320

Dark, Thomas, 230
Dark, Joseph, 230
Dean, Able, 326–328, 364
Deberry Mathias (Madison County, Tennessee sheriff), 219–223, 254, 281, 282, 294
Denmark, Tennessee, vii, 146, 148, 149, 156, 230
Dodridge, 114
Donley, 318, 325
Donovan, Angus L., 318, 318fn, 325, 328, 333, 364
Drayton, 82–86, 92

Earl brothers (William and John), 315, 316, 318, 325, 328, 346–348, 363, 365
Earl, John, 365
Earl, William, 365
Earp, Wyatt, vii
Eason, 103-106, 234
Eastern Tennessee, 6
Erwin, Mr., 182–184, 196, 198, 200–204, 207, 230, 232
Estanaula, Tennessee, 149, 149fn, 150, 212, 283, 285
Evans, Dr., 148
Ewel, 107
Ewing, Maddux & Company, 350

Fayette County, Alabama, 276
Fayette County, Tennessee, 66, 241fn
Florence, Alabama, 103, 267, 274, 275, 278, 279, 280
Forsyth, 105
Fowler, Orson Squire, xix

phrenological assessment of Murrell, xix–xxii
Franklin, Tennessee, 32

Georgia, 35, 44, 45, 147, 156, 157, 302
Gilbert, 296
Glenn (or Glen), 245, 249, 255, 268
Grand Council, *see:* Mystic Clan of the Confederacy

Haines, 76–84, 87, 92, 93, 97, 107, 195
Hare, Joseph Thompson, xviii, 161, 161fn
Hargus, Rev., 182–184, 186, 230
Harris, 19–21, 31, 32
Hatchie River, 149, 168fn
Hawkins, 105
Henderson, 198, 199
Henning family, 144, 145, 147, 194, 212, 216, 254
Henning, John, 127, 127fn, 143, 144, 148, 156, 157, 167, 172, 175, 176, 181, 189, 206, 212, 218, 224, 225, 230, 281, 285, 288
Henning, Richard, 146, 148, 149, 172, 175, 176, 226, 229, 230, 234, 239, 281
Hinds County, Mississippi, 315, 317, 318, 327, 331, 344, 346, 363, 364
History of the Detection, Conviction, Life and Designs of John A. Murrell, the Great Western Land Pirate, viii, 311fn, 312fn, 313, 314, 316

Howard, H.R., ix, x
Hunold, Thomas, 106, 234, 235
Ibberville Parish, Louisiana, 87, 92

Investigating Committee (Livingston, Mississippi), 324
  see also: Committee of Safety (Livingston, Mississippi)

Jackson, Tennessee, 147, 215, 219, 223, 236, 249, 256, 276, 280
James, Jesse, vii
Jasper, Tennessee, 41, 41fn, 43, 44, 45, 46
Jim (slave), 332–333, 335
Joe (slave, blacksmith), 330–333
Johnson, William P., 339, 340

Kentucky, 27, 34, 114, 311

Lafayette County, Mississippi, 268
La Grange, Tennessee, 241, 241fn
Lal Penick, James Jr., x
Landfair, Mr., 321, 322, 329, 332, 336, 339
Latham, Madame, 321, 322, 329
Lee, Harper, 56fn
Lee, Mr., 329
Lexington, Kentucky, 93, 272, 273, 281, 294, 296
Lexington, Tennessee, 25, 25fn
Life on the Mississippi, vii
Livingston, Mississippi, 321, 323, 324, 326, 328, 331, 338, 344, 346, 350, 361, 363, 374
Lofton, 318, 325
Long, Mr., 121, 127
Louisville, Kentucky, 312
Loyd, William, 229, 230
Lunenberg County, Virginia, 1fn

Mabry, Jesse, 329, 329fn, 330, 332
  see also: Sam (slaves of Jesse Mabry)
Madison County, Mississippi, 106, 234, 315, 317–319, 324, 327, 350
Madison County, Tennessee, vii, 62, 66, 94, 103, 104, 114, 117, 123, 144, 147, 156, 158, 159, 172, 173, 204, 206, 210, 220, 229, 230, 235, 236–241, 246, 249, 254, 256, 268, 272, 275, 280, 281, 283fn, 294
Madison County, Tennessee Circuit Court, 233fn, 283
Manchester, Mississippi, 226, 234
Marion County, Alabama, 276
Marshall County, Mississippi, 268
Marvin (Methodist preacher), 88–90, 164
Matamoras, Mexico, 107
Maury County, Tennessee, 62, 62fn, 66, 296
McCorry, Henry W., 233fn
McVey, Reuben, 288
Memphis, Tennessee, 25, 27, 28, 66, 70, 311, 326

JOHN A. MURRELL.

Methodists, 66, 88, 108
Mexico, 107
Middle Tennessee, 1, 34, 62, 158
Milledgeville, Georgia, 93
Miller, 20, 21, 22, 32, 33
Miller, Pleasant M., 283fn
Mississippi, 65, 73, 93, 258, 295, 317
Mississippi River, 30, 73, 95, 116, 117, 145, 171, 177, 186, 197, 226, 230, 260, 312, 344, 362
Mobile, Alabama, 33, 47, 56, 303
Monroeville, Alabama, 56, 56fn
Montgomery, Alabama, 47
Moore, James, 311
Moss, 318, 333
Moulton, Alabama, 102
Murfreesboro, Tennessee, 369
Murrell, Elizabeth (Mangrum) (wife of John A.), 94, 95, 95fn, 99, 210, 219–221, 226, 233, 375, 375fn
  gives secret message from Murrell to his clan, 219–221
  helps Murrell to escape jail, 257
Murrell, Jeffrey (father of John A.), 1, 1fn, 5, 5fn, 71fn
Murrell, Jeffrey G. (brother of John A.), 62, 62fn
Murrell John A.,
  and brother Jeffrey Murrell, 62
  and Carter, 66–68
  and Harry Crenshaw, 13–22, 31–47, 51–66
  and insurrection plans, 56–57, 63–64, 101–102, 110, 130–137
  and John Henning's slaves, 175–176, 225–226
  and Mississippi insurrection, 371–374
  and Richard Henning, 146–147
  and the Mystic Clan of the Confederacy, 128–137
  and Virgil A Stewart, 151–224
  and women, 6, 66, 114
  appearance in prison, 375–376
  arrested, 122–124
  attempt to capture, by Captain Slick's Company, 124–127
  begins stealing, 2–3
  birth, 1
  blacksmith, 369–370, 377
  bound to a tree, 11–14
  burglaries, 79–80
  captured, 210–213, 215–221
  character, 4
  childhood, 2–9
  convicted of horse stealing, 68–69
  convinces a slave to commit arson, 57–60
  death, 377
  death of unknown fiancee, 66
  escape at Muscle Shoals, 102–103
  escape from jail, 257–259
  fight with Drayton, 82–84, 85, 86
  flight from jail, 262–268, 274
  horse stealing, 34, 68–69, 117
  imprisoned, 69–70, 367–376

leaves home, 5
marries Elizabeth Mangrum, 94–95
murder and robbery of Woods, 36–40, 43–47
murder of the fortunate gambler, 48–52
murder of the imposter traveler, 114–116
murders committed by, 75
in New Orleans, 76–84, 109
in Mexico, 107–108
phrenological assessment of, xix–xxii
preacher disguise, 87, 88–90, 94, 98
pursuit of, 273–280
reaction to conviction, 291–292
reads the law, 5, 101
receives letter from antislavery English lecturer, 135–137
release from prison, 376–377
robbing and murdering travelers, 111–114
robbing of a young Kentuckian, 80–81
robbing the mail carrier, 66
sentenced to prison, 289–290
slave stealing, 25–27, 64–66, 73–76, 95–98, 103–106, 121–122, 143–145
stealing from a delusional slave, 57–60
stealing from the brig, 54–56
trial, 282–290
Murrell, William (brother), 71, 71fn, 72–83, 87, 92, 93, 95, 105, 106

Murrell, Zilpha (Andrews) (mother of John A.), 1, 1fn, 2, 5, 19, 71fn
Muscle Shoals, Alabama, 101
Mystic Clan of the Confederacy, vii, 107, 120
and slave insurrection, 314–366
assassination attempt against Virgil A. Stewart, 242–245, 293–300
council house of, 193
Grand Council of the Arkansas, 120, 128–137, 142, 143, 145, 175, 176, 190, 192, 200, 248, 362
initiation, 139–142
journey by Murrell and Stewart to, 190–192
reaction to Murrell's conviction, 292–293

Nashville, Tennessee, 5, 7, 43, 161fn, 214, 292, 296, 326
Natchez, Mississippi, 86, 92, 95, 96, 110, 114, 161fn, 311, 311, 312, 318fn, 319, 331
National Police Gazette, ix, x, xviii
New Lexington, Alabama, 278
New Orleans, Louisiana, 32, 68, 74, 75, 76, 78, 87, 92, 93, 96, 99, 106–109, 350
New York, 365
Nolan, 199, 201

Ohio, 93
Ohio River, 30

Old Agency, Mississippi, 319, 319fn, 325, 326, 327, 344
Old Agency Road, 319fn

Parmer, 45
Patton's Ferry, 296
Pennsylvania, 161fn, 312
Perry County, Tennessee, 293, 294
Perryville, Tennessee, 24, 24fn
Peter (slave of Ruel Blake), 339–342, 356, 363
Phelan, James, vii
Phelps, 76, 84, 87, 92, 93, 97, 107
Pikeville, Tennessee, 377, 377fn
Pontotoc County, Mississippi, 268
Poplar Creek (Tennessee), 161

Rainhart, 189
Raleigh, Tennessee, 27, 27fn
Randolph, Tennessee, 28, 28fn, 101, 145, 147, 148, 164, 168fn, 171
Rankin, 114
Rawson, 318, 325, 328
Raymond, Miss', 363
Red River (Arkansas), 326
Rice, William H., 339
Richmond, Virginia, 93
Ripley, Mississippi, 311
Roberts, 28
Rodgers, 240
Runnels, Col. D.H., 325
Russell (African-American preacher), 331–333, 335

Sabine River (Texas), 107

Sam (slaves of Jesse Mabry), 330, 332, 335, 348, 349, 354, 357
Santa Cruz, 33, 53
Saunders, Dr. William, 253, 326–328, 331, 340, 343–344, 363, 345, 350, 361, 363
  and Murrell, 326
Savannah, Georgia, 93
Shelby, Mr., 177, 178
Slave insurrection in Mississippi (1835), 314–366
Smithville Road, 16
Smyrna Cemetery (Pikeville, Tennessee), 377fn
South Carolina, 36
Sperlock, 194, 196, 197
Springhill, Alabama, 268, 273
Smith, James M., 329
Smith, Lee, 326–328, 364
Stanberry, Capt., 329–330
Stewart, Virgil A., vi, 148, 151–312, 374
  and publication of *History of the Detection, Conviction, Life and Designs of John A. Murrell, the Great Western Land Pirate*, 272–273, 292–294, 312–314, 316, 363, 370
  arrival in Madison County, Tennessee, 147
  assassination attempts against, 242–245, 293–300
  as Adam Hues, 169, 171, 172, 173, 181, 190, 199, 214, 218, 224
  as Cowan, 305
  as Tom Goodin, 248

at Murrell's trial, 283–290
background, 147
escape from potential assassin's home, 307–311
informed of Murrell's recapture, 281
making notes of Murrell's confessions, 286–287
meets Murrell, 151
not known to Murrell beforehand, 283
pursuit of Murrell, 148–150
returns to Madison County, Tennessee, 272
sees Murrell after Murrell's escape, 268–271
testifies at Murrell's trial, 285–288
Sumner County, Tennessee, 327
Surgick, Mother, 78

T.B. Peterson & Brothers, x
Talladega County, Alabama, 129
Tennessee, xix, 5, 35, 36, 64, 65, 72, 196, 234, 238, 258, 280, 311, 326, 327
Tennessee River, 24, 46, 101, 275, 276
Texas, 73, 75, 105, 107, 284
"The Devil's Punch Bowl" (Natchez, Mississippi), 332, 332fn
Tippah County, Mississippi, 267, 268
Tipton County, Tennessee, 95, 97, 98, 169, 326
Tobasco, 108
Tombigbee River (Alabama), 47, 56
Tucker, James, 229, 230, 245

Tuscaloosa, Alabama, 46, 278
Tuscaloosa County, Alabama, 276
Twain, Mark, vii

Vernon, Mississippi, 331, 361
Vess, William, 233, 237–240, 242, 246, 253, 254
Vicksburg, Mississippi, 93, 234, 319, 343, 350, 365
Virginia, vii

Walton, Augustus Q. (fictitious author), 311, 311fn, 312
Warren's tavern (Mississippi), 348
Warren County, Mississippi, 315, 317–319
Waterloo, Alabama, 275, 275fn
Watkins, 220, 226–228
Weaver (African-American preacher), 330–332, 335
Wesley, Tennessee, 168, 168fn, 169, 204–206
Wheeling, West Virginia, 30
Williamson County, Tennessee, vii, 1fn, 18, 62fn, 93
Woods, 43, 44, 64
victim of Murrell and Crenshaw, 36–40

Yallabusha River, 154
Yazoo, Mississippi, 205
Yazoo Pass, 226
Yellow Busha, Mississippi, 230, 231, 236
Yellow Busha County, Mississippi, 231

Titles available from

BRAYBREE
Publishing

History of the Detection, Conviction, Life and Designs of John A. Murrell, the Great Western Land Pirate
by Augustus Q. Walton • ISBN 978-1-940127-02-6

Hawkins' Tories: A Regimental and Social History of the 7th Tennessee Volunteer Cavalry USA in the Civil War
by Peggy Scott Holley • ISBN 978-1-940127-04-0

A Sacred High Place: A History of Mount Carmel Cemetery and Meetinghouse, McNairy County, Tennessee
by John E. Talbott, J.D. • ISBN 978-0-9671251-9-0

Gold is the Key: Murder, Robbery, & the Gold Rush in Jackson, Tennessee
by Thomas L. Aud • ISBN 978-1-940127-09-5

The Peg Leg Politician: Adam Huntsman of Tennessee
by Kevin D. McCann • ISBN 978-0-9671251-4-5

Hurst's Wurst: Colonel Fielding Hurst & the Sixth Tennessee Cavalry U.S.A.
by Kevin D. McCann • ISBN 978-0-9671251-2-1

www.ingramcontent.com/pod-product-compliance
Lightning Source LLC
Chambersburg PA
CBHW032123160426
43197CB00008B/491